DARBY

One hundred years of life in a changing culture

LIAM CAMPBELL

Featuring photography by Scott Duncan

Produced by Warlpiri Media Association Inc.

WARLPIRI MEDIA
ASSOCIATION INC.

ABC
Books

DA

R BY

Published in Australia by ABC Books for the
AUSTRALIAN BROADCASTING CORPORATION
GPO Box 9994 Sydney NSW 2001

ISBN 0 7333 1925 4

Cover and text design by Sandy Cull, gogoGingko
Cover photographs by Scott Duncan Films
Typeset in 11/14.5pt Mrs Eaves by J&M Typsetting and Sandy Cull
Production by Carmen De La Rue, Stella Book Production & Publishing Services
Colour reproduction by Splitting Image, Clayton, Victoria

Printed and bound in China by Imago

5 4 3 2 1

National Library of Australia
Cataloguing-in-Publication data:

Campbell, Liam, 1974– .
Darby: one hundred years of life in a changing culture.

Includes bibliography.
ISBN 0 7333 1925 4.

1. Ross, Darby Jampijinpa. 2. Warlpiri (Australian people)
– Biography. 3. Warlpiri (Australian people) – History. I.
Australian Broadcasting Corporation. II. Warlpiri Media
Association. III. Title.

305.89915092

www.aboriginalstories.com
www.warlpiri.com.au

READER'S NOTE

This is an account of one man's life. It is constructed from stories recorded while
sitting outside his house, or driving through country listening to him singing the *Jukurrpa*
(Dreaming) that resounded in the everyday. At times I found it hard to understand
the stories he told. Stories that appeared to be eyewitness accounts were sometimes a
retelling of events as someone else related them to him. The distinctions between actual
events, rumours and *Jukurrpa* accounts were not always clear. The vagaries of memory
and personality are characteristic of these stories.

This is not a standard biography. It consists of the stories he wanted to tell.
Dates, times and numbers were less important to him than people, places and *Jukurrpa*.
I have attempted to verify the historical details relating to these stories, using written
sources and other oral accounts. I have also included information relating to the
Warlpiri people's story in the twentieth century, to provide a framework for a reading
of the stories. The accompanying audio CD contains examples of the stories, and we
have included transcriptions to follow, so that you can hear some of the words as they
were spoken, and find it easier to read them.

The language contained in the stories is a mixture of Aboriginal and Standard
English, although they also contain some Warlpiri, and a few words from the north
Australian stockman's Kriol. When using Warlpiri words, I have followed the
orthography developed by linguists in consultation with Yuendumu School's Bilingual
Resource Development Unit. However, some writers quoted in the text use their own
spellings of Warlpiri words which can vary significantly from the now standard spellings.

The style of the stories often reflects a blend of English and Warlpiri grammar,
the distinction between gender is not always clear, and the speaker sometimes refers
to himself in the third person. The reason why the majority of these stories were not
recorded in the speaker's first language was because he had a desire to communicate
to a wide audience. Had I been fluent in Warlpiri, the speaker would have been able
to express himself more freely, and through translation could have demonstrated his
storytelling ability. Thus, the majority of quoted text may appear much more simplistic
than the speaker intended and the grammar reflects that of translating his Warlpiri
thought processes into English. I find myself doing the opposite when I try and speak
Warlpiri, and can testify to how difficult it is to move between the two. And his English
was so much better than my Warlpiri.

WARNING

Nyampuju yapa-patu-kurlu. Panukari kalu-wankaru-juku marda nyinami. Panukari mardalu lawa-
nyinajalku. Ngurrjulu-ngalpa wangkaja warlalja milki-yirrarni-njaku photo-ku.

This book contains images of Warlpiri people. Caution should be exercised in viewing
as some of these images are of deceased persons. Permission was granted from their
families for their reproduction.

This book is dedicated to the memory of the following young men and women. We have lost them, like so many others, well before their time:

James Japanangka Brown
Dylan Jungarrayi Brown
Abraham Japaljarri Dickson
Lawrence Jampijinpa Watson
Morrison Japanangka Langdon
Sam Japangardi Marshall
Simeon Jupurrurla Ross
Matthew Jupurrurla White
Annarita Napurrurla Wilson

Central Australia
WARLPIRI COUNTRY (SOUTH)

● Tanami Gold Mine

● Warlarla (Rabbit Flat)

Yinapaka
(Lake Surprise)

Wauchope

● The Granites
Gold Mine

Pirtipirti
(Thompson's
Rockhole)

Jarra Jarra

Lungkardajarra

Wirliya-Jarrayi
(Willowra)

ANMATYERR
COUNTRY

Purturlu
(Mt Theo)

Barrow
Creek

Jila Well

Yumurrpa

Nyurripatu

Wapurtali
(Mt Singleton)

Mt Doreen
(ruins)

Pikilyi
(Vaughan
Springs)

Yurrkuru
(Brooks Soak)

Coniston

Ti Tree

Kunajarrayi

Yuendumu

Yuelamu

Nyirrpi

Napperby
(Laramba)

Ryan's
Well

Karrku

T A N A M I   H I G H W A Y

Karrinyarra
(Mt Wedge)

W A
N T

PINTUPI
COUNTRY

Mt Liebig

Papunya

Walungurru
(Kintore)

Haasts Bluff

Mt Zeil

ARRERNTE
COUNTRY

Alice
Springs

LURITJA
COUNTRY

Hermannsburg

KEY
● mine
significant site
community or outstation
station
Warlpiri Country

Contents

Jampijinparna
purami karnaju
wiyarrpa.

Ngaju-Yimi-
Pulka-lku-rna

I am Jampijinpa.
I'm telling my own true story.
I'm a poor old man now.

Chapter One

The Oldest Man in Australia

I'm Darby.
I'm one hundred and fifty.
I'm the oldest man in Australia.

What is it that we dream about when we are old and grey and full of sleep? When we hear our country crying out for us and we are the last of our generation?

I was thinking about this when I arrived at Hetti Perkins Aboriginal Hostel in Alice Springs. I walked past the courtyard with all the old people in wheelchairs, mouths open, staring up at the sky. The old man's room was at the end of the corridor where it would catch the morning sun. It always made me sad when I walked in. He looked old, lying there flat in the bed, curtains drawn.

I asked him how he was and he laughed and said, 'Not dead yet!' We held hands and talked for a while in his language. Simple talk, using my 'baby Warlpiri' to tell him I had come in from Yuendumu and would visit him over the next couple of days. We switched to English when the nurse came in and I asked her when the old man might return to Yuendumu. The nurse said they don't talk to patients about leaving until the day before, but it was likely he would return soon, weather permitting. The old man indicated that he had come in on the plane and would like to return by road. Then he started talking about how his grandparents got shot. Shot in the head.

The nurse left and I opened the curtains so we could see the sky. I talked about how I was going with the book and how people would be able to read all the stories that he had told me. I showed him some of the photos and began to check the details of some of the stories. But the old man wanted to tell me another story.

We sat and talked for another half an hour before I told him I would return the next day. As I closed the curtains, a peacock walked past the window and the old man smiled. I knew what he was thinking, and as I was walking out I heard him call me back in to ask if I had a rifle? Yes. Did I have bullets for that rifle? Yes. Good. He said he might need that rifle. I smiled and said I might give it to him later. Good. He couldn't walk or see very well anymore, but that old man was always thinking about hunting. He probably lay there most of the day thinking about when he was a youngfella running around with his dogs tracking kangaroos.

Old age had come slowly for him. Most of the men and women he knew as a child, including his brothers, had passed away by the time he was an old man. He even outlived many of the younger members of his family. It was the burden of being very old and was the cause of much sadness for him.

The old man was born into the living heart of the country. He learned the game and developed skills. Then on his own — but never alone — he walked away and encountered those that had come into the country, and discovered that the rules had been broken and the game changed forever. He would spend the rest of his life trying to put things back together.

An independent man, it had frustrated him when he could no longer hunt on foot; his eyesight failed, he lost the strength in his arms, couldn't walk, and finally, when he could no longer look after himself, went to live in the hostel. It was difficult, but he managed to smile and be polite to visitors as he had always done. They would distract him from the sad reality of the situation, separated from his country and his family. They would talk about *Jukurrpa* (Dreaming), or refer to people, places and events that might spark his memory and leave him with images to dream of while sitting in his chair with all the other *purlka-purlka* (old men) in the room.

The Warlpiri, Anmatyerr, Arrernte, Pintupi and Pitjantjatjara men were reunited in their last days at the hostel, sitting, thinking, dreaming, and wanting to go home — their bodies too broken with old age to survive in their own communities. The old man's room-mate, blind Jangala, would keep him awake with his conversation but he knew that it was not much longer until he would claim the promise that was given to him.

He knew that one day he would get a letter from the Queen. But numbers didn't mean a great deal to him. One hundred was much the same as 105, or as he decided was appropriate: 150. He finally received his letter on the day his friends and family gathered at the hostel to celebrate his hundredth birthday in March, 2005. He was also presented with his first official birth certificate. He passed away the next day.

The old man had officiated at, and attended, many funerals, often reflecting on his own longevity, claiming *Wapirra* (God) made him a promise and that it was this promise

that kept him alive. His own funeral was not as big as everyone expected. The Warlpiri community was weary from too much 'sorry business'. But many of those who knew him gathered together to celebrate his life on that little bit of land that the Warlpiri had given back to *Wapirra*. The impact of the wailing that accompanied us as we carried the coffin into the church was lessened by the image of the old man in his country, displayed at the front of the building. The eulogies resonated with interpretations of his familiar cry to 'make it good for the people' – that in death, as in life – there is always hope. Or as Jack Jangala put it, '*Yapa* (Aboriginal people), we have our say, then we move on.' But first we lay on the coffin and asked the old man's spirit to look after us.

Gathered at the gravesite, it was not hard to imagine his spirit leaving his body and lingering for a while, his final visit to his country. Then going 'straight up', and walking on a road, through valleys of green grass, right up to the gates of Jerusalem in that other *walya* (earth), to be reunited with all his Warlpiri brothers and sisters, and all the people who could be found in all the countries 'as soon as the world bin start to turn around'. Just as he said it would be. That old man. That old Darby.

Jukurrpa: Dreaming

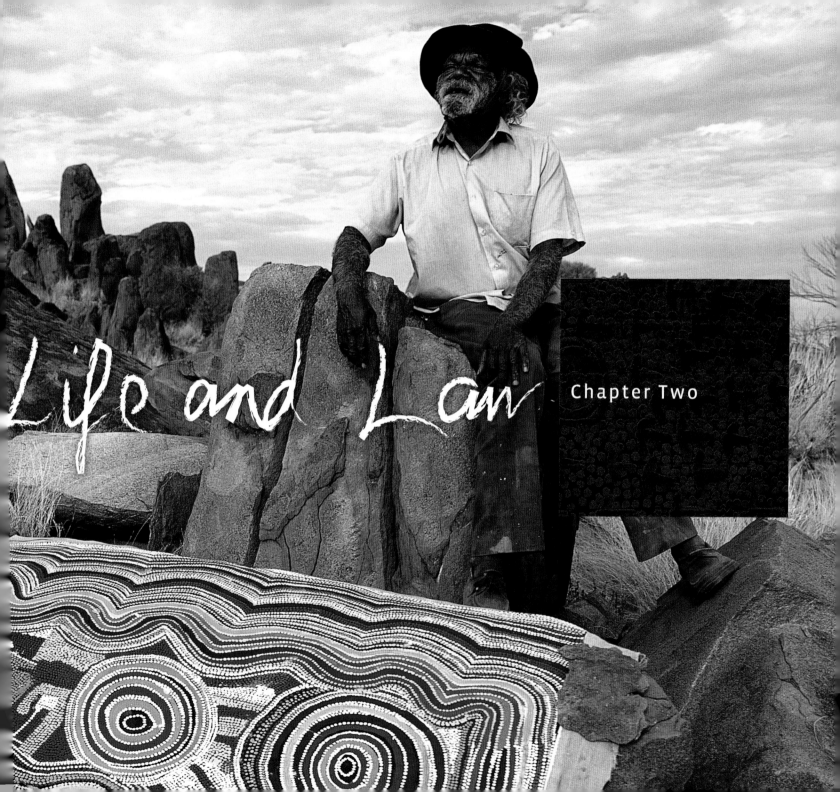

Life and Law

Chapter Two

A Warlpiri man, Darby Jampijinpa Ross was often referred to as one of the last of the old people at Yuendumu to really know the country, the songs, the names of plants and animals, and to have traversed large tracts of land on foot. Many Warlpiri songs, dances, stories, words, pictures and place names have died with him. But the *Jukurrpa* remains.

Jukurrpa can be mapped out on the Warlpiri landscape, and it came to the fore in Darby's thinking whenever he travelled through 'country'. *Jukurrpa* is a Warlpiri word. It does not easily translate into English. Darby spoke of it as Dreaming, the usual translation, and more accurate than Dreamtime, which suggests *Jukurrpa* is limited to a moment in time. Darby also connected *Jukurrpa* to the English words Law and Story, and to that which guides Warlpiri social life. From Darby, in stories, songs and visits to 'country', I understood *Jukurrpa* to be Dreaming, Life and Law.

It is not my intention to present the *Jukurrpa* 'story', but to give the reader a sense of Darby's relationship to it and what it meant to him. It was integrated into his life from an early age and he did not question the stories the old people told him. He had a strong belief in the truth of *Jukurrpa*, its importance for Warlpiri people, and its presence in the landscape. *Jukurrpa* that travelled through 'country' also tied Warlpiri to adjacent groups, like Anmatyerr, Pintupi and Gurindji. To illustrate this, Darby would often remind me that the story of Yarripiri (The Serpent), who passed through Warlpiri country, travelled as far north as Milikapiti (Snake Bay) in the Tiwi Islands. *Jukurrpa* was also a spirit world, seen

PREVIOUS PAGES Darby with
Ngapakurlangu Jukurrpa
(Water Dreaming)
painting at Juka Juka 1989

OPPOSITE Darby dressed
in 'traditional' hairstring
belt 1960s

and unseen, represented by the physical landscape, tangible objects and ceremonies.

It is hard to imagine what life was like in the early days for people like Darby, having grown up with a different sense of the world and little knowledge of life outside the borders of their own 'country'. The sights, sounds and feelings experienced while participating in ceremonies were deeply embedded in his sense of identity and place in the world. Life was affirmed and the world (re)created through the songs and dances. Like his father, Darby was initiated into the deeper knowledge of Warlpiri Law and *Jukurrpa*, attaining wisdom, respect and authority with age. Darby did this during a time of change, yet he continued to develop and maintain a deep connection to Warlpiri Law and *Jukurrpa*. He referred abstractly to his experiences — of ceremonies that he could not talk about in our recordings — often with a hand gesture or sand drawing made after first checking to see if anyone else was watching. He talked about a time when people sang, danced and told stories together, sharing in the commitment of a lived reality. He spoke of sleeping outside, looking up at the stars and the stories told about them while sitting around campfires: of the moon drawing the stars back from the earth to feed in the sky; of Wurdungula frightening the women with his burrowing penis; of love sickness sending the goanna from Mt Theo to Yarripirlangu; of the clouds jostling for position and skidding along the ground as they are blown by Warlura the gecko; of the *Mungamunga* (spirits) who quietly sing and draw men away from their fires to devour them; and of the secret world of men.

Looking north from
Yuendumu hill

There was no escaping these truths. They were in the sky, in the land, in hearts and minds, and in the legs of the dancers and those singing the 'country'. There were no houses to hide in, no electricity to block out the night, no Western tradition to rationalise and explain. It is difficult to imagine a time and place when the most amazing stories, sights and sounds were revealed in the firelight at group gatherings. A time and place where there were places you could not go, people you could not talk to, and where the world was both created and recreated through the songs and dances of those taking part. A time when survival depended upon the knowledge of *Jukurrpa*, Law, 'country', animals, plants and social relationships.

Yuendumu community is in an area of country that holds *Jukurrpa* (Dreaming) belonging to many Warlpiri and Anmatyerr families. For Warlpiri and Anmatyerr people, Yuendumu is on the site known as Yakurrukaji, a soakage associated with the *Yurrampi* (Honey Ant) *Jukurrpa*. Tess Napaljarri Ross explained:

> The name of this place is Yurntumulyu, which is the name of a Dreamtime Woman. Today, everyone calls it Yurntumu (Yuendumu). However, Yurntumu is over there, to the east, where we pass on the road to Alice Springs, beside the hills. Yakurrukaji is the name of the place where the houses stand, where the soakage is. [1]

Yakajirri (Desert Raisin)
sand drawing

There is some contention as to whether the site is on Warlpiri or Anmatyerr land, although the majority concede the actual site of the community is Anmatyerr land. The country around Yuendumu is rich in *Jukurrpa*, including *Janganpa* (Possum) to the south, *Ngapa* (Water) to the north, and *Yurrampi* (Honey Ant) running east–west through Yuendumu. Darby had responsibility and ownership of country to the north, where *Ngapa* travels west, and *Yankirri* (Emu) and *Wardilyka* (Turkey) fight around Ngarliyikirlangu.

The following story is a translation of the Warlpiri version transcribed and edited by Mary Laughren in 1984 and first reproduced in the *Yuendumu Doors* book.

I am telling the story of Turkey who lived at Parirri, and who gathered for himself a big pile of *yakajirri* berries (bush raisins). Now there is a rockhole called Parirri. Jangalas and Jampijinpas lived there. And now it is our country. I have it now.

Turkey was living at Parirri. In the Dreaming, that is. He used to pick berries and make them into big fruit balls. He would gather them and choose the really good ones, the best berries.

Emu was living at Walangkamirirri. Emu lived on the west side while Turkey was living to the east. They used to go gathering fruits around Ngarliyikirlangu. Turkey caught sight of Emu to the west and he thought to himself, 'Yes indeed it looks as though there are some people over there.' Turkey went

and hid in some bushes. 'They might find me and take my fruits away from me.'

So he hid the berries. He dug a hole and buried them. Later on he made them into fruit balls. He got the dried-up fruits and mashed them and made lots and lots of fruit balls out of them. He made really big ones. After that he went off again.

'Oh! I think I'll be able to get some good berries for myself around here. I should always go fruit gathering around here.'

It was that Dreaming who first travelled around in that country. He went a little way south gathering berries. He gathered them into various wooden dishes. 'That's it now. These dishes are full to the top.' Turkey mashed them all and made them into fruit balls.

Just to the west of where Turkey was, Emu was also gathering berries and making them into fruit balls. He was putting them into many piles. When he straightened up he caught sight of Turkey from where he stood on the other side of a tree. He felt very angry towards Turkey, 'I can see him from here all right. He can't see me though. He's not looking this way.'

Indeed Turkey was bent over with his eyes fixed on the ground, busy picking those big ripe juicy berries. He was choosing the best ones and then taking them for himself.

'Ah, this looks like a juicy one!'

He went on gathering berries and making them into big balls. He was hiding them away deep down in the ground. He was acting as though those berries were really his, but in fact they belonged to Emu.

Emu saw Turkey's fruit balls and he thought to himself:

'Well, he's the one who is eating all the best and most juicy berries around here.'

He became very angry with Turkey. 'Here he is walking around in my place. I'll beat him up.' Emu started threatening Turkey. 'He's going to rob me of all my berries,' Emu said. 'How can I eat these ones that he's left? He has taken all the good fruit, only the sour ones are left for me. He comes around here to eat all the nice juicy berries.' So Emu set off to go and have it out with Turkey. 'I'll give him a good hiding right now.'

Emu went east towards where Turkey was. They started arguing first and went on hurling insults at each other. Then Emu took the berries off Turkey. He ran and snatched them away from him and started smashing them to pieces. In his anger he split them into many pieces with his feet and with his digging stick.

He went along smashing all the fruit balls that Turkey had heaped up. Pieces of smashed fruit balls fell all over the place. Those fruit balls which Emu smashed to pieces in the Dreaming turned into those big round boulders which you can see in that country today. After he had smashed all of Turkey's fruit balls and scattered them over the countryside, Emu went away to another place.

Turkey started crying over what Emu had done to all his delicious fruit balls. Turkey felt very sorry for himself and so he set off west to go and find Emu.

'Why did he want to squash all my fruit balls? Why did he want to ruin all my fruits? Well I'll go after him and belt him up right now.'

When he found Emu, they laid into each other. Emu grabbed hold of Turkey and filled his eyes with dirt. Unable to see, Turkey flew away. He headed north across the sky, now blinded. He left all his berries behind and his wooden dishes and shield as well. He left the fruit balls behind him, and now they are still standing there as rocks – rocky hills and boulders which are spread over the ground at that place.

This story which I have related is a true Dreaming story which the old people used to tell, the old Aboriginal people from this place who have gone before us.

There are many other *Jukurrpa* that Darby had responsibility for, always tied to particular sites and often covering a small part of a bigger story. They included the *Pamapardu* (Flying Ants) country to the west of Yuendumu and the *Yankirri* (Emu) sites of Yarlukarri and Rdukarri, an important men's ceremonial area. It is from a *Pamapardu* site that Darby received the name Wanyu. Darby also inherited responsibility for other *Jukurrpa* sites. One of his Jampijinpa brothers was responsible for a section of the *Ngapa* (Rain) *Jukurrpa* to the south of Yuendumu, including an important waterhole called Waturlpunyu. Before he died, Jampijinpa asked Darby to look after his country and his children. Darby recalled the time:

Waturlpunyu (Rain Dreaming place), he's belonga Jampijinpa and Jangala. My brother bin give it, 'You look after all my boy and girl.' Alright, he bin give it (to) me . . . I got 'em here, all my kids.

Darby at Ngarliyikirlangu

Darby had that enthusiasm to go out and be with the children. I remember going out to Ngarliyikirlangu with Darby. On the way, there are some sexy Dreaming sites, part of the Penis Dreaming, where these women cut off this guy's penis and stuck it in the ground. Darby loved telling that story. He reckoned it was a great one to tell white people and a great one to tell kids because it was a really rude one!
ANDREW STOJANOVSKI

It was with some sadness that Darby spoke about this experience because it represented a transaction that would not necessarily have taken place when Warlpiri inhabited the entire landscape. The *Jukurrpa* that Darby had been born into, the responsibilities inherited from his father and mother, and those he was initiated into were the ones that Darby should have been responsible for. The sadness that he spoke about was a breakdown of a tradition: a time when older men and women realised they were not able to pass on their responsibility and knowledge to their children. Many of the ceremonies that Darby spoke about, like the ones that would make the goannas fat or bring the rain, are forgotten, not performed or rarely celebrated today. Darby lamented this. He spoke of whole groups of men dying, and the burden of being old, when your friends and the people you grew up with are no longer with you. He referred to old people in their seventies as 'kids' whom he had known as a young man. He recognised that Warlpiri people were now walking a different road where knowledge of how to survive in the landscape was no longer needed for day-to-day life.

But Darby never questioned the importance of *Jukurrpa*, always hopeful about the possibility of ceremonies being performed, or of visiting *Jukurrpa* sites and collecting the necessary bits and pieces for a particular performance. He spoke of people dancing and singing the *Jukurrpa*, allowing changes within what has always been, and what will be known, where individuals and groups enter a timelessness as the performers collaborate with those that oversee, encourage, chastise, direct, and ultimately blur the distinction between the past and present in the process of (re)creation.

Yarripiri (The Serpent)
painted on *kurdiji* shield
circa 1983

Like many old people, Darby attempted to follow Warlpiri Law with regard to his relationships to others and his responsibilities in holding the *Jukurrpa*. He was at times quite resourceful in his attempts to incorporate less 'traditional' means to achieve these aims. For example, he introduced Christian prayer into the *Jukurrpa* space. The *Ngapa Jukurrpa* tells of an old Jampijinpa man rubbing two white stones together to make rain. Darby was a rainmaker, and like the old Jampijinpa, would rub the stones together to bring the rain. But he would also pray and ask *Wapirra* (God) for rain. This was a different way of 'looking after country', where Darby adopted the ceremony of the church:

We bin ask him, for Father, he want to give me water. Well, he bin give me plenty water. Creeks bin running, rockhole fill it up, soakage fill it up, everything. Green country right up to this way, too. He bin good rain, too. That's why we bin ask 'em Father. Alright, he bin give me water.

Warlpiri ceremonies, including the important men's initiation ceremonies (the *Kurdiji* and *Kajirri*), were to re-enact previous performances, (re)creating the *Jukurrpa* as closely as possible. Ceremony could also be used as a way of resolving disputes and to 'finish

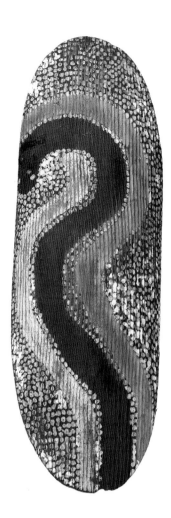

up', to perform the last rites of obligation to a deceased person. One such ceremony is the *Jardiwarnpa* Fire Ceremony that tells of the travels of Yarripiri (The Serpent) across Warlpiri country. In the 1990s, this ceremony was filmed for SBS television. As a senior *kirda* (owner of the ceremony), Darby featured in the telling of the story.

The film opens with aerial location footage of Winparrku (a volcanic plug also known as Blanche Tower) and Warlpiri voices singing (translation), *Winparrku mountain is getting higher...* Darby spoke to the camera as he leaned out of the helicopter circling Winparrku (translation):

The people lifted up that big snake called Yarripiri, and they travelled north. All Yarripiri's people got up and they lifted up that big snake. Dear thing... His name was Yarripiri, that one. They are getting ready and they went that way. They went straight up north.[2]

The singing of the ceremony follows Yarripiri as he travels north. In the film, Darby explained the ceremony to a small group sitting around a large *Jardiwarnpa* painting produced by Warlukurlangu Artists:

This one lying down is called Yarripiri. Where did he come from? He came from Winparrku Mountain. Who followed? The Hare Wallaby followed. He came over to the snake cave. That sacred cave is called Ngama. This one is called Kunyarrpungu. Where is the dog Kunyarrpungu staying? He's also staying at the snake cave at Ngama. Yarripiri is from my father's side. He is both a person and a snake. He is a person. He is my mother's mother's brother. We are very close.

Darby addressed those sitting around the painting:

We are all family and we dance in one group – Jakamarra, Jupurrurla, Jangala, Jampijinpa ('skin' groups). We've got this ceremony, this law, all in one.

During his travels, Yarripiri is tormented by those who prevent him from escaping his nest. He is burnt by fire and grows increasingly angry. In the same way, the *kurdungurlu* (guardians of the ceremony) torment the *kirda* (owners), who are the family of Yarripiri, in their (re)enactment of the *Jukurrpa*.

The Warlpiri sing for days about the travels of Yarripiri and the interaction of the *kirda* (owners) and *kurdungurlu* (guardians) of the ceremony. When Darby was preparing to dance in the climax of the ceremony in the film, he sat with an old man (now deceased), who painted his body, tied a *pukurdi* (headdress) to his head with hair string, branches to his legs and arms, and a flat stone around his neck. The old man spoke about Darby:

Make him 'flash'. He'll be like a young fella! Dance today. Number one. He's older than anybody, this old man. But he's still doing dancing, eh! This one Darby Jampijinpa. He's the one, a good dancer. Good Emu Dreaming. Good on you, my brother! Good one, Darby. You winner!

All night and day they got to dance. All the girl and all the old man got to sing all night. They got to sing right through (to) the daylight. DARBY

Ngajakula ceremony, Yuendumu circa 1969. The Ngajakula is similar to the Jardiwarnpa and is associated with the *Mala Jukurrpa* (Rufous Hare-Wallaby Dreaming) from Mawurrungu. Darby was *kurdungurlu* (guardian) for this ceremony.

Darby was being transformed into the emu that was dancing while the others were burning themselves. Fires were lit, then Darby entered the ceremonial ground, lifting his legs high, pounding the earth with his feet, and dancing as the emu.

Darby knelt down and placed two tightly bound bundles of sticks in the fire. When they caught alight, he lifted them above his head and shook himself as the fire fell on him, while a man stood behind him brushing his body with leaves. Darby placed the fire sticks back into the fire and clasped his hands behind his back before picking them up and burning himself again.

Darby then approached a man who placed a painted *kuturu* (fighting stick) horizontally across his back. Darby clasped it behind his neck and danced, his feet moving fast and body leaning side to side. He walked sideways like a crab, shaking the branches attached to his hips. People were singing (translation): *Yarripiri is getting ready to enter the nest.* More voices joined in. *Jamparli (another snake) is in the nest.*

At the conclusion of his dance, Darby sat down with the Jangala and Jampijinpa men who were singing before the ritual punishment in which the *kurdungurlu* (guardians) for

the ceremony shower the *kirda* (owners) with burning embers.

Following the climax of the ceremony, blankets and money were distributed as payment for the services of the *kurdungurlu* (guardians) and the leader declared: *No argument anymore. Finish!* The film ended with footage of Winparrku mountain and the voices of the Warlpiri singing:

> Winparrku mountain is getting higher
> as it watches Yarripiri
> and all the people travelling into the distance.
> Poor thing.
> It's getting sad for its people.
> Those people travelling look back
> and see Winparrku standing up.
> They are putting yellow ochre on their bodies
> and that mountain makes them feel sad.
> My people are going forever.
> The people are homesick.
> They want to return home.

Darby 'knew' the country and had grown up walking in the places referred to in the *Jukurrpa*. When he danced as the emu in the *Jardiwarnpa*, he was taken to those places in his mind. This 'knowing' of *Jukurrpa* is more than a (re)enactment, or participation as an actor; it is a demonstration and passing on of knowledge, bringing others into understanding and pulling things apart and making them right again.

When Yuendumu was established, and large numbers of Warlpiri were camped together, they had the opportunity to perform ceremonies. But they were removed from the country associated with many of them, and while it was not necessary to visit 'country' to look after it, Darby thought it was important, particularly for the younger generation, that Warlpiri went to *Jukurrpa* sites; that to 'know' them, you had to go there. West of Yuendumu is a place called Mawurrungu. Darby often spoke of it as an important place where 'everyone *kirda* (an owner)' and where many *Jukurrpa* meet. It is also where the important *Mala* (Rufous-Hare Wallaby) *Jukurrpa* begins. Harry Jakamarra Nelson, who has sung the Mawurrungu songs as a ceremonial leader, said it was not until late in his life, when he finally went to Mawurrungu, that he understood them.

Darby had authority over 'country' and ceremonies that he would not have traditionally had, not because he was in direct relationship to them, but because he had participated in the

ceremonies, learnt from the old men, and walked through the country as a child. He knew the country and *Jukurrpa* better than many of their younger Warlpiri owners and guardians. His life participation in these ceremonies connected the *Jukurrpa*, and his presence added an element of depth and experience that was highly valued by those participating.

> There's only one law for Aboriginal people. White people have other law that changes all the time. *(translation)* PADDY JAPALJARRI SIMS

Darby spoke of *Jukurrpa* belonging to everyone — that all Warlpiri had a responsibility to follow Warlpiri Law — and that this could even extend to Whitefellas who visited the community. He often expressed sadness that many of the laws he learnt as a child were less important to young Warlpiri. He saw that land was important to Warlpiri Law, and was concerned about the integration of the 'Two Laws' — Warlpiri Law and Whitefella Law — and that Whitefella Law might one day override Warlpiri Law. Appearing before the Select Committee on Constitutional Development in 1989, Darby said:

> We think the old law is a good law, (but) this time you are mixing both black and white people … They are going to make that law in Darwin in the Northern Territory. If you are going to have this new law we will surely lose everything, including our Dreamings. Well, what are you going to do about the little

boy when he grows up to become a young man? You won't be able to sing at their ceremonies because you don't know. They will also take that from us and the land for good. There are two laws for both black and white people. If they are going to make a decision to have one law, they are going to take everything from Aboriginal people ...

I am telling you now, one day I won't be at Yuendumu. I am just telling you this, you only have one land. Look after it and hold on to it ... Long time ago, in my time, there used to be this law. If we lose it, then they will be after us all the time so that they can take this land from us. The land can't go, the land will always be here ... We have got to have our old law for our land.[3] *(translation)*

Darby acknowledged that initiation ceremonies, commonly referred to as 'men's business', continued to be practised. However, he was concerned that initiation, like the other ceremonies that added the depth and knowledge of *Jukurrpa* and were about caring for the country, might not continue to be performed by the younger generation. He would ask:

What are they going to do? Sit down Whitefella way? They got to think about corroboree now. Learn 'em properly.

Like many of the old men, Darby lamented the lack of interest in ceremonies. Missionary Pat Fleming recalled a time when her husband Tom had returned from a ceremony one afternoon in the 1970s:

I remember the old fellows were having this important 'meeting', as they called it. Some of them were in tears because the younger fellows – the ones say twenty years younger – were not interested.[4]

Rdukarri is a registered sacred site and was an important place for Darby. It holds a remarkable story, illustrated with the marks of many generations of men, and was told and sung with enthusiasm by Darby. He was sad that no one looked after it anymore. He identified strongly with the site, even signing his name on a Warlukurlangu Artists' print depicting *Jukurrpa* associated with Rdukarri by drawing a series of emu's footprints.

Darby did not read or write. When Darby 'writes' it was a figurative or diagrammatic representation related to spatial relationships strongly tied to *Jukurrpa*. He would often draw in the sand when telling stories: concentric circles indicating places, tracks to represent animals, 'U' shapes to represent people, and lines to count numbers. These basic symbols were used to convey more complex meanings when telling *Jukurrpa* stories. At sacred sites, he would rub his hands along the ochre paintings as he sang, or trace the designs in rock engravings as he pondered their significance.

This painting belonga all the old mans. I bin young man sitting around here.
DARBY

The rock shelter at Yamirrringi. Darby claimed the engravings were not made by Warlpiri, but were part of *Jukurrpa*. Although he could recognise many of the symbols, he was not always sure of their significance or their stories. Engravings like these can be found near waterholes, and sometimes etched into low-lying rocks or on nearby walls. They can be found throughout Warlpiri country, but are less common in the 'hungry country' on the northern plain.

When recording stories or sitting at home by the fire, Darby would often break into song. He would sing his *Jukurrpa*: *Ngapa* (Water), *Yankirri* (Emu) and *Pamapardu* (Flying Ant). He told me he knew all the songs and would practise them regularly. He was enthusiastic about teaching them to others, so that they would know how they hold the 'country' and in turn could hold them when he passed on. While travelling, he would use them to navigate, as a commentary, or to evoke a sense of what had occurred over the land. At a sacred site, he would call out to the spirits to announce his presence, then sit and sing the songs. He would talk about how in the past many men would gather at that place to celebrate and maintain their link to the country and its *Jukurrpa*. To the rhythmic accompaniment of the beating of boomerangs, they would sing verse after verse telling the story, (re)creating a spiritual connection to the land and each other. The songs held a special importance and often used language not easily understood by the uninitiated.

It was these songs that Darby would sing to call the country up closer, to evoke a sense of a place and a story if he were unable to go there physically. He would pause to mark the ground, depicting elements of the story to illustrate its movements and the significant sites. But in telling the story, he would always return to the song. He would often lament the loss of these songs, the feeling that he was one of the last old people who still remembered them, and that with his passing they would return to the country, to exist only in memory in the landscape. Those listening to him could not help but feel sad and hope that he was wrong.

When speaking about his support for Warlpiri Media's proposal to film the *Jardiwarnpa* ceremony in the 1990s, Darby said (translation):

That's why we bin learn 'em, learn 'em, learn 'em. So they can't dump away this Dreaming from early days. We don't want to lose this corroboree, the young people have got to hang on. We've been travelling with that Dreaming from early days so that those children don't lose that Dreaming, and so that children from all over the world can see how we still keep that culture and that law . . . we can't lose that corroboree, it's from our grandfather and father. We've got to look after it proper way. We can't lose it. No matter when they take video, that's nothing. It's in the ground, belonging to *Yapa* (Aboriginal people), it's always there. Culture is always kept there, in the ground.

When those old people pass away, those young people can watch that video and they can learn and think about it, and they might dance.[5]

Dental researchers Murray Barrett and T.D. Campbell made a considerable contribution to the recording of Warlpiri *Jukurrpa* and stories in the anthropological tradition in the 1960s. They made audio recordings and facilitated the filming of ceremonies. The archive at the Australian Institute for Aboriginal and Torres Strait Islander Studies (AIATSIS) and Warlpiri Media Association includes many interviews covering a range of topics from the Coniston Massacre and the time before Whitefellas, to the more intensive and detailed recording of *Jukurrpa* songs and ceremonies. Darby is present in many of the recordings, particularly the songs and ceremonies. In 1965, Barrett made several audio recordings of what he called 'The left-handed Emu series' at Rdukarri (Rugari). Roger Sandall, a filmmaker, shot a film at Rdukarri called *Emu Ritual at Rugari*, which is often referred to as recording the last

time the ceremony took place at the site. Darby was present during the filming of the ceremony, the details and content of which are considered 'men's business' and not for public discussion.[6]

Darby worked with a film mob doing a series about Aboriginal culture. Those films are in the Adelaide Museum and some in Canberra. Why did he make that film? It was for young people to look at. He was the main person acting. He made it so the young people can look at them – that's how our people used to walk around and how they lived and how they survived.
OTTO JUNGARRAYI SIMS

We might keep going. Give it to our family. They talk about after, when we finish – our people. PHARLAP JAPANGARDI[7]

Visitors
Recorders and Filmmakers

Thomas Jangala Rice with
Scott Duncan at Juka
Juka 2000

In the 1960s, a group of men, including Darby, gathered at Yuendumu to discuss the problem of keeping men's ceremonial objects at sacred sites and the threat of them being sold or stolen. They decided to establish a museum to house the sacred material. The men contributed some money to the building expenses and work began on constructing the building using local sandstone. They established the Yuendumu Museum Society and obtained a grant from the Aborigines Benefits Trust Fund to complete the work.[8] The Museum was officially opened in 1971 with a special ceremony that included visitors from places as far away as Docker River and the Top End. It was a time for a celebration of Warlpiri ceremony and was enjoyed by the old men like Darby. They created a spectacular ground painting, shared their songs and dances, and played one of the last games of *purlja*, a Warlpiri game played with a hair-string ball.

The Museum became a place where the old men could teach the younger ones, and male visitors could go to learn about Warlpiri *Jukurrpa*. It was maintained by a grant from the Arts Council and visitors to the community would pay fifty cents to enter. Display cabinets, donated by the South Australian Museum, housed various objects, the more sacred ones hidden from view in locked filing cabinets, organised by 'skin' or family groups, and accessed only by the elders. A feature of the museum was the large ground painting that had been carefully created and installed as the centrepiece of the building.

Darby was employed as the museum's curator. He had been a visiting curator at the

In 1988, Darby was photographed in front of the Men's Museum for the 'After 200 years' photographic essay. He was standing next to a pillar painted with his *Ngapa Jukurrpa* (Water Dreaming). Darby spoke about the museum (*translation*): All the old men's things are kept in this one place now. This is not a museum where anyone can go and look. It is a place for men only. These things used to be kept out in the bush. They should not be seen by women and children.[9]

YUENDUMU MUSEUM

South Australian Museum in the 1960s, and now took great pride in showing visitors around the Warlpiri museum and fielding their questions about Law and *Jukurrpa*. It represented an acknowledgement that *Jukurrpa* was important and, even if contained in a building, would survive. But it did not last. After a few years, the museum went into decline. Darby blamed a lack of financial and community support, indicating that the museum's closure was the result of the changing priorities of the younger generation.

When Darby visited the men's museum for the last time in 1997, the door was no longer locked, the roof had rusted out and inside everything was destroyed. He was visibly shaken as he picked through the old cabinets and broken glass, surprised to find two sacred objects. But what to do with them? The people who owned them had passed away. He continued to search and found another broken one, lying in the dust, and wept as he held it.

When researchers recorded audio and visual material of men's ceremonies in the 1950s–70s, Darby was one of the willing informants. Even when Warlpiri became more resistant to researchers and those who would document and photograph their ceremonies and sacred sites, Darby would enthusiastically communicate aspects of Warlpiri *Jukurrpa*, considered by some men to be off-limits to the uninitiated. He had a strong desire to record his knowledge for future generations, in stories and songs, the meaning of Warlpiri words and the significance of *Jukurrpa*. He spoke of *tarruku*, the sacred objects that had been taken from the country, those he had seen in the museum's 'down south', and those that had been returned from the South Australian Museum.

When Thomas Jangala Rice, George Jangala Fry and Johnny Japanangka Williams visited Melbourne Museum in 2002, they saw the statue of Baldwin Spencer encased in a glass cabinet. They were told that he had collected a lot of the museum's Central Australian collection, and were asked to identify the origins of some of the material. They were surprised to see the extent of the off-site collection, which was not reflected in the small amount of material on public display in the museum. They also recognised and identified many of the sacred objects as being from Warlpiri country, and George opened discussions about having them returned for use in ceremonies. He was told such negotiations take time, as the museum must ensure they are returned to their rightful owners. But George was concerned that they be returned soon, while there were still people who could identify them. He has since passed away.

While Darby spoke about young people not caring to learn about *Jukurrpa* or ceremonies, he hoped that there would be more interest in the future. He always made an effort to contribute to and attend Yuendumu School's bilingual and cultural programs. He worked with linguists Mary Laughren, George Jampijinpa and David Nash (among others) to record stories for publication in the school's printery. Darby was an enthusiastic participant in the school cultural days, when the old people would teach children to make boomerangs or paint and dance *Jukurrpa*. He would attend school 'country visits', when the community would spend a week living with family groups at outstations, giving children an opportunity to learn more about Warlpiri culture and history. Darby compared this to the time when he was growing up and the old men were teaching him:

They're following Law, their Dreaming, (they told us), 'Ah, you gotta learn about!' Old peoples, old mans, while they bin learning we (teaching us). They're worrying, long time ago, and they're thinking about for all the 'young man' – they come along and they got to come see 'em that Law … That's what they bin doing, long time ago.

While a belief in *Jukurrpa* continues in the hearts and minds of young Warlpiri, with the passing of each generation, some prior knowledge and understanding are lost. The art centre has become important as a place where the older men and women have the opportunity to record their knowledge for future generations. The artists paint on canvases and record their stories so that young people will learn them and become close to their *Jukurrpa*. But many of the older people lament the loss of the more complex elements of Warlpiri language and social relations, the lack of ceremonies, and the changing priorities of the community. While there remains a great deal of respect for older people and a willingness to learn from them, young people do this with competing interests and obligations. While the older men and women like Darby pass away, they hope that the younger generation will have access to the knowledge that they have recorded in their paintings and stories.

He worked closely with the school with cultural things. Taking the kids out. He used to take us out, all the young boys. And he showed us how to make *palya* (spinifex wax). He showed us how to make spears. He showed us how to keep our culture strong. Corroborees and all that. He done a lot of work with the school, writing a lot of stories, getting them written down for future use. We can look back and see the things that he has done. OTTO JUNGARRAYI SIMS

Chapter Three

walking a

It is rare to meet someone who will take you far from what is familiar and inspire you to walk a different road. Rarer still, when that person is seventy years older than you and whose life experience is very different to your own.

I was fourteen years old and part of a school exchange and language-learning program when I met 'old Darby'. I remember him as the old man who let us camp in his backyard. He gave us all 'skin' names so that we would fit in, and sat on the ground telling stories about his life, at times becoming animated as he related the details of some epic adventure. I enjoyed listening to him, and he told me to come back anytime. So four years later I did. He told me more stories and said I should buy a Toyota – a 'really big one' – and come out to Yuendumu to live and record them. I eventually moved to Yuendumu, bought a Toyota (a big one as it turned out), and began recording and transcribing his stories. I had no idea of what I was getting myself into.

We usually sat on the ground to record the stories – in the sand so that Darby could draw. Or we went out bush, sometimes hunting, sometimes visiting a site he wanted to show me. When Darby told his stories, he constantly referred to 'place', using directional markers or referring to one site in relation to another. He was often concerned with the details of, and relationships between, particular geographic formations. If there was a site Darby and I had not visited, he would tell me he 'had to show' me that place, pointing in its direction or drawing its location in the sand. On these trips it often

Recording stories at Darby's new house, Yuendumu. From left, Banjo Jungarrayi Tex, Darby and Liam

occurred to me that it might be the last time Darby would visit the country.

It was important to Darby that I understood how the country held the stories and that particular places belonged to particular people and how these were the places he walked as a child and knew intimately. While visiting different sites and sitting down and listening to Darby tell stories about them, defining who he was in relation to them, I was conscious that I did not look at the country the same way. I did not know the stories well enough to make connections between them, and I had a different way of conceptualising space. As we drove through 'country', I was marking features and roads and creating a map of the landscape that was very different to the one Darby had in his mind. However, for Darby, there was a sense that I now 'knew' these places, through the process of visiting the country and listening to his stories. This was a different way of 'knowing' or 'learning' to the one I was used to. The 'knowing' Darby was passing on was not usually tested by others — more often, it was affirmed through further participation in a telling of a related story, or on another visit to the site.

We travelled extensively through Warlpiri country, occasionally heading further afield onto Anmatyerr or Pintupi country. Darby once tricked me into taking him on a longer trip. He had been sent reluctantly to Alice Springs for an eye operation, and when I saw him, he told me that it was over and he would like to visit his son Pilot in Alekarenge. So, not knowing that he was avoiding the operation, we headed north. Darby appeared to be well known in the area as we had to stop several times as carloads of people waved us down and Darby got out to sit by the side of the road and talk to them. At Alekarenge, we discovered that Pilot was not there, but met Darby's other 'son', Joe Bird. Joe was a short man who wore a feather in his hat, and was accompanied by eight little chihuahua dogs. He told me that, like a lot of his Jangala brothers, Darby 'grew him up', and that, like Darby, he was a 'rainmaker'.

People used to refer to Darby as a rainmaker. When it was dry and we were sitting in his camp, he would sometimes talk about things I didn't understand, like rubbing these stones together to bring the rain. It was the responsibility of the Jampijinpa and Jangala men.

Over a three-year period, we travelled to the sites associated with the Jangala-Jampijinpa *Ngapa Jukurrpa*, traversing country north of Yuendumu, from Wanulpuru in the east, to Mirawarri in the west. Darby came on the earlier trips, but then it was Thomas Jangala Rice as *kirda* (owner), and Paddy Japaljarri Stewart and Jack Jakamarra Ross as *kurdungurlu* (guardians), who would lead us. Sometimes we drove on the road, and other times we drove in a straight line through mulga scrub and boggy sand for hours to find a rockhole. It was important to the men that we visit the sites. They wanted me to know the country, too. They wanted to put it on a map to 'straighten 'em out properly',

Ngapa Jukurrpa

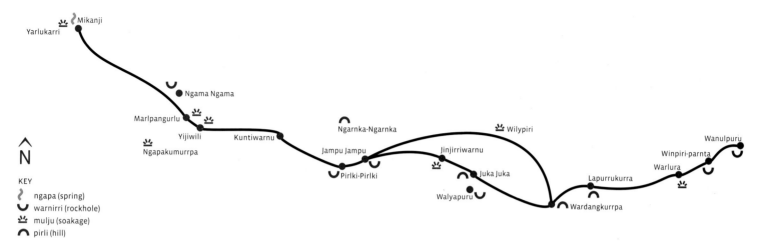

KEY
- ⸜ ngapa (spring)
- ∪ warnirri (rockhole)
- ⸭ mulju (soakage)
- ⌒ pirli (hill)

even though Paddy complained about my GPS (global positioning system) that would record the location of the sites. He thought it was cheating — how I could return to a site without knowing how one place was connected to another. He said, 'Sometimes, *Kardiya* (Whitefellas) are no good, no good at all!' Although, he was the most concerned with finding the GPS when we lost it in the scrub, eventually blaming *mirlalpa*, the spirit beings who look after the country.

It was on these trips that I learnt that *Jukurrpa* exists in more than *kuruwarri* (*Jukurrpa* designs), songs or places. 'Knowing' the *Ngapa Jukurrpa* is not just knowing the story, what the country looks like, or where the sites are located. The *Ngapa Jukurrpa* is also in the experiences of travelling through the country. When I look at *Ngapa* paintings, listen to accounts of *milpirri* (rain clouds) and *mangkurdu-pampa* (blind clouds), hear the songs about Marlpangurlu or Mikanji, or even just stop at a rockhole to drink — that's *Ngapa Jukurrpa* all the way.

The following is written as an account of the *Ngapa Jukurrpa* that begins at Wanulpuru and ends at Palyamilpingi. It is written in a style that reflects contemporary storytelling and my experience of the *Jukurrpa* journey:

To the east of Yuendumu, at a place called Wanulpuru, there is a body of water where Warlpiri people used to stop and drink. It is a deep rockhole set in a low-lying elongated granite outcrop facing south. During 'business' (ceremony) time large groups of people would stop there. Darby used to stop there when he did the mail run from Coniston to Mt Doreen.

Standing by the water, blue hills can be seen in the distance to the east. The *Ngapa* (Water) came from there. From Warlaparnpa and Wanirri, Wurdingirri and Pirlpajilpungu, where lightning struck the ground and created a large rockhole. The *Ngapa* travelled west to Yukurrukurru, where lightning struck again, creating Ngirijarliti. In 1928, this was where the 'big trouble' started. It was also where *kartirli-kartirli* (two female ants) sat down and were struck by lighting, leaving behind two hills called Kurduripa, resembling the mounds made by *kartirli-kartirli*. All this happened to the east of Wanulpuru where another *Ngapa*, a storm from Kalipinpa, travelled through Waturlpunyu and on to Laramba (Napperby).

From Wanulpuru, the *Ngapa* rose up and travelled west to Winpiri-parnta, the place 'where they get that *kurlarda* (spear)'. Another rockhole is there. The spear trees grow all about that place, near where Jack found the Whitefella Frederick Mitchell had perished so close to water a long time ago. Today you can see his white cross from the road.

The storm moved to Warlura, where there is a soakage and a tree which is *larrpa-nyayirni* (real bone), a strange ghost gum with three flat trunks, next to an old one that has fallen over. Not too far away, Warlura the gecko stands with arm bent in the form of *wirrkali*, a bloodwood tree. He stands as if to turn back, as if not to continue heading west, to the place where there was a soakage, now part of Warlura dam.

Warlura, the gecko, who lived there, did not want the rain to stop. He blew the *milpirri* (rain clouds) and *mangkurdu* (clouds) further west. He went to Yinilkimpi, then on to Puntarungarnu, south of Lapurrukurra, where the *mangkurdu-pampa* (blind clouds) attempted to stop. Darby broke into song when we travelled through this *Ngapakurlangu* (Water) country. He pointed to the rock formation you can see from the road; it is where the *mangkurdu* stopped to rest for a while. But Warlura the gecko kept blowing and blowing. Then he stood and watched the storm. But he was struck by lightning and thrown into the air, landing head first in the ground. That tree at Warlura (the place) is this gecko.

The *milpirri* and *mangkurdu* travelled to Wilypiri, where two creeks join and soakage water lies beneath the sandy surface. Downstream is the large waterhole where Warlpiri kids like to swim. From there, *kurdu-kurdu mangkurdu* (small childlike clouds) 'sat down' at Juka Juka to let the larger ones pass. They camped there, leaving the rocks that point to the sky and one that points west, indicating the direction the storm went. Darby was the senior *kirda* (owner) for this site.

At Ngarnka-Ngarnka, the *kurdu-kurdu mangkurdu* sat down again before moving on to Pirlki-Pirlki where there are fourteen rockholes. These rockholes were created by *milpirri* and *mangkurdu* as they skidded along the ground attempting to sit down against the force of Warlura's wind behind them. The *wirnpa* (lightning) followed up the hill to the west of Pirlki-Pirlki.

But before Pirlki-Pirlki, they visited Jinjirriwarnu, and Jampu Jampu, another rockhole. The lines in the rock there are *wirnpa* (lightning). Thomas often walked through here as a child, stopping for a drink with his mother during the time when they worked at the Mt Doreen wolfram mine.

At Kuntiwarnu, the *Ngapa* place to the west of Pirlki-Pirlki, Thomas found a tree he used to sit under as a young boy. It had fallen over and died. In the distance he pointed out a large river red gum in the creek. When he was a boy it was a young sapling. He dug down into the sand in the creek and found the soakage water. There is water in soakages along this creek, all the way through to the country at Kantiwarra, where it 'never dries up'.

It was at Kuntiwarnu that a Whitefella used to keep Warlpiri people in tents. There were three tents. One for Whitefellas, and two for Warlpiri. All the women were camped in their own tent. That Whitefella was really 'cheeky' and wouldn't let the men near the women. Darby remembered trying to sneak into the women's tent and the Whitefella singing out, 'Get out. Get out!'

Darby, Jimija Jungarrayi, and Jack Ross used to take the mailbag from Coniston to Mt Doreen and would stop at Kuntiwarnu on the way. One time, old Jimija was tied up for two days. Old Bullfrog Japanangka used to 'sit down' there with a big mob of nanny-goats. It looks different now that the cattle have made a mess of the country and new trees have grown up.

From Kuntiwarnu, the *Ngapa* went on to Yijiwili where there is a big rockhole on the northern side. Not too far to the west is the large rockhole at Ngama Ngama where the big wind started. To the south is Marlpangurlu, a soakage in a creek. *Ngapa* used to be there too, a long time ago. Mayawunpa, the big wind, came from Ngama Ngama through here, just like that 'cheeky' Whitefella who cut the road. He was a grader driver. His name was Alan Kennedy from Queensland. Thomas used to cut wood for him, and they would have lunch at Marlpangurlu.

A little further south is Ngapakumurrpa, near that big bean tree where there is a soakage. That old road goes there, and you can see emu there, on the other side. To the west, the *Ngapa* travelled through Wirriyajungu, a soakage south of the Tanami road. It's like Wilypiri again, and Whitefellas used to get water from there.

From Pirlki-Pirlki, Marlpangurlu and Wirriyajungu, the *milpirri* and *mangkurdu-pampa* travelled to Mikanji. The water used to be 'right full', and there were lots of soakages. But Wally Braitling had the old station there, among the ghost gum trees. It was Jack that first showed him where it was. Thomas thought, 'that *Kardiya* (Whitefella) bin spoil him', because there is only a dry dam there now. Old nanny-goats used to live in a yard there, not too far away. Darby brought a lot of horses through Mikanji on his way to Pikilyi one time, and people used to walk from Mikanji to Coniston, or even right through to Conner's Well.

To the west of Mikanji is a big sandy creek called Yarlukarri. It was here that the Emus came in from Walanpirri and Karlingkaturu, this side of Yunnga. It was these emu places – Yarlukarri to the west, Ngarliyikirlangu to the north and Rdukarri to the south – that were important to Darby. The Yarlukarri soakage is right in the centre of the creek. It is always 'living there'. All the emus can smell that water, and they dance around that place. That's why they made the open country around Yarlukarri. In Warlpiri, *yarlu* means open place. But, Yarlukarri used to be a dangerous place. Children couldn't look at it. It's covered up now, because a Jampijinpa man once took stones from this place and got sick. His family had to come back and talk to the *kuuku* (spirits) before he got better again.

Back at Mikanji, the *milpirri* and *mangkurdu-pampa* mixed with the spring water and grew strong. They went to Mirawarri, west of Yarlukarri, to fight the Jupurrurla and Jakamarra rain that was coming from the west. They were fighting at Mirawarri when a storm came and stirred everything up. When Warlura, the gecko, joined the fight, a brown falcon called Kirrkarlanji picked up everyone involved: *milpirri* and *mangkurdu*, Warlura, springwater from Mikanji and the Jakamarra and Jupurrurla rain. Kirrkarlanji took them from Mirawarri to Palyamilpingi and dumped them there in the swamp.

Meanwhile, at Kalipinpa, a Jampijinpa man was rubbing two stones (*mikawurru*) together. He mixed the white powder with water in a rockhole, called Pinkapu. Jampijinpa threw the ochre into the air to make the rain, which travelled to Puyurru where it attempted to camp. However, Kirrkarlanji the bird picked up the rain and took it back to Palyamilpingi again.

After visiting the sites, and with Darby's part of the story finished at Mirawarri, we headed

back to Yuendumu as Jangala told us about his father, who was *kirda* (owner) for Milkirriparnta to the north, where there is a large depression and is the place where the *Ngapa* went deep into the ground. But that's another part of the story.

I once visited Darby in hospital in Alice Springs after it had been raining for some time. We could see the MacDonnell Ranges from his window, and they were covered in green grass instead of the usually dry, yellow spinifex. Darby told me all the different names for the grasses. There were so many. I had been 'rained in' at Nyirrpi the week before and I told him about how one of the men there had seen 'bush people' coming into the community and using the taps. One man and two women with no clothes. Darby considered it for a moment, then gave me a serious look and said simply, 'Pintupi mob'. Then he started laughing, and I told him about Japangardi's car that got stuck in the road halfway to Nyirrpi: the road turned into a river and the car got bogged, Jangala knocked himself unconscious with the 'kangaroo jack', and then the water ran through the windows and carried mud that filled the car and silted up around the gearstick. They had to dig it inside-out.

When Darby was too old to continue to record the stories, he handed the responsibility for the project over to others. Adhering to a Warlpiri methodology, he identified Thomas Rice as *kirda* (owner) and Paddy Stewart, Paddy Sims and Jack Ross as *kurdungurlu* (guardians). It was important to know that we were doing things the right way, and that there was a collective ownership over the material. For Darby, it was another example of passing on his knowledge for others to hold.

Darby wanted his stories recorded, written down, and passed on. He wanted them known. His enthusiasm extended to the suggestion that I attach a loudspeaker to my car and drive around the community playing the recordings. That made sense to Darby. Speaking many languages, he understood the power of the spoken word. He was so enthusiastic about recording his stories that he once asked me to leave a tape recorder with him when I went away for the weekend. When I returned and we listened to the recording, it began with Darby concluding a story, then starting another which he addressed to 'all the people in all the countries'. He showed me how he had recorded his 'really big story', enthusiastically turning the tape over and over and over. It was times like these, when I explained to Darby that the tape recorder doesn't work like that, that we would laugh about the differences between us. Darby had a deep knowledge of the country and an understanding of things that I would never know, and I understood the technology and the way things worked in my own culture. It was the cause of much joking between us, and for me they would later be times of reflection. There are many more examples during our time together when I was the one who didn't understand, when I was the 'silly bugger'.

Thomas Jangala Rice at Juka Juka

Visitors

Promoting Warlpiri Culture

Thomas Jangala Rice is Darby's brother's son. In Warlpiri society, he is considered to also be Darby's son. Thomas has inherited much of Darby's responsibility for *Jukurrpa*, is also involved in the Baptist church and sits on various committees at Yuendumu. Like Darby, he has travelled promoting Warlpiri culture. Thomas, Jack Ross, Samson Japaljarri Martin and I travelled to San Francisco in 1999 with Warlukurlangu Artists to create a ground painting installation at the museum. While trips like this are an opportunity to exchange knowledge and understanding, they can also be an opportunity for the travellers to enjoy the freedom that exists outside of Warlpiri society. When we arrived in America, Jack became upset because he thought everyone was tricking him about the time difference. We left on a Monday and, having spent fourteen hours on a plane and crossing the international dateline, arrived on the

same day. How could that be possible? Jack just couldn't accept that. He was quite old then, but he joked about finding an American wife, and Thomas teased him during the two week trip whenever he saw a potential Napaljarri, usually a woman twice Jack's size: 'What about that one, Jakamarra? Might be too big, can't fit 'em long suitcase!'

There was an opportunity for an exchange with the local Native American people in San Francisco. We travelled to the 'woods' outside the city and met an older lady who led us to a waterfall. She stood next to the creek and sang an eagle song. As she finished, an eagle circled overhead, and the men sang a Water Dreaming song to celebrate. Thomas describes the encounter (translation):

We went to a place close to San Francisco with the Indians from there. Their rituals were really interesting. They smoked us with some herb that they waved in the air. They took us to a place where there had been a massacre. We walked quietly to that place. They carried smoking herbs, sacred herbs. They threw a rock that touched the surface of the water. We all took part in this. We went up to a spring where there had been a battle. The Indians had hidden in the hills there. We all sat next to the spring. They smoked us before we could eat. We sat quietly for about half an hour before they would let us eat. Then somebody came along with a branch, sweeping that place. Then a fresh breeze came up. It was calm before that – no wind. The smoke had gone along, following the creek, that's how it looked, up to where the spirits of the dead people were.

We walked about 3kms to another place. We went up several levels to different sites where the Indians had hidden from the *Kardiya* (Whitefellas), we went right up. After the wind came through, I could see lots of horses around. I hadn't noticed them before. It was like there was a haze or fog there and the wind blew it away. There were horses everywhere after the wind. Maybe they had been hiding in the bushes before that. It was late in the afternoon when they came.

A very big eagle came when we got to the top of this place. The eagle came close to us. We sang the *Ngapa* (Water) *Jukurrpa* song. The water ran faster when we sang that song. The further up we went the people looked darker. At first they looked pale like *Kardiya* (Whitefellas), then like *yapukaji* (half-caste), and the higher up we went the people looked darker. The bloke who was their leader put on a traditional outfit and danced for us. They all stood up to say goodbye to us. There were a lot of them. They surrounded us saying goodbye. It was like we were in a mustering yard. We were surrounded by them.[1]

On another trip (to Melbourne), I was asked to introduce a member of the Royal family to Thomas, but as I wasn't really sure who he was, I explained in Warlpiri that he was an important man from England. I later discovered he was Prince Andrew. But Thomas doesn't remember him. Although, he does remember that people were very friendly, particularly the old man with no shoes who talked to him on the street. We walked around the city in single file, one Whitefella leading three men dressed as cowboys. Young men would pull up in their hotted-up cars and, recognising Thomas from the *Bush Mechanics* television series, would get out and shake his hand.

We stayed at Collins Street Baptist Church as a guest of the Rev. Tim Costello. I eventually gave in to George Jangala's pleas to visit the casino, thinking he wanted to play the pokies, but the men simply walked through shaking their heads. Upon our return to the church, we shared the lift with Tim, who asked where we had been, and George proudly told the anti-gambling minister that we had gone to the casino!

One time I arrived at Darby's house surprised to find him reading his Warlpiri bible. Up until then, I had thought he didn't read, but there he was thumbing through the pages. Then I realised he was holding the book upside down. He liked books and would collect them. He would sing as he held them, and touch the photos. He would ask me to find a book he had seen and photocopy some of the photos of places where he had worked. He enjoyed books of Aboriginal art or life stories of people like Clifford Possum and Albert Namatjira. He said that, though they had passed away, people remembered them.

Yuwayi palija, (yes, should I pass away) alright, they can still hear about (my story). One fella from Hermannsburg – that Anmatyerr man. Him bin draw 'em 'bout rock, and a lot of trees, and big waterhole, too. He bin draw 'em 'bout, that Jungarrayi (Namatjira). That good reading that.

At some point — it might have been while we were sitting outside his house, out bush looking for an old soakage water, or exploring a bookshop in Alice Springs — I made a promise to old Darby. This book is the fulfilment of that promise. It is a record of the life of a unique Australian; one who lived for a hundred years through a time of great change.

Darby lived his life attempting to find inclusion and understanding across a cultural divide. He did this with generosity and respect. I called him uncle and friend; he called me nephew and Japanangka. He was a teacher always ready to learn, a leader who encouraged participation and an elder who had the spirit of someone much younger. In *No road (bitumen all the way)*, Stephen Muecke wrote:

... getting to know may mean leaving home and getting lost for a while, to admit that there may not be a road going anywhere that we all agree on, but that somewhere along that road is a local guide who knows a story that leads to a place.[2]

I identify with this statement on a personal level. I often did not understand what Darby was telling me, even though I have spent much of the last ten years talking with him and exploring the Warlpiri landscape, language and culture. However, I hope this book reflects what I always felt the project was about — beyond the academic, the historic, the artistic — a friendship between one man who was willing to share stories about his life and another who was eager to listen and learn. Knowing on the one hand we were communicating across cultural, generational and experiential barriers, Darby and I also just enjoyed sharing our lives — with a good yarn, a cup of tea, a freshly cooked kangaroo, or out bush looking at 'country'.

In 1984, following the introduction of Warlpiri Media's pirate television station at Yuendumu, Darby testified at the Australian Broadcasting Tribunal Hearing at Kintore. He was concerned that outside television broadcasts might undermine tribal law (translation):

In the olden days, Aboriginal people didn't have any satellites. They only had their traditional law on their tribal lands . . . now people chasing after them with satellites to interrupt their tribal law . . . that's why we got the land back, to keep away from European things.[3]

Darby travelled to Kintore in the company of several men, including researcher Eric Michaels and Francis Jupurrurla Kelly, who recalled the trip:

We travelled to Kintore for a conference about satellites and for the ABC film *Fight Fire with Fire*. That car – Toyota FJ45 ute – the clutch got burnt out west of Mt Liebig. Andrew Japaljarri Spencer was driving because he reckoned he knew the country, and we were all sleeping in the back. Next thing we heard this grinding noise – the pressure plate giving out.

I had to take that clutch out and old Darby had an idea. He cut these sticks and made 'em like a little boomerang – little tiny clutch out of mulga. I just put 'em in then and we kept going. We got there and we came back with that same Toyota. Only one gear all the way.

That was the first time I saw it. I got that idea for *Bush Mechanics* – you know that television program we put on the ABC – from old Darby! He was really Bush Mechanic that old man! And old Jack Jakamarra, he told me that story, you know, when he was a youngfella following that car track for the first time. He didn't know what made that track, couldn't understand – no *kuna* (droppings) – he didn't know about cars that time!

Visitors
Bush Mechanics and Satellites

Film still of Francis Jupurrurla Kelly from *Bush Mechanics*

Chapter Four

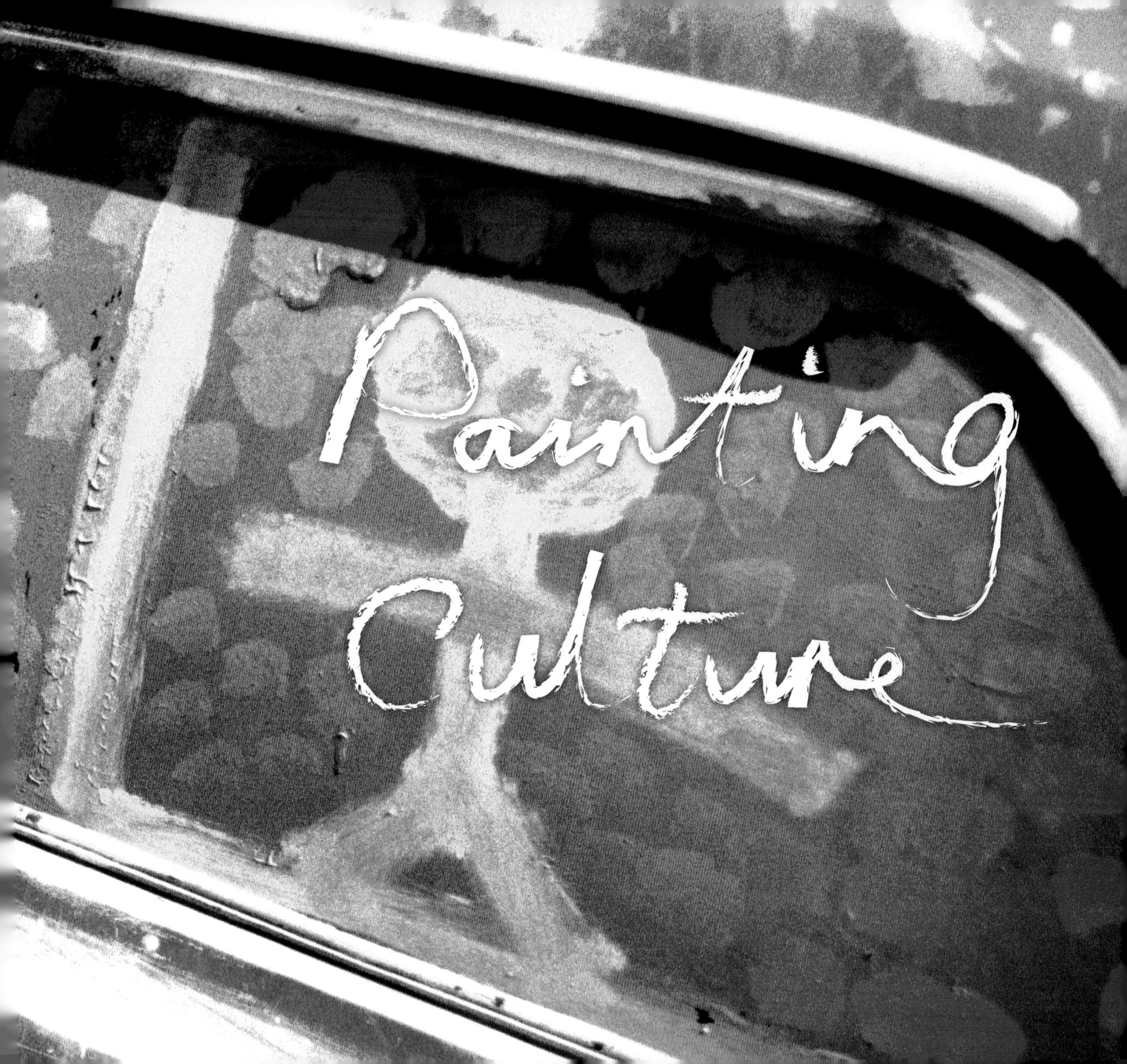
Painting
Culture

Warlukurlangu Artists Aboriginal Association is a Warlpiri-owned arts enterprise of which Darby was a founding member. He saw it as a place where he could document his *Jukurrpa* (Dreaming) on canvas, teach the younger generation about Warlpiri culture and welcome visitors from outside the community. Characteristic of their strong sense of identity, the artists chose a Warlpiri *Jukurrpa* for their name and determined that the art centre would place the interests of its members, drawn from the community, over those of the market or other interested parties.[1]

The name Warlukurlangu comes from a Fire Dreaming to the south and west of Yuendumu and translates as 'belonging to fire'. In the following story, Darby refers to the old Jampijinpa man, who deceived his two sons into thinking he was blind, as Blue Tongue, Lungkarda (the Warlpiri word for blue tongue) and Pampa (the Warlpiri word for blind).

We talk about here for the Law. We're telling that Fire Dreaming from the early days, as soon as this world bin come, long time ago. Whitefella call em Fire Dreaming, and Aboriginal people – *Warlu Jukurrpa*. That's Law, and the Fire Dreaming place where they bin get burnt long time ago. That's why we're telling the story. We're telling Fire Dreaming.

We call 'em Lungkarda. Whitefella call 'em Blue Tongue (Lizard). That's a *cheeky* one, that one. Old man, him bin sitting round over there, not too far away. About eleven miles from Yuendumu. And that's why we're here, telling story.

The painting is one way to show the outside world that we are a surviving culture.
OTTO JUNGARRAYI SIMS

That two man, two Jangala, while they bin travelling around. What they bin do, that two Jangala? They bin get up morning, and carry 'em woomera (spear thrower), and a lot of spear. Carry 'em with the finger. That's the way they bin only do 'em, long time ago. Soon as this world bin come. And that fire, 'Uhm, uhm, uhm, uhmmm' . . .

That kangaroo (is his totem), he belonga that Blue Tongue, belonga that Lungkarda (old man). And that two youngfella never see that kangaroo; they might go and catch another kangaroo – 'outside' kangaroo. Outside kangaroo! And they bring back and give it that old man.

'Hey, blind now! Pampa'. Him blind, that Pampa, that Blue Tongue. He's cunning man that one. He never bin like that two youngfella, that two Jangala. (Even though) any time they bin go catch kangaroo for him. They bring 'em back, give a bit of kangaroo, longa that old man. Oh, big mob of kangaroo! They put 'em *one-a-line* (side by side). And another, his brother again, he put 'em another *one-a-line*.

That old man, him cunning, too. Him bin only go, he got a spear and woomera. Oh, catch how many? Twelve kangaroos! He bring back and cook 'em (for himself). Cook 'em quick! That two youngfella, he don't want (them) to see him.

Him bin all the time look, that old man, that Blue Tongue man, that Lungkarda. That's why we're telling. We dance that story, painted up, long time ago. We bin painted up there, and (the elders) bin show (me).

Alright, that fire, him bin coming out from underground. That fire bin burning there, longa underground. And him bin look, 'hello', he bin light, him bin burning inside. That's Fire Dreaming. From that way, *yatijarra* (north), this side from Tennant Creek. That's Fire Dreaming, too. That same one, him bin coming here now, longa Warlpiri country. And that one, him bin get burnt, longa Warumungu country. Alright, him bin burnt. All over here, he bin coming round underground. Burn all the way. He bin light this one here. He bin have a firestick. He never bin light it. He bin just go like that, and he bin light! Big burn there now.

Alright, make it little bit long way (skip to the end of the story). That two Jangala bin coming (back) from hunting. Another one bin coming here, another one bin coming just behind again. That fire, while he bin light 'em, he bin chasing longa that two. Nother one bin swing 'em round that way, take 'em back. Fire bin chase 'em. Oh, what to do?

That two youngfella, fire bin chasing now all the way. And what to do? Him bin chasing round, burn 'em everything. *Wirliya* (feet) too, this one here, him bin burn 'em. Oh, poor bugger, him bin burn here. Him bin chasing all the way. That fire bin close to him. That Blue Tongue bin looking out: 'Oh, look at this!'

That fire, that two youngfella. Half Warlpiri here, and half Pitjantjatjara people that way. All the 'red ochre' man now. We're telling that one, that story we tell 'em, true word. And from there, him bin burnt 'nother side from Adelaide somewhere. Him bin chasing all the way. And he bin go, bring back again. He bin follow 'em every way. That fire bin burn 'em.

That fire bin chasing round. Right back again, coming right to Fire Dreaming here, longa

My name is Paddy Japaljarri Stewart. We painted the *kuruwarri* (*Jukurrpa* designs) on the Yuendumu School Doors in 1984. It took a long time.

We paint at the Warlukurlangu art centre now. We've been putting our *kuruwarri* on canvas for a long time. We can't leave our *Jukurrpa* behind; we have to keep it alive.

We only paint the *kuruwarri* that belongs to our family, not someone else's. We've been doing this for a long time so that our young people can learn. The young people know their *Jukurrpa*. The *Jukurrpa* that belongs to their mother's father, father's father and mother's mother. (*translation*)

Warlukurlangu (the place). And people, we're frightened from that one, Fire Dreaming. We no want to touch 'em tree there. No good, no good at all.

And from there, all the way from Amata, 'nother side from Ernabella, him bin chasing all the way there. And he bin coming straight into Amata (in) Pitjantjatjara country. And still he bin chasing, that fire bin there. He bin burn all the way. Oh, two fella got a sore everywhere. Swell up everywhere, from fire. And this one nothing now, no skin, that fire bin burn 'em.

Alright, two fella bin come, while they bin coming through to Amata, and coming straight. 'Ah, that fire there!' Same one, that fire bin chasing all the way. And they bin coming straight in (to) Wayililinypa. You know, that outstation over there. They bin coming all the way, longa the desert, that two youngfella there, coming: 'Haaaa, haaaaa, haaaa, haaaaa' (breathing). Alright, two fella bin coming this side from Wayililinypa Outstation. They call 'em Ngarna. There now, (they) bin come there. Alright, big claypan water there, and that Dreaming. And this two fella bin go round there, little bit sore foot. And two fella bin finish (die) right there. Two brothers, two Jangala finish. Rocks there, now. That true word. And very, very no good that one.

The art movement began in the early 1980s. In 1983, Edith Coombs observed Paddy Japaljarri Stewart (who was the school janitor) painting over the graffiti on the doors at Yuendumu School and suggested to the principal that some artists paint them with *Jukurrpa* (Dreaming) designs. They approached Paddy to coordinate the project, as he

The *Yuendumu Doors* painters

From left, Paddy Jupurrurla Nelson, Roy Jupurrurla Curtis, Paddy Japaljarrri Stewart, Paddy Japaljarri Sims and Larry Jungarrayi Spencer

had been involved in painting the Papunya school mural in the 1970s. Paddy agreed, and with the approval of the school council and the support of the teachers, asked some other men to assist him.

Twenty-seven *Jukurrpa*, representing over 200 Warlpiri and Anmatyerr sites, were painted on thirty doors by Paddy Japaljarri Stewart, Paddy Japaljarri Sims, Paddy Jupurrurla Nelson, Larry Jungarrayi Spencer and Roy Jupurrurla Curtis. They worked with big brushes and acrylic paint. Paddy Stewart worked on twenty of the *Doors* and has since become strongly identified with the project.[2] Although Darby was not involved, he often referred to his ownership of some of the designs and thought it was good for the young people to see their *Jukurrpa* in the school. Edith recalled the community feeling about the project:

> Everyone was very pleased with the results, and the idea worked initially. For all the rest of the time I was at the school there was no graffiti or other damage to the doors.[3]

Much has been written since about the meaning of the doors and what they represented, most critics taking a romantic view of the original intention of the project or musing about the cultural meaning of doors to the Warlpiri. Paddy later spoke about what the *Doors* meant to him (translation):

> For the kids to know their own Dreaming, from their own Grandfather. We take the kids out to their countries and tell them their *Jukurrpa* and show them around the sacred sites, so in the future they can pass it on to their children.[4]

Tess Napaljarri Ross expanded on this in the introduction to the *Yuendumu Doors* book (translation):

> Many people told the children about the Dreamtime by drawing on the ground and on paper; they told them a long time ago in the bush by drawing on their bodies, on the ground, and on rocks. This was the way men and women used to teach their children. Now, when children are at school, at a white place, they want to pass on to them their knowledge about this place. They want them to keep and remember it. They want them to learn both ways – European and Aboriginal. They want them to see the designs, the true Dreaming, so they can follow it on the land, hills and on the shields, boomerangs, nulla nullas, spear throwers, and on other things.[5]

For twelve years, the school council rejected outside offers to purchase the *Doors*. However, in 1995, with the *Doors* deteriorating and the graffiti reappearing, they were

Yuendumu Doors before they were taken away, 1995

From left, *Yarlakurlu (Big Yam)* Paddy Jupurrurla Nelson, *Warnakurlu (Snake)* Paddy Japaljarri Sims, *Karntakurlu (Women)* Larry Jungarrayi Spencer, *Watijarrakurlu (Two Men)* Paddy Japaljarri Stewart

acquired to be held in trust by the South Australian Museum. After undergoing extensive restoration, they toured the country as the *Unhinged* exhibition, where they were presented as ominous, floating objects in a dark tomb, with few clues as to their real significance to the Warlpiri.

A small market for paintings developed in Alice Springs in the early 1980s. Françoise Dussart, an anthropologist working with the women at Yuendumu, supported their efforts to paint *Jukurrpa* designs on small boards, *parraja* (coolamons) and *tururru* (clap sticks). Meanwhile, adult educator Peter Toyne, anthropologist Eric Michaels and artist Mark Abbott supported the men in the early stages of their canvas production.

After the painting of the *Doors*, men and women began to paint together and produce small to medium-sized works. According to Paddy Japaljarri Stewart, only men were allowed to use dots in their ceremonial designs, while women used lines in *Yawulyu* (women's ceremonies). It was the men who gave permission for the women to paint with dots.

The colours used by the artists reflected those used in Warlpiri ceremonies and 'ground paintings': *ngunjungunju* (white), *karrku* (dark red), *yurlpa* (red), *karntawarra* (yellow) and *maru* (black). Early works were painted in these ochre colours, imitating the style of the Papunya Tula artists and sold by word of mouth.[6] However, when a small grant for materials was received from the Aboriginal Arts Board, some large colourful paintings were produced, and the Yuendumu artists' distinctive style emerged. A successful joint exhibition with Papunya Tula in Darwin created some controversy over the Yuendumu artists' use of a 'non-traditional' palette.

Ngapa manu Yankirri Jukurrpa (Water and Emu Dreaming) 1999
Darby Jampijinpa Ross
Etching 51 x 61 cm
Printer: Basil Hall,
Northern Editions
Edition: 100

The Warlukurlangu Artists Aboriginal Association was officially incorporated in 1986. It had a strong directive to alleviate:

> ...significant unemployment and the consequent social and economic problems by:
> i. encouraging the production of artwork amongst its members.
> ii. acting as an agent for buying and selling artwork made by its members ... arresting social disintegration within Aboriginal society by supporting the use of traditional designs and methods and arranging the exhibition and explanation of the said products or performances.[7]

An active ceremonial life has been a feature of Yuendumu from the early days, and activity at Warlukurlangu Artists reflected this. Many of the men and women who painted at the art centre were also leaders of men's and women's ceremonies. The artists had a strong desire to paint *Jukurrpa*, ensuring appropriate Warlpiri relationships of *kirda* (owners) and *kurdungurlu* (guardians) were followed and reflected the social and

cultural obligations present in ceremonies and day-to-day life in the community. The *kuruwarri*, the iconographic elements of a painting that held the story, were painted first and scrutinised by others for their adherence to *Jukurrpa*. The dotting that filled the canvases was less important, and many artists developed varying styles of application and experimented with different colours while maintaining a consistency in their presentation of *kuruwarri*.

With the support of Felicity (Flick) Wright as coordinator, and Bronson Jakamarra Nelson as her co-worker, the art centre soon developed into a successful enterprise with group exhibitions in several states. A committee elected by local members was established with a strong sense of community control and collective identity. The domestic Aboriginal art market continued to grow, and the Yuendumu artists became well known for their production of colourful works and their documentation of the *Jukurrpa* that accompanied every painting. As an international market slowly emerged, the artists began producing the large, collaborative works for which they are now well known.

Warlukurlangu Artists developed into a successful enterprise representing over 300 Warlpiri and Anmatyerr artists living in Yuendumu (and to a lesser extent Yuelamu, Willowra and Nyirrpi). The art centre brought money into the community and

ABOVE Warlukurlangu Artists with *Liwirringki Jukurrpa (Burrowing Skink Dreaming)* large canvas.

OPPOSITE *Yankirri Jukurrpa (Emu Dreaming)* 1987 Darby Jampijinpa Ross Synthetic polymer paint on canvas 121 x 91 cm National Gallery of Victoria, Melbourne

became a place where local people could go to talk to the old people or access cultural information. Andrea Nungarrayi Martin provided a consistent administrative presence for subsequent art coordinators, while establishing herself as a successful artist in her own right. Chairman Paddy Japaljarri Stewart became a strong advocate of painting as a means to document *Jukurrpa* for subsequent generations of Warlpiri, as well as to communicate Warlpiri culture to a wider audience (translation):

> Warlukurlangu is for kids, too. Where they can learn their grandmother's and grandfather's
> Dreaming... All the people started painting now. All the women and kids, all come to paint.
> We taught the kids to paint. They come and paint at Warlukurlangu.[8]

Darby was one of the founding and long-term committee members of Warlukurlangu Artists. Before painting for the art centre, Darby produced works for private sale or as gifts. While he occasionally painted iconographic representations of bible stories, it was his *Jukurrpa* works for Warlukurlangu that were widely exhibited and acquired by collectors. However, Darby was little affected by his success, other than occasionally expecting a cheque to come his way. Like many of the older artists, he was not as concerned with painting for market expectations as with communicating the *Jukurrpa* of his paintings. He was an artist who developed further a skill already acquired in Warlpiri ceremony. His

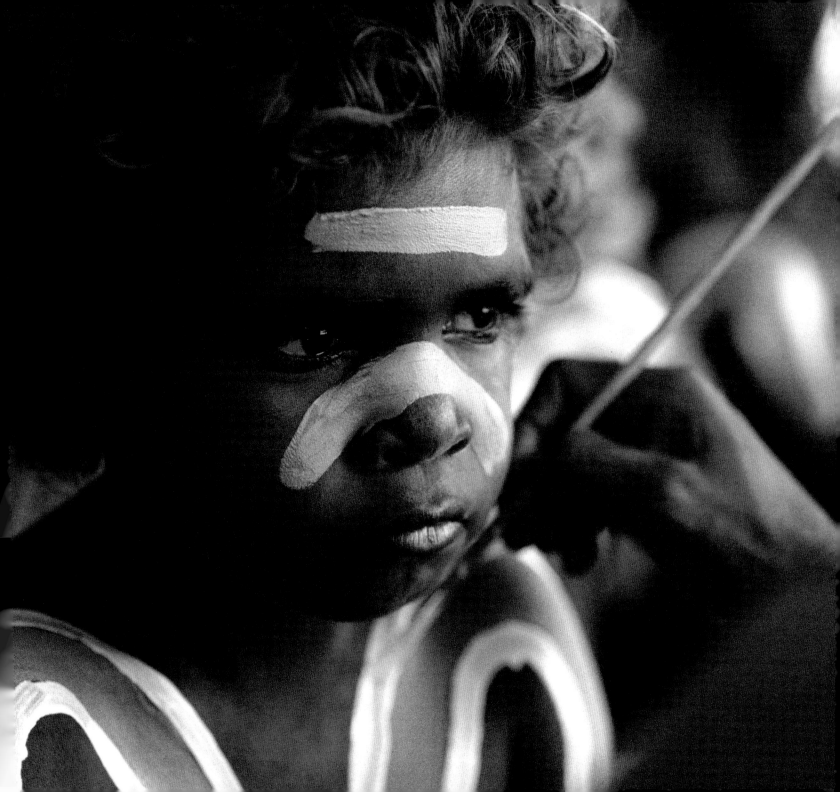

early works resemble Warlpiri ground paintings, although he seldom restricted himself to a 'traditional' ochre palette. Darby developed an enthusiasm for bright colours. His canvases were filled with pinks, yellows, greens and blues; but it was the *kuruwarri* that held the story, the imprint of *Jukurrpa* upon the landscape, that was at the heart of every painting.

> I think the overall impression you get is that all his life he really wanted to understand things and learn about why people are different ... and people look at his paintings and they think they are done by a youngfella, because they look really modern. They say, 'It's not very traditional.' But they don't know that he was one of the most inventive, most educated ... that is the gift Darby had. SUSAN CONGREVE *(art coordinator)*[9]

Darby's commitment to the stories that his paintings depicted was evident in the way he spoke about the landscape. Standing amongst a group of nondescript rocks and spinifex, Darby would declare, through word and song, his 'country'. The hills around Ngarliyikirlangu came alive with his stories. He named the rocks, pointed to a particular tree that was important, a place that was to be avoided, or another to be visited and maintained. It was in this context that Darby would tell the *Jukurrpa*: the emus dancing at Yarlukarri, the floodwater covering the country at Jinjirriwarnu, or the fire that chased the two Jangala men from Warlukurlangu. He would also point to the places where

ABOVE *Kurdiji* shields from Yuendumu circa 1975. The shield on the right was made by Darby and the design represents an emu chick.

OPPOSITE *Ngapa Jukurrpa (Water Dreaming)* circa 1960s
Darby Jampijinpa Ross

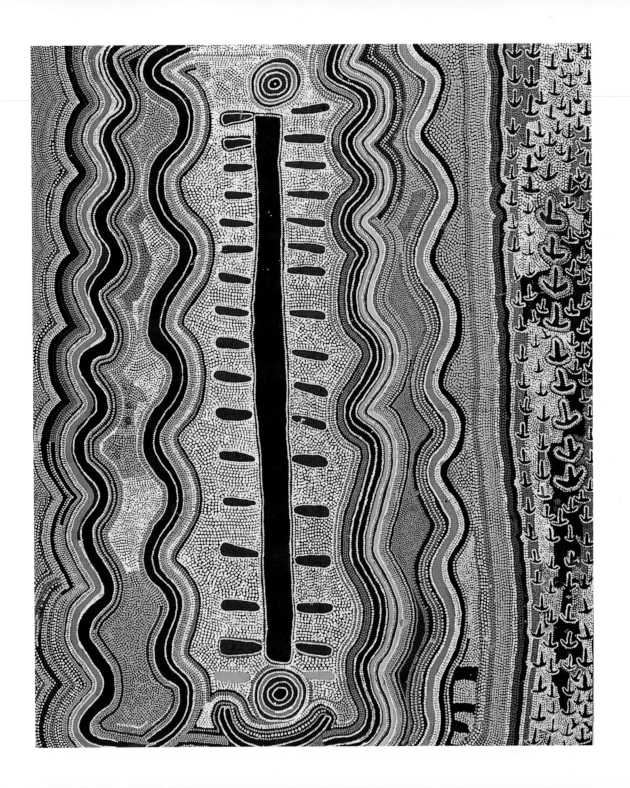

people used to live, collect water, or where ceremonies were once performed.

These are the stories and the country that Darby would paint; country that held many *Jukurrpa*: *Yankirri* (Emu), *Pamapardu* (Flying Ant), *Liwirringki* (Burrowing Lizard), *Yakajirri* (Bush Raisin), *Watiyawarnu* (Acacia Seed) and *Ngapa* (Water). They are the stories that were the *kuruwarri* that formed the basic design of his canvases; each one just a small part of a much bigger story. Sitting outside the art centre, he would often sing and tell these stories as he painted. He would become animated, using hand gestures and sound effects. With paint dripping on the ground, his arms outstretched, Darby would mimic the flight of the giant bush turkey, pointing dramatically in the direction of its flight.

In the 1990s, Darby lived with his wife Ivy in a besser brick flat between the mission house and the art centre. He would shuffle over each morning for a cup of tea. It was a ritual enjoyed by all the old men. The art centre was their place, and removed from the day-to-day politics of the community. If someone brought in some boomerangs to sell, they would want to hold them, rub their hands down the sides, and pass judgment on their quality. If a freshly painted canvas arrived, they would watch and listen as the artist told the story to one of the workers. Once the artist left, the men would either tell the art coordinator that the artist hadn't got the story quite right, or give it the thumbs up: 'Really strong *Jukurrpa* that one!' For the old men like Darby, Jack Ross, Paddy Sims and Paddy Stewart, the painting's real value was in its representation of *Jukurrpa*.

Each day the men would join the women on the back veranda and paint. Jack would sit with his dogs and sing as he painted the *kuruwarri* with a brush. Paddy Stewart would grind his teeth and rock back and forth as he applied the dots with a little stick. Paddy Sims' grandchildren would watch him lay out all his film canisters of paint before he began, then laugh as he knocked them over one by one as he painted. All the old men's clothes were covered in paint: little dots on Paddy Stewart's shoes, thumbprints on Jack's hat, and smudges of colour on Paddy Sims' T-shirt. Darby would often sit with them. They talked about *Jukurrpa*, instructed the children as they painted small boards, drank cups of tea, laughed a lot, and flirted with the women.

Sometimes the artists would ask others to work on their painting. As long as they were the ones who painted the *kuruwarri*, it didn't matter if someone else helped them finish it. This could be quite frustrating for art coordinators who, while sympathetic to the practice, were also trying to sell paintings in an increasingly competitive marketplace, one that didn't always accept two different painting styles on the one canvas. But to the men and women who painted at the art centre, the ownership and responsibility of *Jukurrpa* was a collective one, and did not belong to any one person. This is one of the reasons why the artists enjoyed working on the large, collaborative canvases. This is not

*Ngapa manu Yankirri
Jukurrpa (Water and
Emu Dreaming)* 1989
Darby Jampijinpa Ross
Synthetic polymer paint
on canvas
152 x 183 cm

to say that they were not aware of market expectations; they knew that their works would achieve higher prices if they completed their own canvases.

His eyesight failing, Darby began to rely more on Ivy to help him finish his paintings. Sometimes Ivy would take it upon herself to paint the whole canvas, then not liking the result, would paint over it and start again. She would do this a number of times before the art coordinator arrived to see how Darby's painting was getting on and was presented with Ivy's, by now, very thickly painted original 'Darby'. The art coordinator would then either accept the painting as one of Ivy's, or if Darby had painted the story and Ivy finished it, they would both be acknowledged. On the last ones he did paint, Darby was always concerned with the *kuruwarri*; the vibrant, colourful dotting that usually filled his canvases was less important, and he was content to lay down only the story. Darby's last works for the art centre were a series of etchings, a screen print and a few of these *kuruwarri* canvases. To produce the screen print, Darby painted on twelve sheets of acetate over a period of many months. He found it difficult to see the *kuruwarri* through all the sheets and the dots soon became stacked on top of each other. As a result, it was a painstaking reproduction for the printmakers at Northern Editions but, in the end, was a satisfying result for Darby, evident as he signed them.

By retirement, Darby had produced over 120 documented paintings for the art centre. He exhibited extensively, and many of his works are now held in major public galleries and collections around the world. He left a lasting record of his country and its *Jukurrpa*, and was among Yuendumu's most highly acclaimed artists.

Jack Jakamarra Ross at Warlukurlangu Artists 2001

Visitors
Art Mob

Susan Congreve, art coordinator in the 1990s, recalls Darby's enthusiasm to connect with a wide range of people:

He remembers details about people. I've never met someone so respectful and courteous and interested in what other people have to say. Often when people came into the art centre, they started off with the 'what was your life like' kind of thing to Darby, and they would end up telling Darby their life story ...

The last really big trip I did with him was out to Kunajarrayi. And while he found it really taxing, he was so determined to go out there and be part of it. And he also came out – the diplomat that he is – when (Senator) Richard Alston and Brian Kennedy (National Gallery of Australia) came out. He was there when I first got the phone call and we started to chat about it. He really wanted to go. And when we did go out there, we stayed the night and had Darby wrapped up in these big blankets and a big fire, and he sat down and told Richard Alston all about the place and what an important person he was for it and why ...

Chris Anderson (of the South Australian Museum) promised Darby that he would send up some old display cases for the men's museum ... and actually Darby sent him a fax. Darby came in really, really irate, and – not angry, but really determined – he said, 'Nampijinpa, I need a bit of paper and I need a pen.' I gave him just a plain bit of paper and a pen. 'No, no, no – not that bit of paper. I need a bit of paper with the picture on the top.' The Warlukurlangu picture. So, I pulled out a piece of letterhead and he just wrote 'Darby' in really huge writing across it. I plonked it on the fax machine and sent it off. And Chris is such a busy man – it's rarely ever that I get a reply phone call within two or three hours – and within five minutes he's on the phone going, 'Darby sent me a fax!?' And Darby's like, yeah of course that's going to happen, I need to talk to him. We'd tried a few times on the phone and it hadn't worked. So he must of thought no bugger that ...

Darby painting a plate for *Yankirri Jukurrpa (Emu Dreaming)* 2001

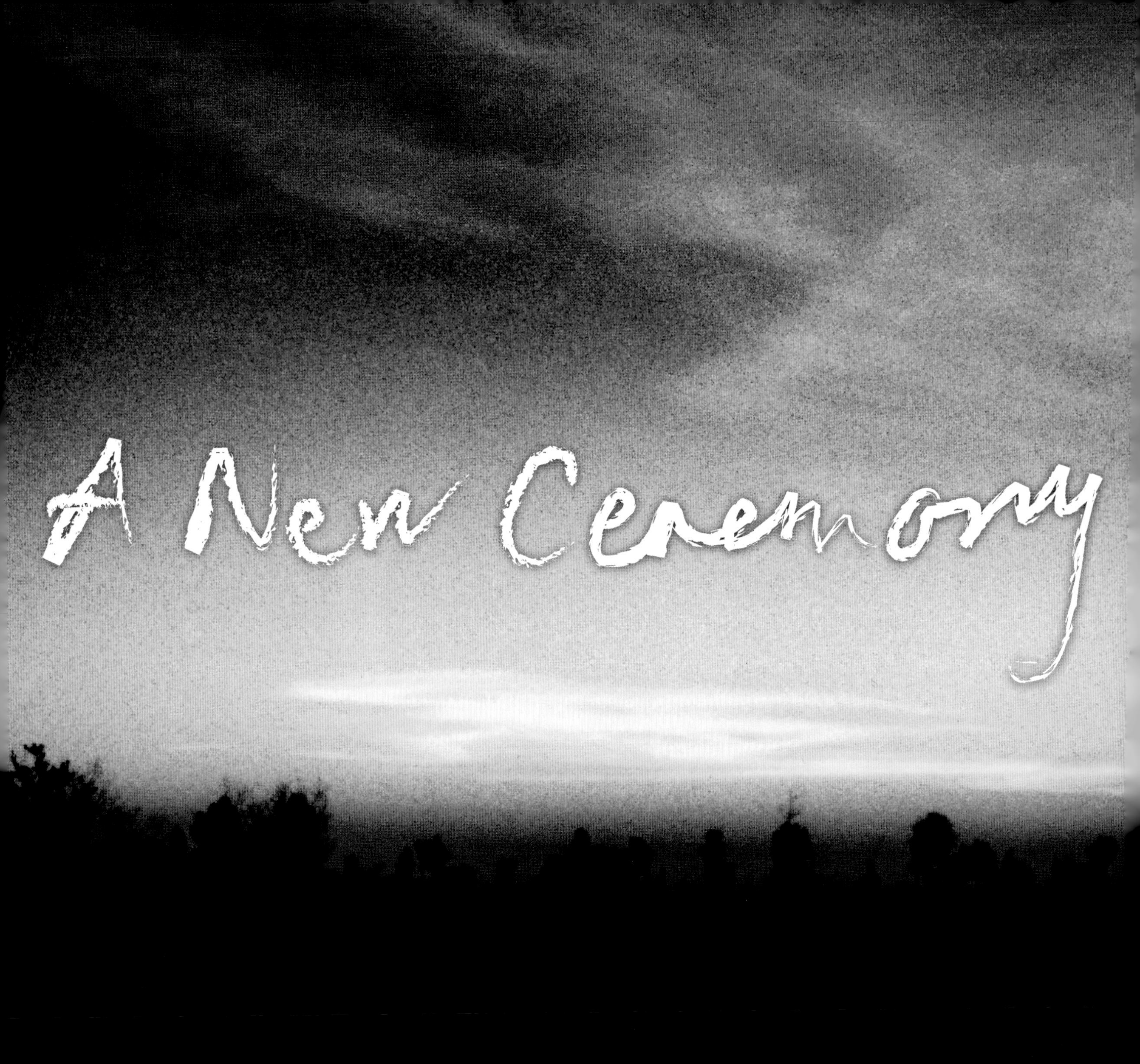
A New Ceremony

Chapter Five

Darby talked about having a cross on his chest that identified him as a Christian and sustained his long life. It was not the visible scars of men's ceremonies, 'sorry business' and knife fights, but a cross 'inside', like a spirit living in him. He prayed to *Wapirra*, the Warlpiri name for Father and God, and embraced Christianity, negotiating his belief with Warlpiri Law and *Jukurrpa* (Dreaming). Darby would draw in the sand to show a road joining 'two *walya*' (two earths): the one in which he was living, where *Jukurrpa* existed in a physical and spiritual dimension and the one to which he would one day go, where he would see his *nguru warlalja* (countrymen) again. It is this second *walya* that Darby associated with the Christian heaven.

When I asked Darby what happened to Warlpiri when they passed away, he told me about how the people at Panma, west of Kunajarrayi, used to build burial platforms in trees — *karntirirri* — for people when they died.

Alright, they're crying. All the old mans reckon he gone, never bin see 'em more. He gone, altogether. He going to *yaru* (up high), longa heaven. Follow 'em all the old mans. They tell 'em, he gone. Your uncle gone. And another one bin say, yeah, your brother finished, now. And they put 'em in the tree. They put (wooden) rail here, from gum tree. Body got to go that way. Got to lay 'em down flat. From there, *munku* (stomach) gone.

That sap (blood) run down the tree, and that body (spirit), he reckon going up – straight up – as soon as they die. That belonga Aboriginal people.

Darby being painted for dancing in the Jardiwarnpa ceremony 1992

Soon as everything finished, they got to sneak up and have a look again (at) that dead man. (Carrying) bushes, they got to look – *manparrpa* (spirit of the dead person). Soon as they look that *manparrpa*, they got to take him down.

They're crying now, everything. They pull 'em out bones. They get 'em out that bones and bury 'em in the ground. Them bones, head and all, they bury 'em good way. After that, they got to get a kangaroo for everybody. They got to have a 'party'. They call 'em *kula-tirnpa*.[1] All right, everybody got to have that meat. And that *pirlirrpa* (live spirit) – Father – he coming back again. He got to pick 'em up that dead man, and take 'em back to *yaru*, longa heaven.

What is yaru?

Yaru we call 'em *yilkari* (sky). *Wapirra* (God) got to take 'em to him. Him go like that (open hands), *kankalarra* (up high), longa heaven.

And old Darby?

I'll be going! Should we die – Christian people – they're going to heaven, longa Father country, good country. While we're here, I'm still feeling strong. I'm not weak, I'm still strong. What to do? He taking our life, and He give it to wind. Power – inside. He got a cross here, inside. That's why we're alive.

What are you going to do in heaven?

Oh, no more anything. No work. Green country, and good place, too. Father standing there, longa gate. Big gate all around. That bitumen (road) there coming, and he got to follow that road. Should me die? I go straight in. They'll be cry about behind now (laughs). Sorry about behind.

Camel train, circa 1942

Rosie Nangala Fleming, Darby's niece who married his friend Jimija, remembered seeing a Whitefella coming to Cockatoo Creek when she was a little girl:

Someone came on camel to Cockatoo Creek. All the girls looked, 'Who's that man travelling on camel?' Come through Coniston to the soakage at Cockatoo Creek. Missionary playing accordion. We bin say, 'What is this?' He was singing Jesus song.

I think missionary – first one – all came to Cockatoo Creek. We bin sitting down there west of the soakage. He was pointing up to the sky. Might be God sitting in the sky? He was clapping (his) hand. He bin point with his finger.

First church travelling from Adelaide, got a camel. Travelling round in the bush. We bin up and down Mt Doreen – Coniston – Napperby. That three. We sold dingo scalps. Before Yuendumu.[2]

Ted Strehlow visited Coniston Station in September, 1932. Strehlow, the son of former Lutheran Pastor Carl Strehlow of Hermannsburg, was officially engaged in academic research at the time. Darby claims Strehlow travelled west to Yurnmaji, and pointed to the Lutherans' interest in establishing a mission on Warlpiri land at nearby Pikilyi, in which case it is possible that Darby is also referring to Lutheran Pastor Albrecht,

who travelled to Pikilyi in 1930, or Pastor Kramer (of the Aborigines Friends Society) who accompanied Strehlow on his journey to Coniston, and would travel to the nearby stations teaching hymns. In any case, Darby would have associated Strehlow with the Hermannsburg mission.

I talk about for Hermannsburg, for Mr Strehlow. Strehlow bin here, coming to catch a big mob of camel. Coming through to Coniston. We're telling story, while we bin see it, long time ago. Early days, before Yuendumu. We seen him down at Coniston. I bin working there.

Alright, him bin coming through to Brooks Soak. Oh, lot of Aboriginal boy bin there. Everybody working. And we keep big mob of camel, longa Randal Stafford's Station. We tell it this story, true word. That's what we learn for work, early days. One hundred years, I'm still alive longa this countries!

That Mr Strehlow, him bin coming to Cockatoo Creek. Him bin camp there, and he bin get the water, and give drink for camel. True, him bin camp there. Morning time, while he bin clean up camp, he bin go and get the camel, and go right up through to Yuendumu. Only this Yuendumu settlement (not) here, before this – early days. He go right through to Yurnmaji. Before the (Mt Doreen) Station, that Mr Strehlow, him bin say they want to make 'em Aboriginal church – Lutheran church there. Long time ago, that's what they bin telling. Him bin put the 'number'. Him bin put 'em down 'number' there. He bin see 'em lot of Aboriginal boy there. They bin running away from him. (They're) only naked, no clothes. All the naked people, they bin running. Reckon they frightened from camel.

Alright, that 'number' – that Mr Strehlow – he bin put 'em in the tree. 'R', him bin put 'em that one. That's long time ago. He bin put 'em down (on) the tree.[3] We bin camping there (later), behind for him (laughing). We bin put 'em same number. Same one! That's straight for you, this word.

Darby's earliest encounters with Christianity were with Lutheran Pastor F.W. Albrecht's Arrernte congregation at Hermannsburg in the 1920s. Darby was a young man then and visited because there was a drought, some of his family were camped there, and he had heard that there was a ration depot. He listened to his countrymen's stories about the Lutheran mission and the Whitefellas that spoke another language and talked about their God. This intrigued Darby and he stayed in the area for some time.

Darby also encountered Christianity at Phillip Creek Settlement. Established in 1944, in response to the large number of Aboriginal people living nearby, Phillip Creek was run as a mission school and ration centre by the Aborigines Inland Mission (AIM) until the Native Affairs Branch took over in 1951.[4] Darby had stopped there occasionally during droving trips and camped with other Warlpiri. He was baptised in the Manga-manda waterhole that was not far from the mud brick buildings of the mission.

We bin longa Phillip Creek, longa Tennant Creek. All the time work there stockman. That's where we have church all the time. Mr Long bin there – Whitefella.

Alright, this story while we bin 'missionary', long time ago, longa Phillip Creek. All my mob Warlpiri there. I say that's where we bin have a church, where we become a Christian. I bin have a baptism down a waterhole. Big mob of people bin there. Some fella they no come to church, (only) little mob bin there. Well just the same here (at Yuendumu). Just the same, little mob. Lot of people sitting round the camp, they never come.

Alright, I come down from Phillip Creek, and we be over longa Tennant Creek town. Nother missionary there, too. All the time we go early in the morning, and work round, longa that mission house, down Tennant Creek. You know, digging (hole) belonga toilet. We fill 'em up bucket, we tip 'em out. Everywhere we digging there, cover 'em up. That's the way we bin only work – Aborigine and Whitefella. There we work to him. Aboriginal 'boy' now I bin working. Early days.

In April 1950, the Rev. Tom Fleming, with wife Pat, took over as Baptist missionaries at Yuendumu. On his return to Yuendumu in the early 1950s, Darby developed an interest in the church and became friends with the Flemings. Pat recalled meeting Darby, and remarked that (at the time) she didn't know '. . . exactly where he came from but he was a very, very clever gentleman'.[5] Although from vastly different backgrounds, it is not hard to imagine why Darby and Tom formed a close bond. They may have

We bin have meeting long time ago, and they bin give it for the Father. This land they bin give it. DARBY

OPPOSITE LEFT Dedication ceremony for the church ground, Yuendumu 1967

OPPOSITE RIGHT Tom Fleming and Darby

initially found it difficult to communicate on a level that satisfied them both, but they would have enjoyed exploring each other's traditions. Darby would have listened to Tom's stories of being in the army, and Tom would have been intrigued by Darby's tales of growing up in the bush and working as a stockman. The bible stories that Tom shared would have resonated with Darby's knowledge of *Jukurrpa*, which he discussed with Tom on their occasional trips out bush.

For fifty years, Darby was a cornerstone of the Warlpiri church and a strong advocate of the Baptist tradition at Yuendumu. In a somewhat practical but also symbolic gesture, Darby eventually made his camp in the missionaries' backyard. People would come for prayer and he would welcome them with a smile and a wave, beckoning them to sit with him and share a cup of tea.

Christianity gave Darby another frame of reference for his life, solidifying his already strong sense of place and purpose. It also gave him common ground on which to establish relationships with people outside his community. They were fascinated by the meeting of his Warlpiri beliefs in *Jukurrpa* and Law, and his Baptist-influenced, yet distinctly Warlpiri, Christian beliefs. Darby reconciled the two in his life and spoke with great conviction and ease about *Wapirra* being 'boss over everything', while firmly believing in *Jukurrpa*. He did not see the two as mutually exclusive or contradictory; he did not feel he had to give up one to believe the other. Darby's sister, Uni Nampijinpa, explained it simply as 'Wapirra is Wapirra' (God is God).

Church services were still being held in the old tin shed when Tom Fleming spoke to the community about building a new church. However, before this could be decided, land needed to be set aside. Tom Fleming tells the story:

> On Sunday evening, April 30th, 1967 almost the entire population gathered as the sun was setting. The Elders sat facing the congregation, but one old man was missing. A hurried visit to his camp found Freddy Japangardi naked and asleep. He was hurriedly awakened, struggled into his clothes, and whisked over to the waiting people. After the service was opened with prayer ... Darby Jambidjinba then said (translation), 'This land to our Father we give it, happy we give it to Him. To our Father, all of us know Him, we give this land to our Father?'
>
> The congregation answered, 'Yes.' 'Do you Elders hear me?' 'Yes,' reply all present.
>
> 'Well then we give the Father this land, of one mind we give it to Him, our land to the Father God.' 'Yes,' reply all the old men.
>
> After he had prayed, Darby then made this further speech. 'Our land we give Him. Let no older brother, mother's mother, or mother's mother's brother, let them not covet or regret. We give it to our Father on high. Do you hear and understand me?' All responded 'Yes.' Darby then prayed, 'This land we give it fully to Him, understanding what we are doing. Let us not regret giving it to our Father. To our Father of eternity we give it to Him, the land to our Father, we give it forever, for good.'[6]

Once the site was chosen and dedicated, the congregation began raising money to build a church. Work began in 1967 and the new church building was opened on March 10, 1968. Over 700 people attended and Darby again officiated and turned the key to open the church. Later that day, it rained and the country flooded, the symbolism not lost on Darby.

On Easter Sunday 1968, Darby was among the first three people baptised in the new church. A week later on April 21, the church was officially constituted with 150 people attending. Darby was among those who became 'foundation members', or perhaps in his view, took his rightful place of leadership following his initiation through baptism. He spoke to the visiting Rev. F.H. Starr (Secretary of the Home Mission Board):

You and me and grandfather (Mr Fleming) are one in Jesus, we are now in one camp.[7]

The design of the new church building was based upon a Western style of architecture and didn't reflect the way in which a group of Warlpiri people would usually meet together. The one concession to Warlpiri social organisation was that the two sides of the church

Yuendumu Baptist Church

were separated by gender: women on the right and men on the left. However, group discussions were held on the church lawns in lieu of a morning service every second Sunday in the late sixties and early seventies. Alcohol began to affect the community, and Darby used the church as a platform to address the issue. He saw it as symptomatic of the young people rebelling against the authority of the old men, and called on them to listen to the elders and respect Warlpiri Law. Darby lamented the situation: the young people had grown up differently to him, they didn't know the *Jukurrpa* and the country like he did, and neither would they come to church. The old men like Darby were deeply hurt that the younger men were not interested in following their traditions and ceremonies.

In response to what was being said by the church leaders like Darby, and in an attempt to develop the Warlpiri character of the church, Tom asked the old men if they would paint some shields with their families' *Jukurrpa* designs and display them in the building.[8] The men took on the task and ceremoniously placed the shields upon the communion table. With building extensions planned, it was decided that these designs should be incorporated in a stained glass window that would be installed in the western wall. Tom sent the designs to a glassmaker in Adelaide, who began to put it together. However, Tom's health was deteriorating. Having collapsed in the pulpit during a sermon, he now sat to take the service, and finally had to retire.

Tom and Pat lived out their final years in Alice Springs. They visited Yuendumu for the last time in 1986, when Tom was saddened by the changes he observed, feeling there was little hope for the future of the Warlpiri community. He told his wife, 'I don't want to see that place again.'[9] And he never did; old Jungarrayi died in 1990. Darby described the funeral, which was attended by many Warlpiri:

Poor bugger finish, my old man. And Nangala (Pat), too. Never mind, I bin go to him, and we bin take 'em down the funeral . . . Good old man Jungarrayi.

The Rev. Ed and Kath Kingston replaced the Flemings as resident missionaries at Yuendumu in 1975. The church window arrived soon after. Nineteen *Jukurrpa* designs represented the church families and depicted the country around Yuendumu; the *Jukurrpa* designs surrounding the cross in the middle reflecting the original intention of the community when they first dedicated the church site to *Wapirra*. Darby produced a design of the *Yakajirri Jukurrpa* (Bush Raisin Dreaming) from his country around Ngarliyikirlangu to the north of Yuendumu.

In the mid-1970s, there was a 'heightened God-consciousness' in the western desert, and as a result the Yuendumu church attracted many new members.[10] At the same time, the church leaders adopted new 'cultural' methods of communication. Jimija Jungarrayi told the story of Abraham (Genesis 12) using Warlpiri iconography in August 1975.[11] At Lajamanu (north of Yuendumu), Baptist missionary Ivan Jordan began to use Warlpiri iconography to illustrate his sermons, and church leader Jerry Jangala Patrick organised shields to be painted with bible stories. In October 1977 a Christmas *Purlapa* (public ceremony) was performed by the Lajamanu church. Inspired by their northern counterparts, who had shared the Christmas *Purlapa* with them, the Yuendumu church members decided to develop their own interpretation of the Easter story. Over 400 people travelled from as far away as Halls Creek and Fitzroy Crossing to attend the Easter *Purlapa* at Yuendumu in 1978. Kath Kingston described the time as she remembered it:

Darby (centre) and church members preparing the cross for the Easter *Purlapa* (Corroboree) at Yuendumu, 1986

The first corroboree was at Tanami, on the right hand side of the road, with the mine set a little back amongst the gum trees. The Yuendumu people came back and decided they wanted to 'dance' Easter. They'd sit in the back of the church with a tape recorder. They really wanted it to be right according to Scripture – that everything they sang would be just right. They didn't want to have to change things, because once it's set, it's set forever.

That Easter they had their dance. On Good Friday they did a ground painting, a huge one. Then they took it all away and had a whole new one by Sunday. It wasn't just old people from the church, but everyone.

The old ones like Darby and Paddy were the key dancers. Darby was always a soldier.
He'd have his spears, and they'd light a fire stick and wrap cloth around the end of it and dip
it in kerosene. They'd dance with these fire sticks and their spears. And he was one of those
people that always put a lot of action into his dance. Just so animated, he was wonderful to
watch. The whole community was really involved, and Darby was one of the leaders.[12]

Twenty years later, when Darby was in his nineties, the annual Easter *Purlapa* was held
in Lajamanu, and was a much smaller event. The men cleared the ground and placed
a painted *mingkirri* (ant hill) in the centre, and constructed a wooden cross and a *yunta*
(windbreak) that would function as the cave. Sergeant Jupurrurla danced and died as
Jesus on the Friday night. Then at sunrise on Sunday morning, the old men prepared
to dance the resurrection. Darby and Thomas Rice painted each other's bodies with red
and white paint and applied feathers while they were still wet. They tied red cloth about
their waists, placed *pukurdi* (head-dresses) on their heads, attached branches to their legs,
and selected their boomerangs.

Darby was saddened by the absence of the young men who had chosen instead to
play in the football carnival in Alice Springs. There weren't enough men to dance,
and participation was important to imbue the ceremony with meaning. School teacher
Andrew Cowen and I were asked to join in, and Sergeant ordered us Whitefellas, and

everyone else participating, to 'dance really good for those missionaries'. As Darby practised his steps, obviously enjoying himself, the Rev. Ed Kingston sat on the ground, taking his place with the men who had begun to sing. Meanwhile, Sergeant complained that the white crosses we were painting on his body weren't of sufficient quality to indicate the important transformation that was about to take place.

After further instructions from Sergeant, we all formed two lines facing each other, and began dancing to the beat of the boomerangs (as the disciples). When Sergeant (Jesus) emerged from the cave, the other dancers fell back and lay on the ground, followed by Andrew and I, who were struggling to keep up. When he retreated again, Darby and Thomas danced, doubting what they had seen, communicating with hand signals, and finally disappearing in the dust from the stamping of their feet. Three women entered and danced towards the cave and Sergeant came out to meet them. We all returned and the dancing reached a climax as we faced the singers. Then it was finished. Jesus had risen for another year, and Darby had danced Easter for the last time.

Some commentators point to the Christian *Purlapa* as evidence that the Warlpiri have 'indigenised' Christianity. According to the Rev. Laurie Reece, the early efforts of missionaries were aided by the existing Warlpiri belief in the creation of the physical world. Warlpiri spoke of the world being created *nyurru-wiyi*, in the beginning, and having been around for *tarnngangku*, a long, long time.[13] Reece saw further confirmation in parallels between the Warlpiri story of Napaljarri-warnu, the Seven Sisters, and Pleiades, the Greek version. He believed the association of the constellation with women was a 'good indication of the origin of the constellation names prior to the tower of Babel'. Reece also wrote of a Warlpiri belief in reincarnation and the entering of the realm of *Jukurrpa* during sleep. He acknowledged within Warlpiri belief the recognition of parallel spiritual and physical worlds, above and beyond which is *Jukurrpa-warnu*, 'who is the ultimate, superlative, creator, originator of all that there is'. He suggests this as an explanation of the Warlpiri belief that *Jukurrpa-warnu* can reveal things to people in their sleep. However, when discussing the term with Darby and other Warlpiri, the best translation of *Jukurrpa-warnu* we were able to come up with was 'things related to Dreamings'. No doubt Reece was searching for a way to fit the Christian concept of God into a Warlpiri worldview.[14] Reece also pointed out that many of the bible stories describe God speaking to people in dreams.

Liam and Darby, Easter
Purlapa, Lajamanu, 1998

Visitors
Missionaries

The Lutherans at Hermannsburg were among the first to demonstrate an interest in the welfare of the Warlpiri. After a 1930 expedition to Pikilyi in the heart of Warlpiri country, Pastor Albrecht planned another trip in 1931 to follow up on the idea of placing Aboriginal evangelists in bush camps where they would live a nomadic existence and share the gospel.[15] Two days into the trip Albrecht got sick and had to pull out, although the expedition continued without him. Albert Namatjira, later to become a renowned landscape painter, was among the group who spent several weeks in the bush at Pikilyi before returning to Hermannsburg.

Albrecht and the Lutheran Mission were key players in the establishment of Haasts Bluff Reserve in 1942. Albrecht had originally advocated an extension of the proposed reserve to include the area to the north around Pikilyi to ensure pastoral interests did not continue to override those of the Warlpiri.[16] However, Bill Braitling already held a pastoral lease over the area that included Pikilyi. The fight for a reserve for the Warlpiri was a complex affair, involving several other protagonists besides Albrecht and Braitling. Not least among them was Olive Pink, a much maligned and misunderstood anthropologist who had lived with the Warlpiri at various sites in the 1930s. Known as Talkinjiya to the Warlpiri, she has since become somewhat of a mythical figure in Central Australia.

While Albrecht and Pink became temporary allies in their fight to establish a 'native reserve' at Pikilyi, Pink eventually proposed a 'secular sanctuary' for the Warlpiri, one that would exclude missionaries, government officials and other interested parties.[17] It would be a place for the Warlpiri to make their own choices about how they wanted to live, albeit under the guidance of Pink herself. However, she faced strong opposition from Braitling, who exploited the story of how he had rescued her from dying out at Yurnmaji. No doubt, in the male-dominated Northern Territory of the time, many people would have questioned the ability of a single woman to survive in the harsh climate of the Tanami Desert.

In the ensuing drama, heightened by Pink's criticism of the establishment, Patrol Officer Ted Strehlow was asked to make a report to the authorities.[18] This was unfortunate for Pink, and consequently the Warlpiri. While Strehlow sympathised with the plight of the Warlpiri, he could not easily accept the idea of a 'secular sanctuary'. Nor could Strehlow abide the fact that Pink, who had become something of a nemesis due to her work with the Arrernte, was the one who was proposing it.[19] It appears that Strehlow let his personal feelings about Pink influence his report, delivering a scathing criticism of her activities. Strehlow's biographer Barry Hill suggests that, taking into account the obvious personal nature of Strehlow's attack on Pink, politically it was what the authorities wanted to hear.[20] As a consequence, Strehlow (along with Braitling and the administration of the Native Affairs Branch) denied the Warlpiri their chance for a reserve that included Pikilyi, a place he had previously recognised as 'perhaps the greatest ceremonial centre in the Ngalia area'.[21] Albrecht later reflected on this time:

I believe the number of people affected there was in the vicinity of 200 … There, too, the one white man was worth more than all the Natives who lived there before.[22]

In the 1940s, the Baptists of South Australia had expressed an interest in starting a mission amongst the 'Aboriginal people of the north'. This was largely the result of the efforts of the Rev. E.H. Watson who was based in Alice Springs as an army chaplain

during the Second World War and had contact with members of the Aboriginal Labour Corps. At this time, another Baptist minister, the Rev. Laurie Reece, wrote to Albrecht at Hermannsburg for advice on finding a post in Central Australia. Albrecht suggested he investigate the country northwest of Haasts Bluff and offered to organise guides and camels for a survey of Warlpiri country. Reece, with guides (whose names were recorded as Titus, Ezekiel and Pardipatu) left Haasts Bluff on May 26, 1944.[23] It was a six-week journey and Reece was deeply moved by the experience. He had discovered many more Aboriginal people living in the area than the authorities had assumed.[24] Reece also had cause for concern after observing Warlpiri working for Braitling at Luurnpakurlangu (Mt Doreen), and was troubled by what he saw at Pikilyi, an important water source for the Warlpiri, where he echoed Albrecht's thoughts that bullocks were being given preference to the Warlpiri.[25] On an earlier journey in 1932, Strehlow documented similar evidence from two Warlpiri women whom he met east of Pikilyi:

The two women alleged that Braitling was now hunting the Ngalia (Warlpiri) people from their springs at Pikilji (Pikilyi), and had begun to shift his cattle to these waters.[26]

Reece presented his survey to the South Australian Home Mission Board. While his report was passed around the various committees, Yuendumu government settlement was established at Rock Hill Bore by the Native Affairs Branch in April, 1946.

A number of bores had been sunk northwest of Alice Springs to Luurnpakurlangu (Mt Doreen) on a newly established stock route. Reece had noted Rock Hill Bore, near the site Warlpiri refer to as 'Yurntumu' and approximately 290kms northwest of Alice Springs, showed promise of a good, reliable water supply. D.D. Smith, Director of Works at Alice Springs, suggested to the Native Affairs Branch that it would be a possible site for a settlement.[27] After a few failed attempts to settle people at Tanami and The Granites, Frank McGarry (Native Affairs Branch) relocated Warlpiri to Rock Hill Bore. The initial population also included some of the Warlpiri and Anmatyerr who had been living at Luurnpakurlangu and Bullocky Soak near Ti Tree. Warlpiri people had never lived together in such large numbers and Patrol Officer Gordon Sweeney (Native Affairs Branch) recalled groups of Warlpiri meeting for the first time at Yuendumu and performing a 'peacemaking ceremony' to settle old conflicts.[28]

A delegation of Baptists visited Yuendumu in July 1946, and the Rev. Phillip Steer and Rev. Laurie Reece subsequently arrived in Yuendumu on February 13, 1947. At this time, the population was about four hundred. The Native Affairs Branch designated the new arrivals as welfare workers, which increased the scope of their activities.

Steer quickly made friends with two Warlpiri men, including Jimija Jungarrayi. Using material from Alice Springs, a mission house was built over a period of forty-two days with a team of Warlpiri men lead by Jimija. There was no electricity then and all buildings were constructed with secondhand materials. They eventually built a second mission house, a store, a school and a hospital. The Baptists also facilitated the staffing of the hospital, kindergarten and school.[29]

The Steers and Reeces began conducting church services. Steer recalled the first service:

We had no bell to call the people to church nor did we have a building in which to meet. For the first service we simply gathered them around us in the scanty shade of a mulga tree. Just a handful of men and boys, but only five weeks later a mixed group of over 140 people gathered on the site that we had chosen for the church.[30]

A Salvation Army welfare hut from Alice Springs was soon dismantled and erected at Yuendumu as a building for the congregation to meet in. Services were relatively short and pictures were used to illustrate Bible stories. Mostly children attended, and after returning to their camps, recounted the stories and sang the songs to their parents. Reflecting on the Baptist missionaries' early efforts, Steer wrote:

Pre-school children receiving porridge from missionary Pat Fleming 1953

Our task was to identify with them, to understand them and to show a sincere and genuine friendship and receive in return their acceptance.

It has often been said, maybe no one will listen to what you have to say but remember they will watch the way you live. In God's hands and by the power of the Holy Spirit our lives lived out before these people was the way God had planned to reach these people for himself.[31]

Reece on the other hand believed that, as a missionary, the only way he could adequately discuss subjects such as the 'Origin of Life' or the 'Creation of the World' was to understand Warlpiri culture and language. Something of a lay anthropologist, he advocated in *Oceania*:

… learning the language of the Wailbri, for it is virtually bound up in their way of thinking and living. We come to a people whose culture, history, language, customs and practices are far removed from ours, and unless we meet them on a common ground we become builders of a superstructure on a foundation of which we know nothing.[32]

Reece did not necessarily believe that the God the Baptists were talking about with the Warlpiri was not known to them, as he believed it was embodied in the Warlpiri *Jukurrpa-warnu*, which

he translated as 'Creator Being'. Reece saw the mission's role to bring 'further revelation' of *Jukurrpa-warnu*, which included the gospel:

The Warlpiri use the word *tjukurrpa* to mean 'dream, dreaming, eternity, or the eternal spirit world.' They add the suffix *-warnu* to give a word its ultimate or superlative meaning; its highest or supreme characteristic. Adding this suffix indicates they are referring to the one above all others indicated by the word. Hence when they say *Tjukurrpawarnu* they mean the highest or supreme one in the spirit world. They referred to *Tjukurrpawarnu* as the One who originated or made all the other *tjukurrpa*, each of which was given the power to make a separate kind of animal or bird life. For example, *Wanatjukurrpa* was the one responsible for making and maintaining all snake life; or *Wawirritjukurrpa* was responsible for all kangaroo life. Thus *Tjukurrpawarnu* is the Supreme Being, the ultimate originator and creator of everything, for the physical features of the countryside also were formed by the actions of the various *tjukurrpa*.[33]

In April 1950, the Rev. Tom Fleming, with his wife Pat, replaced Reece and Steer as Baptist missionaries at Yuendumu. Fleming had been ordained in 1937 and joined the army in 1939 as a YMCA representative. He was sent to Singapore

with the Eighth Division in July, 1941. When Singapore fell to the Japanese in February, 1942 Fleming was taken as a prisoner of war to Changi for six months before being transferred to a Japanese war camp in Borneo where he spent the next three years. While in prison, Fleming prayed, promising if he got out alive, he would spend the rest of his life working for God anywhere he was sent. The prisoners were released in September, 1945 and Tom returned to Melbourne in poor health. After he had recovered, Tom pastored the Moonee Ponds Baptist Church from 1946 to 1949, before transferring to Yuendumu in 1950.

Tom found his early years at Yuendumu (during which time the government pursued a policy of assimilation) to be very challenging. He wrote:

Communication was somewhat difficult in the early years. Unfortunately no opportunity was given the early missionaries to attend a language school. There was no Warlpiri dictionary, no grammar, and with the multitude of jobs to occupy their time the missionaries had no hope of learning the language. Furthermore Government authorities decreed that all instruction should be in English.[34]

In 1956, following the example of Albrecht, Tom began to visit the surrounding cattle stations where Darby occasionally worked.[35] Tom would conduct services in the afternoon and at night

From left, Rosie Nangala
Fleming, Pat Fleming,
Tom Fleming and Jimija
Jungarrayi, Yuendumu
Sports Weekend 1978.

would show a film or slides lit by a lantern. In 1958, he began flying once a month to Hooker Creek (Lajamanu). He would preach in English with some Warlpiri, and people would learn the stories through repetition.

D.D. Smith, who then ran Mt Allan Station, 50kms east of Yuendumu, remembered Tom visiting consistently every two weeks. According to his wife Pat, Tom rarely missed a fortnightly visit in nineteen years. Smith recalled the pressure Tom was under (from the Baptist Mission Board) to baptise people at Yuendumu, and that Tom didn't believe in simply running people 'through the dip' to create 'immediate Christians', but was willing to baptise anyone who came to him.[36] Pat recalled Tom's frustration, saying 'God doesn't count heads', and that he wasn't interested in supplying the Mission Board with numbers of converts.[37]

Although very conservative in his style of service and instruction of Christianity, Tom focused on communicating the gospel orally, and was later enthusiastic about the success of the 'Tell Australia Campaign' of 1973-74. This he regarded as reflecting the methods used by the early Christian Church, which he described as having 'gossiped the gospel wherever they went'.[38] Pat remembered some young men coming to services, but largely attributed the growth of the church to the children, pointing out that most of the long-term church members were young children in 1950, and that this reflected Tom's belief in educating and growing up Christians from childhood.

Tom lived in the community for twenty-five years, baptised thirty-three people, and having fulfilled his promise to God, reluctantly decided it was time to leave in 1975. Reflecting upon their time at Yuendumu, Pat recalled that Tom spent five years forgetting the things he had learnt at Theological College and finding out how best to speak to the people at Yuendumu. It then took another ten years for the adults to be interested in what he was talking about.[39] The Rev. Ivan Jordan, a long-term missionary in Lajamanu (and later Yuendumu), wrote of the Flemings as 'people of their times', acknowledging that in hindsight they could be considered 'rather paternalistic, but they greatly endeared themselves to the Warlpiris'.[40]

In November 1975 twelve people were baptised in Yuendumu, and testified to the way *Wapirra* (God) had spoken to them. Tim Japangardi Langdon, '. . . dreamed that God had taken away a flagon of wine and told him not to touch it again'.[41] In October 1979 during a five-day training camp for church leaders at Rabbit Flat, the Warlpiri and Gurindji church leaders, including Darby, testified to the ways *Wapirra* had spoken to them in dreams. Darby often spoke of his visions. In one of these dreams he was paralysed, and saw *Wapirra* appearing at Yuendumu hill coming through a gate, beyond which was Heaven and the city of Jerusalem, where the land was rich with green grass. He said this inspired him to continue to pray and follow *Wapirra*, who in response sustained his long life.

When researcher Tony Swain visited Yuendumu in the early 1980s, he recorded the following story with Darby (referred to as J. in the text):

A long time ago J. had a frightening dream. In retrospect he thought it was God punishing him for his unChristian behaviour. In it he heard a loud rush of wind, like an aeroplane. Two large doors appeared in the sky (c.50 x 50 metres) and opened to reveal a lush, green city which was equated with Jerusalem (also located by the man to the south). Jesus (*Wapirra*) emerged from the gates. He was young (c.30), white and had a glistening neat red beard. He wore a yellow jumper and shirt and white trousers and shoes. All his clothes were new. He was approximately 4 metres tall.

He carried a chair with him and sat to look at the world below. Four red beams 'like torches' shone from his chair. The world turned red. From the trees hung small shiny objects shaped like bullroarers. J. said that when he dies he will go to that city. J. then added that Jesus had 'come to Yuendumu twice'. On the other occasion the earth was again turned red and was washed by a 'really clean rain'. J. was hit in the back of the neck by lightning which put Jesus' power into him. This power explained why he is still alive today although most of his peers have died. The lightning is still inside him.[42]

In the following story, Darby describes his vision of Jesus delivered to him in a dream in the 1960s. He describes *Wapirra* appearing near Yuendumu, and travelling through the sky to visit the earth.

He bin come here. Him bin coming on a big cloud. Him bin (sound effects) lightning. Just like alongside of me. Not the proper lightning, only belonga Father, longa 'nother side from Yuendumu. This side from Yuendumu hill.

Another (time), him bin travelling moonlight, longa moon. Only little spear, he bin have him. Looking around, 'Oh, him not here.' That Father bin coming through the gate. Big gate over there. Long way down, longa heaven. The Father bin coming to me, now. Straight ahead, and him bin coming right up to moonlight. Moon bin here – *kakarrara* (east); and he bin here. And from there, he bin look down to me. Oh, he bin making me paralysed! *Yuwayi* (yes), him bin making me paralysed. What to do? I bin, 'Oh, look this!' I bin shivering. I never bin sleep after that, while that Father bin come, while he bin make everything cold down here. Yeah, that's why me pray for everybody. That's true word.

We bin big mob camping round there. I bin dream he bin come out through the big, big, big fence. He going right up to top, and he got a big gate here, and can't take 'em off iron. All the time him stand up there.

He's the Father's country, this Yuendumu. That's not nothing. That's a good day while he bin travelling round here – about three days. That Father bin come through this way, from Heaven. I'll be there, too. Never mind – should me finish longa this country – I'll be going to him. That's my promise. That's all me say for the Lord Jesus Christ. We'll be going to Heaven.

That Father bin coming here. He bin travelling, carrying little spear. He bin travelling footwalks. He bin sitting there, look back to me, old Darby! 'That's *Wapirra*!'

That Father – while he bin coming, longa this country, longa desert – we bin ask him, want to give me water. Well, he bin give me plenty water. Creeks bin running, rockhole fill it up, soakage fill it up, everything. Green country. That's why we bin ask Father.

To the Warlpiri, *Wapirra* communicates in dreams, and for Darby these dreams were revelations of *Wapirra* visiting the Warlpiri landscape. In the chronological biblical narrative, *Wapirra*'s interaction with humanity occurred in a country that Darby had not visited, and whose *Jukurrpa* was not known. For *Wapirra* to enter the Warlpiri landscape, he must reveal himself in dreams, and become part of the same process that Warlpiri acknowledged was the way in which *Jukurrpa* was revealed.[43]

Swain argues that Warlpiri can only accept Christianity and God in a utopian form without connecting the biblical narrative to time and place:

> ... while the Warlpiri have rejected the notion of a God involved with a lineal history they
> have nonetheless been influenced by the Christian notion of a utopian, undifferentiated world
> Space. God then is manifest neither in historical time (the orthodox Christian view), nor place
> (the unsuccessful Warlpiri view), but is, in Bergson's evocative words, the ghost of Space ...
> the intrusion is best understood not as a conquest, but as an alliance – an alliance socially
> between Aborigines and Whites, cosmologically between Dreaming and God, and ontologically
> between place and Space.[44]

Swain attempted to record a Warlpiri understanding of the chronological biblical narrative. While impressed by his informants' knowledge of biblical events, when he asked them about Adam, Moses and Jesus, he was told that they all lived on the 'one day'. This led him to the view that, for the Warlpiri, 'God's prophets and son had been dislodged from a lineal history and incorporated into an atemporal Dreaming.'[45] When Darby spoke of *Jukurrpa*, it was always in relation to 'known' places and a horizontal organisation of space in *walya* (earth); when he spoke of Christianity and the stories contained in the Bible, it was in relation to 'unknown' places and a vertical organisation of space crossing over into the other *walya* (heaven) where *Wapirra* resided and to where Darby would one day go when he passed away. This does not mean that *Wapirra* did not also interact with the Warlpiri landscape. Like many of the older people, Darby would speak of how *Wapirra* had looked after the Warlpiri when they were living a nomadic life in the bush:

Who was giving all this food? The Father in heaven – *Wapirra*, our Father – was providing our people with bush food. *Wapirra* gave us bush potatoes.[46]

While some of the church members claimed *Wapirra* for themselves, other community members charged them with becoming like Whitefellas. Tom Fleming challenged this by stating that the emphasis of the church at Yuendumu was that Christianity was not a white man's religion but was for all people.[47] However, it was the Whitefella missionaries who had established the Baptist tradition at Yuendumu, and Darby clearly associated the origins of the church with Whitefellas. Although he was familiar with the events in the story of Moses, (when asked in old age) Darby suggested Moses was a Whitefella who had come from England. This is not to say that he did not understand his Christian faith, rather it gives some clues as to his interpretation.

Yuendumu hill

You got to go to good place. No more singing out, nothing, longa heaven. That *yaru* (up high) (is) green country. No more argument. No more fighting round. No more singing out.

Father take 'em me, and (I'll be) sitting there. I might see 'em there – my countrymen, whole lot! All my family will be there sitting round, whole lot. Moses – he's the leader man – he's there. We got to see Adam and Eve.

Lloyd Ollerenshaw, Baptist missionary at Yuendumu in the 1980s, spoke of Warlpiri *Jukurrpa* being 'very close to eternity', and reflected on the Baptist teaching:

We used to teach about God existing before the world was created, even before *Jukurrpa*. However, it is possible the Warlpiri understand Eternity better than the linear way we look at time. God has always existed in Eternity-*Jukurrpa*. He always will. The past becomes the present when we participate in the Dreaming, or at a communion ceremony, eating and drinking Jesus.[48]

In 1995, Darby attended Church every Sunday and would stand and pray in a mixture of Warlpiri and English. He had developed a style, rhythmically repeating phrases, and raising and lowering his voice. He regularly lamented the lack of attendance. He prayed for the church, the country around Yuendumu, and for the young people who were not there.

Wapirra, thank you *karna wangka jalangu* (while I talk to you here today) . . . We're worrying for the everybody. No more fighting round. Everybody got to know the Father. Father and Son and Spirit. Amen.

When I visited Darby at his house to talk, he would sometimes finish the conversation with a prayer. He would thank *Wapirra* for the rain, or ask that he would 'make it good for the people'. In public, Darby's prayers would sometimes seem like sermons. He would refer to himself in the third person and remind everyone that he was not much longer for this world and would soon be joining *Wapirra*. Darby also spoke of being reunited with all the people who had gone before, like his friend Jimija. He spoke of his spirit going 'straight up', his 'number' being looked at, and joining all the 'mob' from Central Australia.

Darby spoke of the compromise he had made with regard to his involvement in Warlpiri ceremonies. As his Warlpiri beliefs had influenced his Christian beliefs and their practice, so had his Christian beliefs affected his level of participation in some Warlpiri ceremonies, including those known as *Juju*.[49] Dave Price explained:

Paradoxically Darby's generation also agreed to a lot of changes by accepting Christianity. *Juju* was part of the Law. However, it is now interpreted as 'evil'. People like Darby, and my father-in-law, rejected aspects of the Law that they interpreted as evil under the influence of Christianity. It was part of that Law that was denied to women, not all of men's business, but the part that related to sorcery. The Warlpiri dictionary gives these definitions as well as more neutral ones that relate to supernatural knowledge and abilities. It quotes 'juju-ngarliya' as being a man or woman who fully understands the meaning of *Jukurrpa*. I think it is a word like the English 'magic' that has a wide variety of meanings, menacing or otherwise depending on context and how it is qualified. I think that the old fellas were a bit overwhelmed by all of the changes and didn't always appreciate how much they had changed themselves to accommodate the new. The result has been increasing confusion.

Darby spoke of being 'two ways'. Being Warlpiri, following Warlpiri Law, and being *Wapirra-kurlangu*, belonging to God's family, which included *Yapa* (Aboriginal people) and *Kardiya* (Whitefellas). He did not see them as mutually exclusive; adhering to both was a way to hold on to tradition, Law, ceremony and *Jukurrpa*. It provided him with a definitive understanding and recognition of his place in this world, and the next.

Darby believed that the church could be a place where Warlpiri could resolve disputes and 'live a good life'. He also saw the church as a place where *Yapa* and *Kardiya* could be reconciled under *Wapirra's* Law. In the early 1970s, Darby travelled to Adelaide, Sydney and Brisbane and attended church services as a representative of Yuendumu. Darby travelled on evangelistic trips to other Warlpiri communities. He also travelled to the Mardu communities of Punmu and Jigalong in Western Australia representing the Yuendumu church. In old age, Darby continued travelling interstate to attend Baptist conventions, and regularly welcomed visiting church members and school groups at Yuendumu. He spoke of the 'millions of white mans' that he saw in the churches in Adelaide, Melbourne, Brisbane, Sydney and Hobart. All the 'church mob' were his family:

And that's why we talk about now for the Father and Son and Spirit. He's all in one, no matter every church. No matter 'nother place church. Lutheran, Catholic, all that. All true, only one. We got 'em Father – one ... That's why this church (is) everybody's church. Thousand, thousand people. I've seen 'em everywhere. Right up to Darwin, all that country up to Cloncurry, Brisbane, Sydney.

Darby also considered himself an elder with a responsibility for the worldwide church. He would pray for people in other countries, whom he saw as worse off than himself, even though he lived most of his life in humpies or tin sheds and owned very little. He identified strongly with people from Papua New Guinea or India, whom he considered *Yapa* like himself. Inspired by Mr Oris, who had told him the story of his people in India, Darby would collect money for the 'hungry people' of Africa and Asia on behalf of the church.

We put 'em on longa offering money ... and we send 'em on to – oh, might we think about for hungry people – might (be) Africa? Might for Bangladesh? Got a big trouble down New Guinea, too ... Poor bugger. And nother one Africa – they're dying – no food. We got to think about for that people ...

As he got older, and was less mobile, Darby was unable to attend church every Sunday. But he would sit and pray, or sing the Warlpiri 'bible songs' in his camp, thinking about *Wapirra* and the promise that would be fulfilled for him when he passed away.

In the early days of the Baptist church, English hymns were sung with the accompaniment of an organ. Some of these songs were translated into Warlpiri, and other original songs in a similar style were written in Warlpiri and accompanied by a guitar. But, it was the 'bible songs' that best expressed the Warlpiri character of the churches at Yuendumu and Lajamanu. These songs were sung in a similar style to those used in ceremonies, and were accompanied with the rhythmic beating of boomerangs. Short statements were introduced by the men, and repeated as the women joined in, until all the voices reached a climax and then gradually faded away. There was a pause before moving on to the next song:

Kaaturluju nyanunguju nyinami-ka jukurrarnu *(God is eternal)*
Kaaturluju ngurrju-manu nyiya-kanti-kanti lawa jangkaju *(God made everything from nothing)*
Yapa panungku yirrarnulu Jijaji watiya warnta-warntarla *(People put Jesus on a cross)*

These songs are a liturgical expression of Warlpiri Christianity, unusual in the Baptist tradition, and are an indication of the way in which the older men and women, like Darby, have integrated Christian faith with their pre-existing Warlpiri beliefs.

The Christian community at Yuendumu now includes those who identify as Baptist, Catholic, Lutheran and Pentecostal. While the Baptist church remains the cornerstone of the Christian community, the Pentecostal congregation continues to grow in popularity and some tension has developed between the two congregations.

In the 1990s, an enthusiastic group of younger gospel musicians, of both denominations, emerged. There were already lots of musicians playing different styles in Yuendumu: reggae, country, rock and instrumental. But it was only the gospel concerts that regularly went until 4am. Even if the PA was broken or the speakers blown, the 'gospel mob' would play. Most were middle-aged men and women, but as participation was encouraged, occasionally some of the younger men would take the stage.

'Gospel' has emerged as a genre in its own right in the western desert. The 'gospel mob' believe in *Wapirra*, but a lot of them don't attend regular church services. Their services are music sessions with a particular style and groove — a blend of Baptist, Lutheran and Pentecostal hymns, rock and roll, country and reggae. At Yuendumu, it was common to hear lyrics like 'Who's gonna be the one gonna set me free?', accompanied by the laid-back sounds of gospel guitar, bass and drums several nights a week. Competing congregations, increasingly louder and more enthusiastic, were characteristic of the 'gospel wars' at this time. Short sermons ('Smile if you got royalty. But if you got Jesus, praise him.'), impromptu prayers and 'God bless everyone out there' were delivered to your door through the night air from a small group sitting on amps and tyre rims on a concrete slab at midnight. The message was much the same, but it was a different ceremony to the one that was known to the older people like Darby, who would often contest the late night prayers of those with microphones with their own quiet pleas to *Wapirra* to make them stop, please make them stop.

Australian Rules football was introduced to Yuendumu by Superintendent Ted Egan in the late 1950s, and the Yuendumu football team played its first games against Hermannsburg and Alekarenge (Warrabri) in 1960.[1] Darby enjoyed the 'ceremony' of football and liked the boomerang that was on the first jumpers. Johnny Japanangka Williams was one of the men who played then. He said they didn't have to train because they were already fit and strong, and that the game was enjoyed by the young men as an opportunity to prove themselves as warriors. On their first trip to Darwin they beat all the other teams except for St Marys, a Darwin based club. Ex-player and long-term President of the club, Eddie Jampijinpa Robertson, recalled the time:

It was rough football in those days. Not like today. You would run with the ball and knock

the magpie – became their mascot. In 1962, they wrote to the Collingwood Football Club (Magpies) in Melbourne and requested support for uniforms. Collingwood sent jumpers, shorts and boots, and the Yuendumu Magpies have claimed them as family ever since.

Yuendumu hosted its own Sports Weekend for the first time as a football carnival between Areyonga, Hermannsburg and Yuendumu in 1961. The Yuendumu Sports Weekend soon developed into a major sports carnival with football, softball, basketball and athletics. There were also cultural events like fire making and boomerang and spear throwing. Women competed in races carrying buckets of sand balanced on their heads and men climbed a greasy pole to win a bag of flour attached to the top. Older people would also perform *purlapa* (public ceremonies). In 1970, over 1200 people attended the Saturday night concert and Yuendumu Sports Weekend became known as the Aboriginal Olympics. At the opening ceremony, sportsmen and women dressed in team colours and marched behind flags representing their respective 'countries'. As always, Yuendumu was in black and white.

Warlpiri Warriors

Darby was an enthusiastic Sports Weekend committee member and participant, excelling in the spear throwing and fire making, organising *purlapa* and umpiring football games. Dick Kimber (known as Jakamarra to the Warlpiri) remembers watching one of the football games, sitting on the boundary behind Darby and the goal line:

In the early 1970s, Yuendumu Football Team was favoured to win the title in the August weekend Yuendumu Olympics. The games progressed over the weekend, and sure enough Yuendumu was in the final. In those days of just one central umpire, the man in white was Shane Woolf, a very fit umpire who lived in The Alice and had volunteered his services. Coach of Yuendumu was Harry Nelson, and as one of the goal umpires there was Old Darby. Even in 1972 he

was called Old Darby. He was probably about 55-60 years old at the time of the 'Olympics' and, as with most of the senior and middle-aged men, had taken part in the dancing and the spear throwing competition.

Darby loved the sense of occasion, and delighted in his role as umpire, but though he had witnessed modern Aussie Rules since Ted Egan had introduced it in the mid-1950s, he had never played it. Thus, he had been instructed what to do, and knew that if the ball went untouched through the big posts he had to wave two flags for a goal, and otherwise it was a point. All went well, and Darby was as alert as the players. His eyes were good, and he enthusiastically waved the flags.

The scores were very close with but a minute or two to go. The players on both sides were desperate, with Eddie Robertson like greased lightning for Yuendumu. Harry Nelson was urging them on. The crowd was barracking. The dogs were barking.

At this stage, with the ball at the other end of the ground, the opposition full-forward and the Yuendumu full-back had moved out towards the centre circle. Suddenly, the ball was whipped down the ground and kicked far over their heads towards the goal. It bounced and bounced towards the goal line, with the two players racing neck-and-neck as they desperately tried to reach it. And Old Darby watched like an eaglehawk.

The players were still too far away to see exactly what happened, but it hit a stone, jumped in the air and crossed the white goal line. Darby, who had the flags under his arms, reached for them. And then something extraordinary happened. The ball, having bounced over the line, bounced out onto the oval again! Darby paused. Never before had such a thing happened! And while he paused Shane, the central umpire, strained to see what had happened and awaited Darby's signal.

Darby was so momentarily nonplussed that he simply watched the ball, which was still doing little bounces near the goal line. And at this stage the Yuendumu full-back, thinking that it probably had crossed the goal line, kicked it in disgust – and it sailed out along the boundary. As it did so, Shane, not receiving a signal from

Darby, called, 'Play on! Play on!', and as no other players were clear about what had happened, the contest began again. And now the ball was rapidly kicked towards the Yuendumu goal, and right on the bell a goal was scored. Jubilation! Yuendumu had won!

However, there were opposition players who were angry, and they moved towards the central umpire, Shane, who had umpired every game that long weekend, and was very fatigued, suddenly found that he had the speed of an Olympic sprinter. He took off for the boundary, with the opposition team in pursuit, and the opposition's supporters retrieving spears from the surrounding bushes.

It was David Odling-Smee, then the head master at Yuendumu, and a key organiser during the weekend, who used the megaphone to calm the situation. 'We will not resort to spears,' he said. 'We will not use the old way to settle things. Leave your spears behind.' Every time Shane heard the words 'spears', his legs moved faster! He leapt into his car, locked the doors, and began praying. As his mate, I walked casually over to the car, and suggested that he drive gently away, as though unperturbed, and enjoy a shower.

Eventually things calmed down, and the trophies were awarded. Later Old Darby explained what had happened:

'That football, he's got a Law, Jakamarra.
Him bin bouncin' this way, him bin bouncin'
that way. And that's the Law.
That's the Law of the Football.
Him got a Law.
And that's the Law of the Football.'[2]

Today, football is immensely popular in Central Australia and nearly every Aboriginal community has its own annual Sports Weekend, but the Yuendumu Sports Weekend continues to be one of the largest, with its competitive football and softball competitions, gospel nights and infamous Battle of the Bands

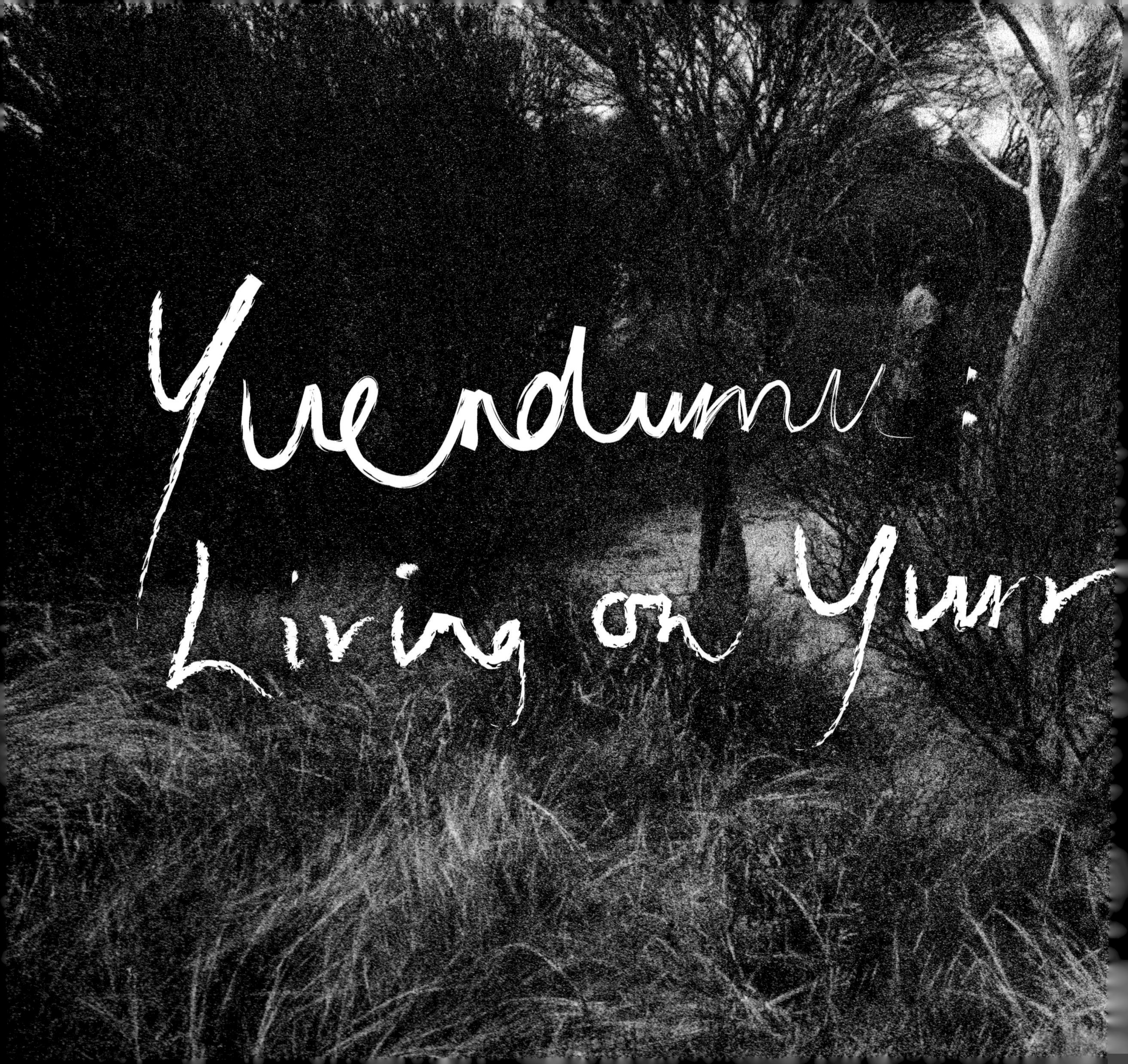
Yuendumu:
Living on Yurr

ampi

Chapter Six

Darby worked in various occupations until his retirement in the 1970s when he settled permanently in Yuendumu, on the site of the *Yurrampi Jukurrpa* (Honey Ant Dreaming). During this time, government policy towards Aboriginal people changed significantly. Land Rights legislation was introduced, and Warlpiri made claims for recognition of ownership of their land. Outstations were established and bilingual education introduced to the school. The skills and experiences Darby gained in his younger years were a valuable asset to the community. He was involved in various community organisations, worked with visiting researchers, was a consultant to the Parks and Wildlife Commission, and became a highly sought after elder of the tribe.

Warlpiri at Yuendumu refer to life on the settlement during the 1960s and 1970s as a relatively ordered and regimented existence where life revolved around work programs. Harry Giese, Director of Welfare for the Northern Territory Administration, claimed Yuendumu was one of the show communities with regard to employment up until the late 1960s.[1] There was an orchard and park (complete with fountain and stones arranged in the shape of boomerangs) in the centre of the community, and considerable effort was expended in placing rocks throughout the community and coating them with white paint. A cattle station, vegetable garden and piggery were established within the Yuendumu Reserve. Men were employed as gardeners, station hands and labourers in occupations usually overseen by a Whitefella manager. The Yuendumu Mining Company (established 1969) also employed men on a copper mining project, prospecting and

Darby with bush potatoes,
southwest of Yuendumu
1979

mining raw material west of Yuendumu. Ore from the Mt Hardy mine was taken to a treatment plant in Yuendumu, where it was processed before being trucked to Port Pirie in South Australia.[2] After attending a Home Management Course, women worked as domestics, kitchen hands, teacher assistants and trainee nurses. Or as Dolly Nampijinpa Daniels remembered it: 'We were proper Whitefellas back then!'

When Paul Hasluck became the Federal Minister for the Territories in 1951, and the *Aboriginals Ordinance (NT)* was replaced by the *Welfare Ordinance (NT)* in 1953, the provision of Aboriginal housing became an important part of the government's policy of assimilation. The first houses for Warlpiri at Yuendumu were one-room dwellings with a veranda and no power or water.[3] These houses were only available to a few families and most people still camped outside the settlement in 'humpies' or other makeshift dwellings made of bushes or leftover material, in areas relative to the direction of their respective countries. Darby and his (then) wife Polly lived in a humpy.

When houses were built for Warlpiri, they were fairly basic compared to those provided for Whitefellas. Long-term resident Wendy Baarda recalled the situation in 1972:

There was a central area of houses for white people ... all with nice lawns and gardens.
Aboriginal people were not allowed in this area except for school and work. Every white
household was allotted a gardener and a housegirl ...

Only one Aboriginal family had a Stage 3 house, that is a house with rooms, windows, taps and electricity. There were Stage 1 houses for the rest, very small one-room tin or concrete brick sheds with a concrete floor and two openings for doors and one window. Most people preferred to live in humpies.[4]

However, Bess Nungarrayi Price remembers her excitement when her family moved into one of the small 'donkey' houses for the first time. She also recalled moving freely throughout the Whitefellas' houses, and often visited her aunty who worked for the Cowens, a family she still keeps in contact with.

When Warlpiri got the land back under the NT Land Rights legislation in the 1970s, it was cause for celebration. Today over half of the land in Central Australia is Aboriginal-owned. However, Warlpiri have been unsuccessful in their attempts to claim the land held under pastoral lease by the Braitling family. Mt Doreen/Vaughan Springs Station covers an area of country that is dear to many Warlpiri, and has been the object of considerable debate since the 1930s. When Daisy Napanangka Nelson and her sisters, who had lived in the area as children, visited the waters at Pikilyi during the annual school 'country visits' in 1995, they danced around the stones of the *Yuparli* (Bush Banana) *Jukurrpa*. They told their grandchildren stories about the place, and visited the spring where water comes up from under the ground, expressing disappointment that it had been capped by a concrete slab. They sang love songs as they travelled past Yurnmaji, and laughed as they recalled the stories of their childhood. They talked about one day getting the land back. But this was not to be. Daisy died a few years later, the Warlpiri dream of regaining Pikilyi not yet realised.

Whitefella call 'em 'humpy'. We call 'em 'yujuku'. DARBY

Darby and his wife at their bush home, Yuendumu 1960s.

Nguru Warlalja *(Our Family Home Land)*

GORDON JANGALA ROBERTSON

Yapa-lpalu nyinaja *(The people were)*
Nguru warlaljarla *(in our family's land)*
Ngurrangka *(at home)*
Nyurru-wiyi *(a long time ago)*

Yapa Warlpiri-patu *(Warlpiri people)*
Wapaja-lpalu *(were walking around)*
Warla-nyampungka *(everything they needed was here)*
Nyurru-wiyi *(a long time ago)*

Nyurnu-wangu pirrjirdi *(healthy and strong)*
Nguru warlaljarla *(in our family home)*

Nganimpaku yapa *(Our people)*
Nganimpaku-palanguku *(our 'close' ancestors)*
Ngajuku Warringiyi *(my paternal grandfather)*
Ngajuku Jamirdi *(my maternal grandfather)*
Ngajuku Yaparla *(my paternal grandmother)*
Ngajuku Jaja *(my maternal grandmother)*
Pinaja-Ipalu *(were knowledgeable)*
Wapaja-Ipalu *(they walked around)*
Pirrjirdi-nyayirni *(really strong)*

Nguru warlaljarla *(in our family home)*

Yapa kalpalu wirlinyi *(The people went hunting)*
Wanta wiringka *(under a big sun)*
Wirliya-juku *(always on foot)*

Yapa Warlpiri-patu *(Warlpiri people)*
Yapa nganimpaku *(our people)*
Wiyarrpa *(the poor things)*
Nyurru-wiyi *(a long ago time ago)*

Nguru warlaljarla *(in our family homeland)*

In 1978, the *Northern Territory Crown Lands Ordinance (1978)* was introduced. It ensured Aboriginal rights to country held under pastoral leases were reasserted. Under the Ordinance, Aboriginal owners were allowed ('in accordance with Aboriginal tradition') to enter the land, access natural waters, hunt for animals and gather plants.[5] They had the right to do this without being prevented by the lessees. Warlpiri like Darby had never permanently left their respective 'countries', though they were separated at times by distance and enforced settlement or intimidated by pastoralists. Darby always maintained a link with his country, visiting whenever possible and performing ceremonies associated with its *Jukurrpa*. But for some of the older men and women, there remained some confusion about Land Rights.

Francis Jupurrurla Kelly remembered the Land Rights marches and one incident involving Darby's friend Jimija Jungarrayi at the bicentenary march in 1988:

> In those old days, they went for that Land Rights march past in Canberra, you know. They went from Kintore, Yuendumu, Papunya – all over. And they went there – marching for legislation you know, in Canberra. And this old bloke (Jimija) was singing out, marching with that flag and everything. They was talking, 'We want Land Rights!' Everybody saying 'Land Rights', you know.
>
> But this old bloke was with them – Lindsay Turner was with him – and he (Jimija) was saying, 'We want 'em Land Rover! We want 'em Land Rover!' And that Lindsay said, 'Nah, not Land Rover, you got to say Land Rights.'
>
> 'Oh that true, you gotta say we want 'em Land Rover now!' (Jimija) He was talking and singing out.
>
> And next thing they change the topic, 'Oh, we like to talk to Bob Hawke, you know' – 'We want Bob Hawke!' And he (Jimija) was saying, 'We wanna go war! We wanna go war!' He was saying like that instead of 'Bob Hawke', he wanted to go war or something, you know. 'We wanna go war!' He was the President of Yuendumu that old bloke and he was really tough old man that one. I'll call him his name – he's Jimija.[6]

When Pastor Albrecht of Hermannsburg proposed that the government 'Give the Aboriginal people some of their land back' in 1968, he recommended 'excising Aboriginal living areas from pastoral leases'.[7] The 1998 Reeves Report of the *Aboriginal Land Rights (1976) Act* referred to this recommendation as 'the genesis of the excisions debate that has raged to this day'.[8] A similar idea was expressed in Coombs and Stanner's argument that Warlpiri who wanted to live a more 'traditional' life should be assisted to 'decentralise':

> Aborigines should be assisted and efforts made to keep the new groupings small and closer in style to the traditional Aboriginal way . . . the Walbiri country be seen as a whole and a plan be worked out for its development in small decentralised Aboriginal communities serviced from larger, but still small, towns . . .[9]

Coombs and Stanner recommended that 'policy be directed to facilitating this movement for those who wished to take part'.[10] They referred to Mt Theo (Purturlu) as a place where up to 130 people, approximately ten percent of the Yuendumu population, said they would move permanently if given the opportunity.[11] Warlpiri refer to this as the 'Outstation Movement'.

Money became available for outstations when the Department of Aboriginal Affairs guidelines were finalised in 1979. Most of the potential outstations identified by

Coombs and Stanner at Yuendumu were established. Some Warlpiri were able to access vehicles to facilitate travel to and from their outstations. Darby was a strong supporter of outstations. In the 1980s, he spent considerable time living at Bean Tree (Yuwali) Outstation (in his country near Ngarliyikirlangu) to the north of Yuendumu. In 1984, during the Yuendumu Council election speeches, Darby took the microphone when it was alleged that Yuendumu Council didn't look after outstations properly. He was speaking as Chairperson of the Yuendumu Outstation Council and began speaking in fast Warlpiri, introducing some English at the request of those present. He spoke about how the Yuendumu Council should look after people, and threatened to leave Yuendumu and live in his 'country' permanently:

I'll get outside *kapurnalu nyinami Ngarliyikirlangurla!* (we will stay at Ngarliyikirlangu).[12]

Having made his point, Darby sat down amidst applause from the crowd. But by the late 1990s, the Outstation Resource Centre had gone into decline and funding for outstations was difficult to obtain. However, there were some fifteen outstations associated with Yuendumu, and several others with Nyirrpi (originally an outstation of Yuendumu), regularly visited by Warlpiri. Mt Theo, which became the location of a respite centre for petrol sniffers in the 1990s, was the only outstation where people now live on a semi-permanent basis.

Visitors

Government

In 1966, the Gurindji stockmen on Wave Hill Station, led by Vincent Lingiari, walked off in protest against their poor employment conditions.[13] The strike soon developed into a demand for the land to be returned to the Gurindji. Prime Minister Gough Whitlam travelled to the Northern Territory, after many years of struggle for the Gurindji, and made a promise to return the land to Vincent Lingiari's people by pouring sand into his hands. The photo depicting this ceremony became a symbol of the birth of the Land Rights movement.[14]

In 1954, the government introduced the *Welfare Ordinance 1953 (NT)* that formed the legislative basis for statements of policy, such as the following from the NT Welfare Branch Report 1958/59:

The policy of the Commonwealth Government with respect to aborigines in the Northern

Territory is to promote and direct social change amongst them in such a way that, whilst retaining connections with and pride in their aboriginal ancestry, they will become indistinguishable from other members of the Australian community in manner of life, standards of living, occupations, and participation in community affairs. It is important for the success of this process of assimilation that ... aborigines should be encouraged to detach themselves from their present position of group separateness and solidarity and become merged as individuals in the general community.[15]

The dominant government philosophy of the 1950s and 60s regarding Indigenous Australians was assimilation and centralisation, which was followed by a policy of voluntary 'integration'. When the Whitlam government created the Department of Aboriginal Affairs in 1972, they implemented a new era of self-determination that they described as:

Aboriginal communities deciding the basis and nature of their future development within the legal, social and economic constraints of Australian society.[16]

The Whitlam government appointed Justice Woodward, who had previously acted as Counsel

Yuendumu Old People's
Programme opening, 2001.
From left, Darby, Gough
Whitlam and Francis
Jupurrurla Kelly

for the Aboriginal plaintiffs in the Gove Land
Rights case, to head an inquiry into Aboriginal
Land Rights in the Northern Territory.[17] In 1974,
the Whitlam government accepted, 'in principle',
the recommendations contained in Justice
Woodward's Second Report, then introduced the
Aboriginal Land (NT) Bill 1975 into Parliament.[18]
However, after Whitlam's dismissal and the
subsequent election of Malcolm Fraser as Prime
Minister, it was the new Coalition government
which redrafted the legislation and passed the
bill as the *Aboriginal Land Rights (NT) Act 1976*.
However, the Fraser government's legislation
only allowed for 'claims by, and grants of land to,
Aboriginal people based on traditional affiliations'
rather than 'needs-based claims'.[19] Fortunately,
this was still of benefit to the Warlpiri, who still
occupied much of their traditional land, yet lacked
any formal recognition in Australian Law.

With the support of lawyers, anthropologists,
and the newly formed Land Councils, Warlpiri
applied for, and were granted, inalienable,
community freehold title to their land under
the new Land Rights legislation in the 1970s.[20]
Hearings were held in the Warlpiri communities,
and while they involved some of the trappings of
the Australian legal system, Warlpiri participated
in a process that took as evidence Warlpiri
Jukurrpa (Dreaming) and the importance of
Warlpiri relationships to land. Darby and his
friend Jimija Jungarrayi are listed as claimants

on many of the reports, and along with other
'traditional owners', gave evidence at the hearings.
Rosie Nangala Fleming remembered the time:

My husband (Jimija) was fighting in the court
for this place. Winner for this one! And (then)
everybody came in. Bush-*wardingki* (bush
people). Everybody – Anmatyerr, Warlpiri,
Pintupu.[21]

Darby loved to talk about the way he used to live as a young man, moving from place to place, hunting kangaroos and collecting bushtucker. He enjoyed 'going bush', and searching for old soakages or animals that Warlpiri used to hunt. He was always concerned that those accompanying him should remember the places they visited, their names, their *Jukurrpa*, which plants grew there, or which animals could be found at certain times of the year. Academics, Parks and Wildlife Officers, the Central Land Council, and visitors from other communities often called upon Darby for his extensive knowledge of Warlpiri flora and fauna. He featured in an episode of Les Hiddins' ABC television series *The Bush Tucker Man*. He went on many trips with Parks and Wildlife Officers looking for rare or extinct animals. In the 1970s and 80s, they searched for *jajirdi* (western quoll), *janganpa* (possum), *pakuru* (golden bandicoot), *walpajirri* (bilby) and *mala* (rufous hare-wallaby). They caught *walpajirri* near Jila Well, and *mala* near Sangster's Bore. Parks and Wildlife Officer Ken Johnson credits Darby's role in the ABC documentary *The Walpajirri Dreaming* as bringing the plight of the bilby to the attention of all Australians. Ken's work with Darby contributed significantly to the introduction and acceptance of Aboriginal knowledge in the scientific community.

Darby participated in a wildlife survey with Ken in August 1979. They travelled to country northwest of Yuendumu looking for *walpajirri*. They saw many animals, some now rare or possibly extinct, and Darby names them in the following story. The recording was made by Mary Laughren the day after Darby returned to Yuendumu, and the text is a summary of the 1988 English translation by David Nash.

I'm telling how we went from here, from Yuendumu. I'm telling you this story about when we went to Jila Well. The Whitefellas from Alice Springs came out. They enlisted my help.

At Jila Well we turned east. We went along the waterless spinifex plain. It was dry. We went around in the spinifex, and saw *walpajirri*, the spinifex dweller. I'll tell you about that animal, the *walpajirri* that we got. It was a female one, and we put it in a box.

After rising in the morning, we travelled north to Jarrardajarrayi.[22] We were a long way north in the middle of the spinifex plain. We got a *nyinjirri* (ridge-tailed monitor), which was travelling in the spinifex. We continued travelling, and got four (tyre) punctures. After that, we fixed them, and camped on the spinifex plain.

We set out the next morning. We saw the *milpa-rtiri* (spectacled hare-wallaby), which was on the spinifex plain. We saw it, then we kept going along. I saw some dingo pups at a soakage. After that we saw something that looked like a *wakulyarri* (black-footed rock-wallaby).

We went west to Pirtipirti. We stopped there, and filled up with water. We stayed the night there. In the morning we set off looking for kangaroos. The dogs scared one away.

We went a long way west to Yawulyawulu. We went and went and went. No *mala* (rufous

hare-wallaby), no *pakuru* (golden bandicoot), nothing at all. We saw only *milpa-rtiri*. There were a lot of them. The old people used to eat that animal. We got a snake, a dangerous snake, which was on the spinifex plain. It was a very long one. After that we got two *pirntina* (woma pythons). We went a long way from Pirtipirti. After that, we went north. We camped halfway, on the spinifex plain, at a place where there was no water. We went a long way. We were going westward. I was walking. We were looking for animals, for *mala* and for *pakuru*. After that, we went west. We shot a large *wardilyka* (bush turkey). I shot it myself.

After that, we saw a soakage. It was just a clump of green grass. We didn't dig it, poor thing. We left it. We got six *lungkarda* (blue-tongued lizards), a lot. I brought them back and gave them to (my wife) Napangardi. We got a lot of *wanakiji* (bush tomatoes), and *yarla* (bush potatoes). We dug up a lot. We dug with a shovel.

After that, we went half way. We dug for *walpajirri*, dug and dug. 'It's gone right in!' Dug and dug and dug. 'Really down here somewhere!' It still went digging down. I listened to it, 'It's really digging there, that *walpajirri*.' I sent it off yesterday. I sent several to Alice Springs: two female, one male *walpajirri*. There might be a number on the spinifex plain there, in pairs. There are many of them, a group here, a group there. Later, I'll go west to Lapi Lapi, for *pakuru*, *mala*, *nyintarn-nyintarnpa* (quoll) – that animal like a cat. We went west to the termite mounds. Really big termite mounds. They stand up very high like a hill. No *pakuru*, no *janganpa* (possum) there, but there are dingoes at that place.

After that we went to Japanangka and Japangardi country that stands there to the north – name of Yawulyawulu. From there, we continued travelling, and saw many kangaroos. They ran away when they saw us.

From there, we went along and got some *wanakiji*. We put them in a bucket and a box. I got many in my hat. Old (George) Japangardi got a lot, too. That *warrarna* (great desert skink) that lives on the spinifex plain is like a fish – similar skin. Its skin is like a fish's. We got very many *warrarna*-like animals: *warlura* (gecko), and *pirirrpa* (spiny-tailed gecko) – we got everything. And *yurdiwaruwaru* (long-nosed dragon), *jalupa* (desert skink), *lungkarda*, and *nyinjirri*. They are light-coloured there, on the spinifex plain, many of them. There's a snake we call *mukurulypa-mukurulypa* (python), very big, like *yurnturrkunyu* (black-headed python) or *pirntina*, with markings.

In the following story, Darby describes another trip with Parks and Wildlife staff in search of wildlife in the Tanami. He was saddened to find many of the animals he hunted as a child were endangered or possibly extinct.

Pakuru (golden bandicoot), we call 'em *pakuru*. Finish, whole lot. Dead! That's all. We bin have a big mob of *pakuru* (before). This time (when) we're travelling, nothing now we never find 'em.

That far we bin going round everywhere. From there, we bin go right in to Gurindji country now, me and Ken Johnson. We bin walking round there, what they call Suplejack Station, just west from

FROM LEFT Judy Nampijinpa Granites with bush potato; George Japangardi and Darby with *walpajirri* (bilbies) in 1979; Peggy Nampijinpa Brown collecting firewood; and *wanakiji* (bush tomatoes)

Kartarra. Alright, we bin there all around longa desert, look (for) *mala*. We never find 'em, nothing. We bin all through. We never find 'em possum, nothing. We never find 'em *jajirdi* (western quoll), nothing.

The 1970s were a period of rapid change in Yuendumu. The administration of the settlement now involved Warlpiri. Government policy, and terms associated with it, also changed: self-determination became self-management, and both were supported by the concept of Aboriginalisation. A male-dominated Aboriginal Council initially represented Warlpiri interests. Then Yuendumu Council was established in 1974 and by 1977, twenty-five (predominantly middle-aged male) councillors were elected to represent what was now referred to as Yuendumu Community. The Warnayaka Tribal Council, of which Darby was a member, was also in existence as a means of acknowledging and maintaining the authority of the older men.

Back then he was involved with the tribal elders, and still takes part sometimes, by getting young people and helping them in court. But now he's getting older. It's different to the Community Council, the Tribal Council was actually talking with the court mob, with the judge, about how to deal with Aboriginal Law and Whiteman's Law. So he was the main person. He was very much involved in that issue. Now, he's given it to someone else. – OTTO JUNGARRYI SIMS

Visitors
Naturalists

A decline in numbers of marsupials in Central Australia was acknowledged as early as 1932, and, by the 1970s, some researchers thought fourteen identified species may have been extinct.[23] Ken Johnson estimated that one third of the mammals in the area had disappeared in the last fifty years, and that *mala* were close to extinction in the Tanami.[24] In the 1980s, Parks and Wildlife staff bred *mala* in captivity, and with the involvement of the Warlpiri community, released a small group into a fenced-off paddock near Willowra, on land associated with the *Mala Jukurrpa*. Unfortunately, they did not survive, perhaps due to the particularly hot summer in 1986. Darby thought dingoes or eagles killed them. A larger, electrified enclosure was subsequently constructed and a program of controlled burning implemented.

Les Hiddins, the Bush Tucker Man, wrote:

Darby Jampijinpa is a great old bloke. The first time that I met him, he was living in a small tin shed behind the local minister's house. At the time, I had never worked in the desert country so everything that Darby cared to show me was brand new. Looking back on it now, I guess my complete ignorance of the desert may to some extent have been compensated for by my desire to learn. I was a pretty thirsty student in those days. As far as my job was concerned, I was only interested in learning about bush tucker and survival. But that old man from Yuendumu made sure that my education was much broader than that.

He felt that I had to understand the country and what it stood for. I had to understand why an outcrop of rocks on a flat landscape attracted the rain clouds and broke them up to capture precious water in the crevices. He was teaching me the theory behind things. He was teaching me survival in a way that only a desert man could.

As the years went by, the teaching continued and Darby never gave up on his pupil, always proud to show off his country. Sometimes we got into areas that were beyond me, and other times, things were interesting but of little relevance to my work at the time.

I remember once we travelled for about 150km through the open desert country to find a particular bush that Darby had in mind. He knew exactly where to find it and in what direction. On and on we drove, across the vast open edges of the Tanami. Whenever I asked him how much further it was, he simply pointed with the blade of his hand and said 'more further'.

After a good three hours' drive we finally arrived, with the fuel gauge touching half a tank. We got out of the Land Rover and trudged over to a green-coloured bush almost two metres tall. I peered at it, looking for some sort of fruit or berry or anything. Nothing. Just the bright green leaves. Then Darby began to proudly explain the bush to me. Apparently the green leaves of the bush were burnt to produce a thick smoke, and the smoke was used as some sort of post-natal medicine by Aboriginal women. I couldn't help but smile to myself as I began to photograph and catalogue Darby's bush. The Army Chief of the General Staff would be thrilled to bits about this!

But this has been part and parcel of the learning process, part of learning about the country. At times we spent days exploring Darby's land, visiting his birthplace, or the rock shelter in which he lived as a young man, hunting kangaroos with a woomera and spear. In the process he taught me how to find the honey ants hidden in amongst the stunted acacias, or just where to dig a water soak in this parched landscape. And, of course, through all of this we yarned a lot. Darby told me about the time he worked for the Army during the 'Japanee War', droving cattle up around Borroloola in the Gulf Country.

We talked about other trips, about the time when we found the 'biggest mob' of native tobacco growing way to the south, down near the sand country, or when we shot that big red kangaroo and we carried it back to the camp, draped over the jerry cans on the Land Rover.

These days Darby hardly ever uses the old tin shed. He's now got his own outstation up and running, just a few miles out from Yuendumu. It's his own country, not far from where he was born. He's very proud of his country, and his country is obviously very proud of him.[25]

One of the functions of the Tribal Council was to resolve problems that were considered tribal matters. The old men like Darby thought a lot of the social problems could be resolved by enforcing Warlpiri Law. However, the Tribal Council found it difficult to deal with some issues that were considered Whitefella problems. This included the increasing amounts of alcohol entering the community and the practice of grog running.

We never take anything from white mans ... This people here, while they're every minute – Whitefella drink – grog, they bin bringing more trouble. They're fighting round, stick 'em in the knife, cutting one another. Bleeding head, and poke 'em right in the heart. Poor bugger him get killed for nothing. Wasting people! That knife belonga only cutting meat ...

I hear about travelling, 'They're cutting one another (in) Alice Springs!' They stick 'em in longa rib. That's not right. He'll kill a man. We hear about trouble all the time. Long time ago, we never do that. We sitting and feeding kangaroos for my mother, grandmother and my grandfather again, and my old man, my father. Give it meat for everybody ...

That drink only belonga Whitefellas. I bin only grow up (with) wild sugarbag, and wild honey ants. That's all we bin grow up (with). That lot is good. That's why we bin grow up good. I don't know about this time. We bin go meeting (the) Queen, down Alice Springs. (She) bin give it, 'Oh, Aboriginal people can drink.' No good. No good at all! That drink belonga white man, not Aboriginal people ... That drink – throw 'em out altogether! We no want to see 'em more!

Susan Congreve, art coordinator at Warlukurlangu Artists, recalled an incident in the 1990s when one of Darby's relatives was drunk:

> We were sitting in the art centre, and I looked out the back window, and Ivy (Darby's wife) was there going, 'guns, bullets, guns, bullets...' so fast that I couldn't understand what she was saying. It was only later that I realised that's what she had been screaming. And then we heard a gun go off. And I looked out the back window, and I saw Darby trying to wrestle the gun off someone. Bessie came racing down the side of the art centre. She was screaming out in Warlpiri, 'My grandchildren are over there. Never let guns off there. How dare you.' She was saying it a lot more strongly than that, but it was really like, 'I'm going to kill you for that, all my kids are here, my whole family, how dare you.' And Darby was just begging him to give him the gun back. Really upset. And Ivy was hysterical. And I got into a panic because I saw Bessie go. I thought, I'm going to see two people that I really care about shot. So, I went out there, too. And I thought, oh no, now I've really done it, we'll all get shot. And when the policeman came around, that man had locked himself in the house. Darby was so brave. He could have shuffled quickly away and hidden, but he actually took it upon himself to get the gun. And the horrible thing was that it was his gun.
>
> I found out later that the argument had started when somebody had seen the 'payments to artists' book in the art centre and seen that Darby had some money from a painting and they'd gone off and spoken about it. And that man decided that he wanted to go to Alice Springs. He went to get some money off Darby. And Darby wouldn't give it to him... Darby was shaking the whole day, trying to explain the man's behaviour, with all of us saying, you don't have to explain, that's not your responsibility.

Yuendumu Council adopted a solution to designate the Yuendumu Land Trust a dry area, where alcohol was prohibited, unless a resident held a liquor permit. This system continues today, and those carrying alcohol into the community without a permit risk having their cars impounded by the police and then sold by the Liquor Commission. It was perhaps a result of the ineffectiveness of dealing with the social problems in the community that the Tribal Council became increasingly marginalised and eventually dissolved. The new governance structures relied upon community members who had a good understanding of English and were able to read and write. This effectively excluded the older men like Darby, who saw it as further evidence that the old ways were not valued as much as they should be. Colonisation and the subsequent social experiment of settlement and passive welfare had eroded their authority. Darby expressed some of his frustrations when he spoke to the Select Committee on Constitutional Development in 1989 (translation):

Big city now! DARBY
Yuendumu 2001

All you who can read paper will write and send this to Darwin and it should be a good law, (but) the old law is a good one because that's where everything started before. Think about the ceremony for the young men. Think about it, it will be a problem because that used to be in the old law for a long time and now you want to shut it out altogether . . . All these government men come to us and you've got to try to talk to them, and think about changing the old law for this new one . . . (but) they will argue a lot like they do inside parliament. They argue and they fight like a wallaby.[26]

Eddie Jampijinpa Robertson proposed some solutions in response (translation):

> The Land Rights Law and the Tribal Council Law, maybe we can put those old laws into this law . . . then we will have the law all the time, (then) they can't change anything and they can't take it from us.[27]

Reflecting on Darby's frustration, Thomas Jangala Rice said that the Tribal Council is no more because now the strong old men are all gone and many who are left are either corrupt or frightened.[28]

Yuendumu Council was constituted under the *Local Government Act (NT)* in 1993, and today the community has a local government council of elected members with an elected president. An administrator is employed to negotiate the day-to-day running of the community in consultation with councillors and local government guidelines. Darby never became a prominent member of the new governance structures in the community. But he was a long-term contributor and participant on many committees, including the Baptist Church, Men's Museum, Art Centre, Yuendumu Outstation Council and to a lesser extent, the School, Warlpiri Media, Mining Company and Social Club Store. In the 1980s, Darby was still very much involved in the Church, the School's cultural program and general community matters, but as Otto Jungarrayi Sims observed:

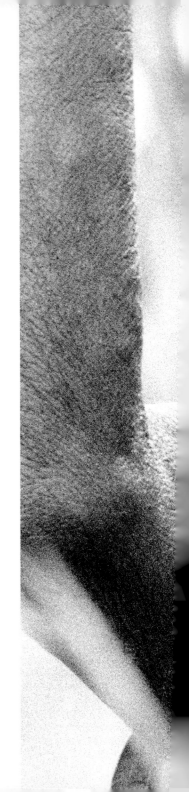

Bessie Nakamarra Sims

> He just worked quietly, doing good things. They'll see the outcome of what he's done. I think it's good to work quietly. I think he learnt that from all the old missionaries. I think in the future a lot of people will like to remember him as a respected old man who's done a lot of things for this community.

Visitors

Researchers

Whitefellas have been writing about Warlpiri people for over one hundred years, since the explorers Gosse and Warburton travelled through the country. Variously referred to as Wailbri, Walbiri, Ilpara, Walmulla, Warramulla, Ngalia, Warnayaka and Ngalpari (some of which refer to subdivisions), the people of the Tanami are now generally referred to as Warlpiri.[29] As academics and anthropologists began to visit Warlpiri country, a tradition was established that has continued to the present, and research amongst the Warlpiri has become somewhat institutionalised. Simon Japangardi Fisher, the first Warlpiri man to obtain his Master's degree, claims that the Warlpiri are the most studied group of people in Central Australia.

The first academic researchers to visit Warlpiri land include the 1931 South Australian Board for Anthropological Research expedition through the Cockatoo Creek area, and Ted Strehlow's early journeys to collect information from informants for his studies of Aboriginal language and culture. Olive Pink, an anthropologist, camped with Warlpiri people at Yurnmaji and Pirtipirti (Thompson's Rockhole) in the 1930s and 40s. However, it was not until the establishment of Yuendumu that academics and researchers consistently visited the Warlpiri. Over the last fifty years, anthropologists, linguists, musicologists, dental researchers, art critics, geologists, botanists, filmmakers and historians have spent considerable time with the Warlpiri community at Yuendumu. There are literally hundreds of books relating directly to the Warlpiri. Not surprisingly, Darby, as a charismatic and willing informant, is often present in this research.

One of the first researchers that Darby worked with was Nancy Munn, an American social anthropologist.[30] It was to investigate the Warlpiri coding of information in graphic representation that brought Munn to Yuendumu in 1956 to carry out fieldwork. Her particular interest involved a structural analysis of the cultural symbolism and associated theoretical problems among the Warlpiri.[31] Munn, whom Warlpiri refer to as Nangala, endeared herself to her subjects by choosing to live in a tent rather than a house in Yuendumu. She collected graphic designs by observing sand drawings or iconographic representations used in men's and women's ceremonies. She also collected

Ngapa Jukurrpa (Water Dreaming) drawings by Darby for anthropologist Nancy Munn 1957

drawings from informants. Munn collected two such drawings from Darby in 1957. Although Darby was not one of her main informants, Munn said she remembered him because of his friendliness, and because of the two *Ngapa Jukurrpa* (*Water Dreaming*) drawings he produced:

> They seemed to me quite distinctive, especially the second one in which he printed his own name on the rock (I don't recall any other instance in which a man printed or wrote his own name within the drawing like this – identifying himself with the place and the drawing in this way) . . . It is among my favourite paper drawings from Yuendumu.[32]

Over a period of twenty years, dental researcher Murray Barrett visited Yuendumu on behalf of the University of Adelaide. His ongoing research and data collection aimed to provide information about 'dental diseases under settlement conditions' and to acquire an 'accumulation of information on facial growth and dental development'.[33] Researchers accompanied Barrett on occasion from places as far away as Denmark, Japan and the United Kingdom.

Initially, Barrett's research focused on how environmental factors and eating habits amongst the Warlpiri had changed after settlement. Water quality was tested and a dental survey begun. This survey was quite extensive, and included photos, measurements, casts and x-rays. Warlpiri were also asked about their beliefs relating to teeth. Darby, Jimija Jungarrayi, Pharlap Japangardi and Tim Japangardi Langdon were Barrett's main informants. In an observation of Warlpiri explanations of toothache, Barrett wrote:

> Darby stated that toothache is caused by a little brown snake with a soft nose and a long tail who lives in the grass. This snake is called *wilka ngarunu* and he 'sings' the tooth or bites ('fights') the tooth and makes a hole in the tooth. 'After that one he cries – *murumuru kulgalga*.' Darby knows this to be true because the old men who told him about it said that it was true.[34]

Barrett concluded that:

> Accounts given by the four men made it quite apparent that they still believe in the efficacy of magic. They hold the strong conviction that in days gone by it was possible for toothache to be cured by knowledgeable old men who were thoroughly conversant with details of the necessary magic songs and acts.[35]

Discussing Barrett's research, Ted Strehlow drew attention to Tim's comments that such men were dead and that many of these songs had been lost.[36] Tim explained it simply:

Mirnirri (thorny devil)

These days we have doctors and dentists – nobody uses these songs now.[37]

Darby's grandparents told him that eating *mirnirri* (thorny devils) could prevent toothache, and Jimija claimed to eat them for this reason.[38]

When Barrett and his colleagues visited Yuendumu, they would stay with resident missionaries Tom and Pat Fleming, with whom Barrett became good friends. Barrett's first visit in 1951 lasted three weeks, and included the Head of the Department of Dental Science, T. D. Campbell, and nineteen others, all of whom camped in tents at the mission house. Pat worked with Barrett recording family trees, and eventually collected between 600-700 family records, including births, deaths, marriages and other historical information.[39] Barrett estimated the ages of Warlpiri, and another researcher verified the dates, which were usually within six months of Barrett's estimates.[40] Darby's birth date was recorded as 1905. Pat's records, collected and maintained in Barrett's absence, were part of the supporting material for widening the research program in 1961 to incorporate further data, including face, skull and body measurements

This was not the first time Warlpiri had been the subjects of medical examination. In 1931, the Board for Anthropological Research, with members from the University of Adelaide and the South Australian Museum, travelled to the Cockatoo Creek (Yanartilyi) area, to the east of Yuendumu. They made face and breast casts. They also collected boomerangs and other implements. It was this early research, facilitated by missionary Ernie Kramer, and the subsequent expedition to The Granites in 1936, that resulted in University of Adelaide researchers travelling to Yuendumu in 1951. Twenty years later, Barrett and his co-researchers had accumulated 1,717 sets of dental casts of 446 people, skull measurements of 288 people, hand and wrist measurements of 250 people, and many photos.[41] Much of this data was compared with skulls of Aboriginal people held at the South Australian Museum. Warlpiri remember the research with a mixture of humour and disdain at being 'treated like animals', but also express a feeling of *wiyarrpa* (sympathy) for their family whose dignity they feel was denied by the researchers.

The late Ken Hale was a talented American linguist who first worked on the Warlpiri language in 1959.[42] Long-term Yuendumu resident Frank Baarda remembered Ken's remarkable talent for learning languages, and how 'he just seemed to be able to pick them up'. In his first two years in Australia, Hale documented the core vocabulary of seventy languages.[43] He returned in 1966-67 for an in-depth study of Warlpiri, and again in 1974, at the commencement of Yuendumu School's bilingual program. This visit was an intensive six-week period when Ken taught Warlpiri courses to school staff, discussed a Warlpiri curriculum, and worked with Robin Japanangka Granites on a series of taped lessons. Considering the small amount of time he spent in the community, he had an extraordinary ability with the Warlpiri language, and was able to converse freely with Warlpiri speakers. In the next twenty years, he visited three more times for relatively short periods, yet had a significant impact on local linguists. He encouraged the study of linguistics in the Warlpiri community by first language speakers, and continued his strong support of bilingual school programs.

Hale also expended considerable effort in recording and documenting the names of flora, fauna and significant sites in Warlpiri country. It is not surprising that he and Darby became friends. Darby loved to teach people the Warlpiri words of plants and animals, and Ken and Darby both shared a love of languages. Darby spoke several Central Australian languages fluently, including the languages of neighbouring Anmatyerr and Pintupi. Having travelled extensively, he claimed also to be able to converse with speakers of Warumungu, Warlmanpa, Gurindji, Pitjantjatjara, Kaytetye, Alyawarr, Arrernte, Jingili, Mudbara and Kriol. Responding to the older Warlpiri generation's use of English, Dave Price, married for over twenty-five years to Bess Nungarrayi, a Warlpiri woman, , wrote:

I am always telling people how lousy my Warlpiri is compared with Bess' mastery of English. There is also the extreme deliberately imposed difficulty that was put in the way of young men learning *jila wiri*, the sacred Warlpiri language used by the old men. They were expected to learn it by hearing it, with no instruction. There was a key to mastering it that required an uncommon level of understanding of how languages work. They learnt through brief exposure. Ken Hale talks about it in one of his papers. He was deeply impressed by the intellectual achievement it represented. I don't know if it is still learnt but it certainly was in Darby's time.[44]

Over a period of twenty years, after Ken had returned to America, he and Darby corresponded by sending each other cassettes recorded in Warlpiri. Linguists Mary Laughren and David Nash recorded many of these 'letters' for Darby, and Ken transcribed some of them. He thought they could one day form an interesting archive of Letters from Darby. Before his death, Ken (whom Darby called Japanangka) returned some of Darby's tapes:

Here I am, good afternoon. You are listening to me Japanangka, you are listening to my story. My name is Darby. Here I am talking all that way to you. I am talking to you my child, my sister's son, Japanangka. You are listening to me here at Yuendumu where I live. I have been worrying for you, of course, my sister's son.[45]

An eclectic mix of history, *Jukurrpa* and social comment, Darby's letters to Ken are further evidence of his desire to communicate and build lasting relationships with Whitefellas:[46]

Japanangka, you are now in your own country. I am talking to you here. Maybe you are well. Maybe you've gone to the war . . . Japanangka, you might tell me, maybe you might tell me good news, whether you've gone to the war or maybe you stayed. This is Darby talking to you. It's terrible to think that you might be going to the war. You make me sorry for you poor thing, Japanangka, you who were once here, you whose car we used to ride around in . . . Well goodbye Japanangka.[47]

Reflecting on Ken's correspondence with Darby, Dave Price writes:

Ken did this with Bess' Dad as well. When Bess and (sister) Jeannie visited Ken in his home a couple of years before his death all of their conversation was in Warlpiri, and he had taught his wife and kids to speak it as well. We were told that he was successfully tested for fluency in thirty languages and was known to speak many more. Bess heard him use Chinese in a restaurant for example. He told Bess that Warlpiri was one of his favourites and challenging for him. He was a quiet and thoroughly decent genius. If Warlpiri was challenging for him then we've all got an excuse.

1931 Cockatoo Creek expedition

Visitors
The White Toyota Mob

The metaphor is that of theatre. The script is written in Canberra, experts travel outback to build a 'stage'; the Aborigines are 'actors' on the stage of the State. GILLIAN COWLISHAW[48]

Every day in Yuendumu, consultants, researchers and 'government mob' drive in and out of the community in White Toyotas. They come to talk about service delivery, cultural protocol and government policy. They come to consult, direct, research and educate and are often met by the same group of people, many of whom sit on several committees. Warlpiri who sit on these committees often joke that their 'job' is to attend committee meetings, and that there is one every day for most of the year. Ideas are discussed, plans made, and procedures followed. Some Warlpiri use the occasion as a forum to air their grievances about a separate community issue, and many

of the more experienced visitors are somewhat cynical, and express their frustrations about the process. They realise that they are also 'actors' on the 'stage of the State'. There are also those that some people refer to as the 'white saviours', people who work for Aboriginal organisations and come to help the community solve their problems. An often quoted adage relating to non-Aboriginal community workers is that they are either 'misfits, missionaries or mercenaries'.

To Darby, these meetings were just like a ceremony: there were rules to follow, those who led the proceedings, and those who participated. And there were those who sometimes observed the meetings just because they were entertaining, or they had been dragged in and were too far from the door to quietly slip away.

When Gough Whitlam came to open the Old People's Programme building he was an old man himself. He sat with Darby before making his speech, when he re-enacted the pouring of sand into Vincent Lingiari's hand, spoke at length about the Labor Party's achievements, and a lot of other things not particularly relevant to the occasion. But, that was alright, he was an old man like Darby and used to be the Prime Minister, and everyone expected him to talk for a long time.

Sometimes the White Toyotas give way to light aircraft, and Senators and Parliamentary Secretaries come to discuss some issue. A 'public meeting' is called and people asked to attend at the council building. A makeshift wall is often constructed in the middle of the room, and the women sit on one side and the men on the other. This is because some of the men and women are required to avoid each other under Warlpiri Law – they have what Warlpiri call 'no room' for each other. The visitors often sit at the front and ask questions in English and wait for responses. These usually come from those with the best English. Misinterpretation and miscommunication are common. Then the visitors leave, and sometimes they talk to the media and tell them about the meeting, often drawing conclusions and solutions to problems taken at face value from their informants. But, this is usually of little concern to those who had attended as they would likely be preparing for another important meeting. Or if the Central Land Council have organised a 'royalty' meeting, then all other meetings are off, and everyone heads down to what they jokingly refer to as the 'big argument' building.

As Darby used to say, might be government mob, might be health mob, might be land council mob . . . You can see their White Toyotas coming in every day.

Darby was a strong believer in the importance of maintaining the Warlpiri 'skin' system and adhering to appropriate Warlpiri marriage of 'right skins'. A Jampijinpa man, like Darby, could marry a Napangardi woman as his 'first choice'. However, he could also marry a Nakamarra or Napaljarri woman in an acceptable union. When Darby was a young man, Warlpiri men would be given a 'promised wife' at the time of their initiation, and would sometimes be required to take their brother's wives if they passed away. Only under special circumstances could they negotiate their own marriage. When a man was 'promised' a wife by his father-in-law, the woman was often very young, or in some cases, had yet to be born. As a result, the young unmarried men often competed for the attention of women married to older men, like Darby's father, who had accumulated many wives by old age.

Darby said this was the cause of much conflict, particularly when Warlpiri moved into the settlement, as the young men and women had more opportunity to establish and maintain their secret love affairs. Since then, fewer Warlpiri have chosen to follow the 'promised wife' system, and most men marry women more or less their same age. Some Warlpiri now even marry outside the traditional boundaries of the 'skin' system. In doing so, they say they marry 'for love'. Darby, however, was always quick to point out that he thought Warlpiri should only marry 'right skin', and would refer to *Jukurrpa* stories warning of the negative consequences of marrying 'wrong skin'. But, Warlpiri people don't usually get married in the same way as Whitefellas, in a ceremony in a church. Warlpiri joke about getting 'kangaroo married', the ceremony of marriage sometimes represented by picking up one's swag (mattress) and moving from one camp to another to live together. Such unions exist outside of Australian common law marriage, and are officially designated as de facto relationships, yet are recognised as marriages under Warlpiri customary law.

Warlpiri marriages, particularly for older men like Darby, often involve negotiation with the wife's family. When Darby showed an interest in Ivy Napangardi in the 1980s, there was some opposition in the community to the two forming a relationship. Darby was much older than Ivy, although this was not unusual at Yuendumu in those days. Ivy's mother opposed the union, apparently concerned that Ivy could not look after Darby. However, Darby disagreed and, in frustration, arranged for he and Ivy to travel by car to the remote Jila Well Outstation and then continue on foot to Puyurru Outstation.

A lot of goanna we bin kill 'em. Ivy bin there standing, looking out, never follow (the) track. Goanna run longside Ivy, (she) never bin see 'em. Only I bin see 'em track. And from there – one, two, three, four, five, six, seven – seven goannas. Oh, very good!

We bin travelling (through) all that country right up to Yumurrpa. *Wirliya* (footwalk), from Puyurru.

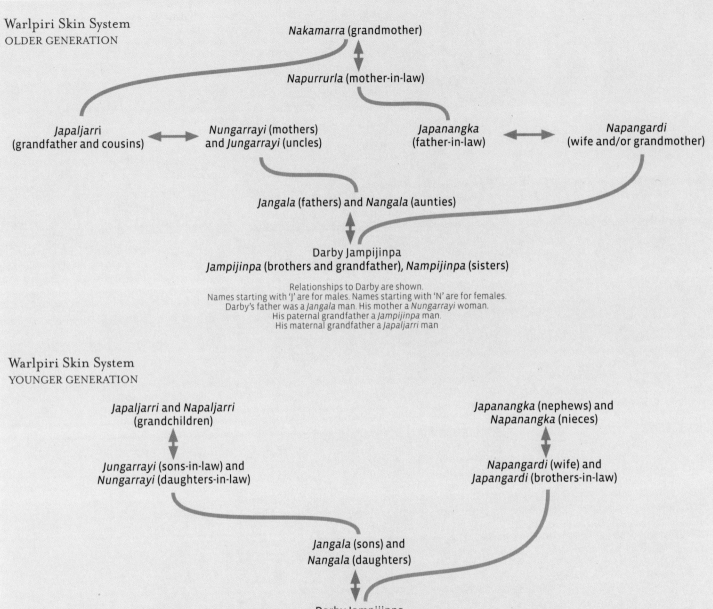

Warlpiri Skin System
OLDER GENERATION

Nakamarra (grandmother)

Napurrurla (mother-in-law)

Japaljarri (grandfather and cousins)

Nungarrayi (mothers) and *Jungarrayi* (uncles)

Japanangka (father-in-law)

Napangardi (wife and/or grandmother)

Jangala (fathers) and *Nangala* (aunties)

Darby Jampijinpa
Jampijinpa (brothers and grandfather), *Nampijinpa* (sisters)

Relationships to Darby are shown.
Names starting with 'J' are for males. Names starting with 'N' are for females.
Darby's father was a *Jangala* man. His mother a *Nungarrayi* woman.
His paternal grandfather a *Jampijinpa* man.
His maternal grandfather a *Japaljarri* man

Warlpiri Skin System
YOUNGER GENERATION

Japaljarri and *Napaljarri* (grandchildren)

Japanangka (nephews) and *Napanangka* (nieces)

Jungarrayi (sons-in-law) and *Nungarrayi* (daughters-in-law)

Napangardi (wife) and *Japangardi* (brothers-in-law)

Jangala (sons) and *Nangala* (daughters)

Darby Jampijinpa
Jampijinpa (brothers and grandchildren), *Nampijinpa* (sisters and grandchildren)

Darby's ideal marriage partner is a *Napangardi* woman.
His children will then be *Jangala* and *Nangala*.
His brothers' children are the same and considered as his own.
His sisters' children are his nephews and nieces.
His sons' children are *Jampijinpa* and *Nampijinpa*.
His daughters' children are *Japaljarri* and *Napaljarri*.

KEY

First choice marriage

Patrilineal descent

Darby and wife Ivy
Napangardi Poulson

I bin about four weeks there. Ivy bin there sitting – nothing. And (she) never cook damper. I bin cook damper.

(Ivy) still young. Mother-in-law, (she) tell 'em me – right, (she) might like take (her) away from me. And I bin keep going, 'No, I got to take (her).' Take (her to) bush. Alright, we bin going travelling now. All the way right up to Jila Well. We're camping around there. And we're travelling right up to that big hole, longa Jila. We camp there. We move again, afternoon we look about goanna – not kangaroo. After that, we bin come back, and me and Ivy bin looking around for goanna. How many goanna we bin get 'em? Four. And from there, we bin cooking right in the Jila Well, longa old bore, *karlarra* (west) side. We bin camping there. How many days we bin camp? Four days.

Somebody bin come along – alright, we bin jump on longa that one (car). We bin go right up to Yuendumu. Sitting round there. Mother-in-law bin here (at Yuendumu). (She) never bin after me more. That Japanangka (father-in-law), him bin say, 'Alright, you two fella go!'

Old Japanangka, Ivy's father, gave his permission for them to live together. They spent the next twenty years together. Darby treated her like a princess, and in return,

(She) never run away from me. Napangardi look after me properly.

Chapter Seven

Proper Head
Drover Man

When Darby sat with old Warlpiri stockmen at Yuendumu and talked about the people and places they worked, a common theme emerged. They discussed the landscape and the various *Jukurrpa* of that country, mapping the droving routes and cattle properties in relation to language and 'skin' groups and *kuruwarri*.[1] As a group, these men appeared to frame — not only their identities, relationships and histories within their complex religious and social system — but also their experiences of the pastoral industry. Ann McGrath wrote that for old stockmen (like Darby):

> Aboriginal society was not truly colonised, for Aboriginal station people had a firm footing on either side of the frontier.[2]

Darby had fond memories of his working life; he enjoyed working with cattle, travelling and meeting people, and seeing new country. He liked to tell these stories to young people, thinking that they would benefit from similar experiences. They would joke about 'old Darby' having done everything. 'You know, old Darby, he was a stockman. Yeah, a drover man! He's been everywhere. Maybe he was a cook, too? Yeah, and he was working at the gold mining . . . ' And so on.

When telling the stories of his working life, Darby did not always use chronological order. Places and people were the markers that he would use to tell his stories; time and

They bin have 'em big
truck longa Coniston.
DARBY

dates were not necessary. Some people said that 'Darby liked the big numbers'. He was prone to exaggeration when it came to numbers; a thousand could easily be a million for Darby. He would also use words like 'behind', 'fresh one', 'and from there' to indicate time. He would use them interchangeably and in different ways depending on the context. This presented particular problems in reconstructing this period of his life.

I have used Darby's stories as a guide, referring to historical records to substantiate the time and place of events as much as possible in this account of Darby's working life up until the 1960s. I refer to some of the people with whom Darby worked, including prospector Jack Saxby, pastoralists Randal Stafford and Bill Braitling, and Darby's friend Jimija Jungarrayi. I begin at Coniston Station, where Darby had returned after the events of 1928 which are recounted in the next chapter.

When the long drought finally broke, Darby joined Jack Saxby on two prospecting journeys in the early 1930s. On the first of these, he was put in charge of the camels, and prepared them for the long journey to the goldfields.

That's early days. I got to ride a horse. Learn straight away. Sometime he drop down the ground. No saddle, only bareback. Ride him bareback, and we got to take 'em back big mob of camel down Coniston. Randal Stafford, him bin give me job.

From there, another job I get 'em from old Jack Saxby. We bin working there, now. I bin working to him, long time ago, old Saxby. This we can talk about, and I bin learn for riding camel. And making a yard, long Coniston. Randal Stafford, long time ago, he bin have (one of my) grandmother, Aboriginal girl. Everybody bin have an Aboriginal girl. Not white girl. No, nothing.

We work all the time there, riding horse. Put 'em on bridle and put 'em saddle and riding round. I got to go mustering round a lot of camel there. Four, five, six, seven camel. From there, we bring 'em into the station ... that's where we bin learn everything for the camel work. How to bring back a camel and put 'em in the house (yard). And 'whoosha, whoosha', make 'em lay down now, one-a-line. From there, longa big tree we tie 'em round. We put 'em on tail – behind here – lead 'em on. And one, two, three, four, five, six, seven. Seven altogether. And from there, we take 'em into the yard. Put 'em in the big Coniston yard.

Alright, we bin work and we bin learn, and we bin grow up to Whitefella, now. We (learn) bit of English, we get 'em from white man. I bin working to old Jack Saxby, long Coniston. Big mob of camel bin there. All the time, big mob of Aboriginal people travelling. Naked, no clothes. That far, while we bin there looking around.

From there, soon as I bin grow up there big boy, we get young man (initiated) straight away (at) Coniston. I bin sitting round proper man, now. And some girl, they bin want me. While we bin single man, they running away girl for we. They want to like (get) 'married' for me, now.

We bin cutting timber down, lot of timber. We going to build 'em that big yard, right near station.

That's where we bin learn work. We bin work there for clothes and blanket, food – everything – sugar, tea. That's long time ago.

Whitefella, they pull 'em the big truck, while he want to give *kuka* (meat) for we, while we bin sitting round there working. And we cutting down (timber), make 'em clear for that yard.

While we working there all the time, we knock off only five o'clock. That old man got to ring 'em bell, for while we want to knock off. After that, we go back and have everything food. Good food. They're cooking damper. That's longa station. Some girls bin work round there – Aboriginal girls.

Right, from there, people coming up everyway, hungry fella, you know. Hungry fella, they come everyways. They looking for the food, and we give it to hungry fella, while they sitting round the camp. They got a killer (bullock) alright. They bin only kill it two killer: one for Aboriginal peoples, one for the Whitefella – European people. That two killer, they got to use their cattle.

Alright, from there, they thinking about for that one. Cutting everything now, salt 'em up. Aboriginal girl there, and Aboriginal boy there, too. They work, cutting meat for that lot. And some they take 'em – what they call one quarter shoulder, and another quarter leg. They take 'em leg, and one cut of rib bone. They eat 'em everything bone there, too. Can't waste 'em cattle, long time ago. Hungry fella!

Alright, some fella we got to load him up and bring back in whole lot of stuff. Oh, might carry 'em a lot of cattle, too – while he bin kill 'em down the Coniston slaughterhouse. Bring back there and put 'em longa every backpack. And horse got to carry 'em, too. And give it for everybody, too. That's hungry people, while they bin living around there. Another lot bin there now, sitting around. And we give it meat, and we're telling, 'Don't look about trouble.' Whitefella might finish for whole lot. That true word.

Alright, from there, we get 'em more boy. One called Yikinyanu Japaljarri. He belonga Kunajarrayi (country). That's why I pick him up. And him not man, (only) boy.

Saxby, Darby and his young cousin Yikinyanu travelled northwest through Warlpiri country, passing Luurnpakurlangu (Mt Doreen), before heading west to Mikanji and Wapurtali (Mt Singleton). They prospected along the way before eventually arriving at The Granites goldfield.

Darby worked for Saxby at The Granites for about two years around the time of the 1931-32 gold rush. It was dry, barren country with few trees, and water was scarce. According to Charles (Pat) Chapman the water in the government well gave you diarrhoea unless you distilled it:

Then one day we were getting firewood and we went out and only about a mile and a half away I came across a little rockhole underground. It was only about three foot wide but eventually about eight foot, ten foot deep and it was full to the brim. It was beautiful water. It was fairly dry but it was full to the brim. We got our water from that for a long time, about six of us, but never told anybody else about it because they'd drain it out. Eventually they did find it and they drained the lot out of it. It was no good after.[3]

Darby would spend most days carting water from the well several miles away for Saxby and fellow prospector 'old Jack' Atherton. He would use a windlass to lift water up by the bucketful. Sometimes he would get water from a rockhole at Yarturlu-Yarturlu, the granite boulders to the south. He would also catch rainwater in drums.

That well down Granites, that's *bedy* (about) nearly seven mile from that hill. Long way, longa desert. All that country right up to (Granite) hill. Old Jack (Atherton), him bin cooking bread there. Big mob of *warlu* (fire), and plenty rain water. Fill 'em up every drum. That's no bore, only rain water. Big rain bin longa that place. Got to fill 'em up longa bucket, longa big drum all about. How many drum? Nine drums. Big drums. And we got to fill 'em up (with) rain water. He got to use it for tea.

That windmill down Granites, that's where we bin camp. Right longa that big hill. Two Jacks there, now. Saxby and old Jack. We work there now, longa Saxby. How many year? *Bedy* (about) two years. We bin have Christmas there.

Darby remembered a lot of Warlpiri camped at The Granites, and some women catching syphilis from Whitefellas. The Whitefellas lived in tents, and the Warlpiri camped some distance away. It was rough living for those Whitefellas, and the Chapmans made some little huts out of mud and stone. The weather was extreme: it was either very hot or very cold, and it rained only on rare occasions.

Stafford spoke to Ted Strehlow in 1932:

> I've been good to them on every station I've
> been on – I've fed them – I've treated them well.
> I've never interfered with them much on their
> walkabouts; and yet I feel sure that they don't
> like me much any more than they like those
> other whites who treat them as though they
> were dogs. But it doesn't matter to me. I know
> that these myalls (bush people) sometimes spear
> one of my bullocks; but as long as it doesn't
> happen too often, I say nothing about it. It was
> their country before I came into it, and I know
> they often have a pretty tough time in making
> a living for themselves.[6]

Visitors

Pastoralists and Prospectors

Coniston Station was taken up by Randal Stafford
in 1917 and stocked three or four years later.[4]
Stafford built his simple homestead of wooden
poles and spinifex by the Warburton Creek at the
Anmatyerr site of Yimampi, where he lived with
Alice, an Anmatyerr woman. Stafford was among
the first Whitefellas Darby met. He was an older
man, short, with a white bushy beard. Speaking
with a broad English accent, he was admired by
some of the white population for his tenacity
to survive on the frontier, and for his generosity
to prospectors who would stop at his homestead
on their way to and from The Granites goldfield.
One such visitor was Michael Terry, who recorded
this information about Stafford:

> His great-grandfather led the charge of the
> Inniskilling Dragoons at Waterloo; his uncle
> was the first white child born in Victoria.[5]

In the late 1920s and early 1930s, Michael
Terry – prospector, author and self-styled
'last explorer' – journeyed for a time in the 'big
paddock' of remote Central Australia.[7] The Warlpiri,
Pintupi and Anmatyerr people of his populist
accounts blend into the background
of a frontier landscape as childlike black
caricatures. They are the 'niggers', 'boys', 'bucks',
'lubras' and 'gins' of typical 1930s literature.
In 1928, Terry and his team set out to cross the
Tanami in six-wheel Morris trucks, prospecting
along the way. At the end of their journey, they
met Jack Saxby at Coniston Station, whom Terry
described as 'a tall dark cattleman-prospector'.[8]
Saxby accompanied Terry on his return to the

Randal Stafford

prospect near The Granites goldfield.

Although Saxby was implicated in the shooting at Nguntaru (Waterloo Rockhole), where several members of Darby's family were killed, Darby referred to Saxby as his friend, whom he had known since he first worked at Coniston Station before the massacre. But he did not say much more about the man, and there is not much detail about Saxby in the historical record. However, Saxby gave a few clues as to his character, in relation to his role in the events at Coniston, to the Board of Enquiry in 1929:

I am a prospector at present well sinking at Coniston ... I fired three shots at the leaders of the mob. I could not see whether I hit anyone ... I always carry a revolver on my tours and consider it necessary. I have had occasion to shoot at blacks before this trouble. I have had to shoot to kill.[9]

Saxby later worked on Mt Riddock Station. Peter Latz met an Aboriginal stockmen at Mt Riddock who remembered Saxby coming from Queensland and being a 'flash cowboy-type' dressed in black with stars on his saddle and his rifle in a sheath.[10] Latz knew Saxby was implicated in the Coniston shooting and thought that he was anxious to avoid the Warlpiri. He went to see him one day and found him dead in his hut, lying in the fireplace:

So, he got his just reward I think – he fell into the fire and died.[11]

At the age of twenty, William (Bill) Braitling had gone in search of gold at The Granites during the 1910 gold rush. After leaving the field and working in the Top End, he returned to the Tanami in search of cattle country. He was granted a grazing licence over an area of Warlpiri country in 1926, which was converted to a pastoral lease in 1930.[12]

Jack Jakamarra Ross saw Braitling, whom Warlpiri call Pirlini, at Kampalypa (Mission Creek). He was the first Whitefella Ross had seen. Lisa Watts and Simon Fisher relate the incident:

Ross was terrified, believing that a white ghost was approaching him. Braitling talked to Ross in an unintelligible language. However, Ross understood from Braitling's gestures that he was looking for water. Ross walked approximately 80kms out of fear, leading Braitling, who rode on horse back, to Mikanji Creek (McKenzie Well). Ross showed him a soakage filled with water, and he said that it was from that very day that Braitling settled permanently and 'made his home there for good'.[13]

In 1932, Braitling erected his tent camp at Mikanji, an important water source for the Warlpiri associated with the Water Dreaming.

Darby recalled Braitling raising goats, and

Thomas Jangala Rice, wolfram mine shaft at Luurnpakurlangu

exploring and prospecting through Warlpiri country on horseback. He appears to have done this at the expense of fulfilling the terms of his pastoral lease. A damning report by a 1935 NT Pastoral Lease Investigation Committee found the lease to be 'practically unstocked: 400 goats, 33 sheep and 50 horses'.[14]

In 1938, Braitling relocated to Luurnpakurlangu, which he called Mt Doreen after his wife. Oral accounts suggest that Braitling actively disrupted the traditional way of life for many Warlpiri by coercing them in from the bush to work for him as manual labourers mining wolfram by hand at Luurnpakurlangu. Others simply walked in. Some Warlpiri say they were attracted by the supply of food, the presence of family members, and that they thought they would be safe from any further reprisals after the Coniston massacre. Thomas Jangala Rice was a

child when he lived there (translation):

We were living at Mt Doreen Station. They used to give us food. That Whitefella Braitling was a 'cheeky' one. After we ate we used to go and work picking up wolfram.

We used to eat meat and flour. After lunch, we would go again to pick up more wolfram until late afternoon when we would hear the bell ring and we would come back to eat supper. When the other kids used to come back without any wolfram, or even just a little bit, Mrs Braitling used to put those kids to the side. She would say, 'You're too lazy, you have to sit on the side.' Mrs Braitling used to look after us, feed us and give us clothes. When the boys got older they would be sent away to work with the stockmen.

In 1944, hundreds of Warlpiri were in the vicinity

of the mines.[15] When Patrol Officer Gordon Sweeney investigated the reports of Braitling's mistreatment of workers at Luurnpakurlangu, he found evidence of several incidents, including the flogging of Jimija Jungarrayi. Darby was himself lucky to avoid punishment, as he said Braitling didn't like the men chasing the women, and he had been a bit of a 'lover boy' at Luurnpakurlangu on occasion. In 1945, Sweeney prosecuted Braitling for the assault on Jimija in the Supreme Court.[16] However, the presiding judge questioned Sweeney's integrity and refused to accept the reliability of the Warlpiri witnesses (including Jimija who denied that the incident had occurred, possibly intimidated by Braitling and the proceedings), and dismissed the case, despite the pressure applied by newspaper reports. However, serious concerns were raised independently by Baptist Minister Laurie Reece, and enough evidence was presented at the trial to merit a Federal investigation under Justice Simpson. The Simpson Enquiry vindicated Sweeney, but did not recommend taking any further action, or resolve the allegations that Braitling actively prevented Warlpiri from accessing their important water sources at Pikilyi. However, further attention was drawn to the need for an independent settlement for the Warlpiri where they would not be exploited by pastoralists like Braitling.[17]

At one stage, up to 400 Warlpiri worked at Luurnpakurlangu digging the shafts and picking up small pieces of wolfram.[18] The mine operated for nearly forty years, the price of wolfram fluctuating with demand. During the Korean War, wolfram prices were pound for pound: one pound of wolfram buying one monetary pound.[19] Between 1939 and 1959 Braitling's wolfram production was valued close to £100,000.[20]

The Granites and nearby Tanami goldfields, were initially accessed from Halls Creek in the northwest, and occasionally along the chain of wells from Wave Hill in the north. However, after Terry's crossing of the Tanami, traffic along the now infamous Tragedy Track from Coniston Station increased – the northwest stock route (later to become the Tanami Highway) being incomplete in the 1930s. It was still very remote, dry country and many would-be prospectors died attempting to reach the field.

The Tanami's gold bearing potential was first recognised by geologist Alan Davidson when he prospected through Warlpiri country in 1900 with a camel team. He discovered gold at Janami, recording its name as Tanami.[21] A week later he arrived at Yarturlu-Yarturlu, naming the area Granite Hill after the large orange boulders in the area.[22] Although Davidson had not found the field profitable, several parties subsequently prospected at Tanami with varying degrees of success.[23] A gold rush occurred in 1910–11 when more than 500 people were reportedly on the field.[24] The Warden Lionel Gee recorded sixty men there in 1911 and ten others having died while travelling to and from Tanami. The men were in Warlpiri country, using their water and mining near a sacred site. Dick Kimber wrote:

From a Warlpiri perspective they should have reciprocated with gifts of food and prized items, but by not announcing their travelling presence by lines of smokes, and by taking rather than giving, the intruders were acting as enemies.

That British rule, and a belief in benign conquest and settlement, prevailed in the capital cities, was unknown to the Warlpiri, and also had limited relevance to the cattle-men and gold-seekers on the frontiers.[25]

In 1910/11, a prospector was speared by a group of Warlpiri. Dave Price writes:

Several Warlpiri were arrested, tried in Darwin, acquitted for lack of evidence, released on the outskirts of Darwin and 'disappeared'. Others seized by miners also 'disappeared'.[26]

The field went into decline soon after. However, another small rush occurred at The Granites in 1925-26 and a five-stamp battery crusher was transported by a team of donkeys to the field by Tanami Gold Mining N.L.[27] But it did not last as the drought conditions of subsequent years made life hard at Tanami and The Granites, and Michael Terry's reports had not been encouraging. However, interest in the field developed again in the early 1930s after the drought broke. In 1932, prospectors Jimmy Escreet and Jack Atherton found rich alluvial gold in the Burdekin Duck at The Granites. News of their find reached Charles Chapman (Snr) in Queensland who eventually purchased the Burdekin Duck lease for £5000.[28] Geologist Cecil Madigan was sent to the field in 1932 to investigate. He was followed by Melbourne print journalist F.E. Baume who was sent in response to a rise of The Granites share price.[29] Baume wrote an unfavourable report, expressed in the typically bleak language of 1930s Australian journalism, and the share price plummeted. At the height of the rush there were an estimated 200 people on the field.[30] Charles (Pat) Chapman described the rush:

Warlukurlangu Artists
visit to Kurra (Dead
Bullock Soak) open cut
gold mine 2001

They pegged all over the area. It would be flat ground with the sand and the spinifex and not even a stone on it. It was a silly thing if they ever saw anything out of it. Anyhow, it didn't last very long. They disappeared.[31]

By the end of 1932, only Chapman, whose plot showed the best potential, and a few others remained. However, they also eventually abandoned the field. It wasn't until later, at the end of the century, that The Granites gold mine was re-established. With new methods allowing for an economical extraction of gold from large amounts of extraneous material, it soon evolved into a large-scale, multi-million dollar enterprise, with Warlpiri sharing in the profits. Operated by Normandy-North Flinders Mining, the mine and associated Callie deposit was the largest in the Tanami Desert and reportedly the first gold mine in Australia developed in consultation with and permission from Aboriginal Owners. The old gold diggings were still visible: a five-stamp battery, a windmill, a few water tanks, the ruins of a stone house, and a few old shafts and mullock heaps. But, it was the new mine at Kurra (Dead Bullock Soak), 40km to the west, that showed the most potential. It was a series of large open cuts and underground shafts with a steady stream of trucks carrying rock to the surface. By 2004, Newmont Mining, one of the world's largest gold producing companies, had taken over the operation and the gold price increased to over $400 an ounce. Production is maintained at a steady pace, and royalties continue to flow into the Warlpiri communities.

Darby returned to Coniston Station with Saxby in 1932. However, they soon returned to the goldfields, this time travelling on the infamous 'Tragedy Track', past Mt Theo (Purturlu) and on to Tanami (Janami) where they spent their time looking for new prospects. Darby described crushing the stone with the battery:

I get 'em white stone, break 'em up. Fill 'em up stone and wash 'em in the water. We get 'em plenty of stone and break 'em up. Wash 'em in the water, longa dish.

Their efforts were mildly successful and they returned to Coniston with some gold. On his return to Coniston Station, Darby jumped on a truck to Alice Springs (previously Stuart Town). When he arrived, Darby discovered the police were investigating the murder of an Aboriginal woman west of Karrinyarra (Mt Wedge). They asked him to join them:

I bin police tracker, and we bin take prisoner now – that mob. Right up to Darwin . . . All that Pitjantjatjara. Ten fella, altogether. (After the trial) they let go again. No witness.

Darby once again returned to Coniston to work as a stockman. Although pastoralist Bill Braitling's main camp was at Mikanji, some Warlpiri were working in his wolfram mine at Luurnpakurlangu. Darby would occasionally visit Mikanji and Luurnpakurlangu in the 1930s, delivering mail from Coniston. He considered the mailman's job important, and to some degree it reflected the prestigious role of messenger within the Warlpiri community. Sometimes Darby would walk and occasionally Stafford or Braitling would provide him with a camel. This was in the mid-1930s, some years before Connellan Airways began their regular mail run to Mt Doreen, The Granites and Tanami.

I carry 'em mailbag from Coniston. Taking this way – *karlarra* – west. We bin have dinner down (at) the rockhole Wanulpuru. And after dinner, me travelling right through to that place called Ngapakurlangu. From there, we travelling right through to Wilypiri. We camp longa Wilypiri, and (next day) travelling from there right up to Mt Doreen (Luurnpakurlangu). I camp there.

Take 'em down mailbag, give it for Whitefella – Billy Braitling. (He) bin have nanny-goat. How many they bin kill 'em? Two nanny-goat. They bin get a killer there. No bullock. From there, we wait, have dinner. We bin get a little bit of flour. That Billy Braitling, he's a bushman.

We bin camp there. Old man Jimija (Jungarrayi), he bin working to him (Braitling). How many girl bin stop there? All the girl bin stop there. Sometime, they're robbing that man, too – Billy Braitling. Get tucker from him. Robbing him flour. They cook, make a dish, make a damper. They boil 'em tea and a little bit of sugar, longa Mikanji.

Randal Stafford bin there (at) Coniston. That's where we bin learn, long time ago. Sitting round there, and pick 'em up camel. Alright, we bin travelling right up to Mikanji. We camp there, and look after 'em proper way, and lead 'em back this way again, long Coniston. That's where we bin learn everything.

In the mid-1930s, Saxby convinced Darby to join him on another prospecting journey, offering to provide him with riding boots, clothes, rations and a riding camel. After learning the basics of station life at Coniston, and travelling to and from Mikanji, Luurnpakurlangu and The Granites, Darby headed east with Saxby to Kurundi Station and Hatches Creek in Alyawarr and Warumungu country. In explanation of his decision to follow Saxby, Darby said he was upset at his mother's passing and that he wanted to go away for a while:

I lose 'em my mother and my grandmother. All there, all bush, all finish. No food for everybody. That's where they bin finish – Kunajarrayi way – dry time. Before the war (and) after that (Coniston) trouble. I lose my family! I bin (go) down Kurundi (Station), working there, longa stockcamp, longa Saxby.

Darby and Saxby arrived at Kurundi Station and worked in the stockcamp. However, Saxby soon left for Queensland and Darby never saw him again.

Old mine site with battery crusher, The Granites

At Kurundi Station, Darby worked for George Birchmore, who had arrived in 1918 with Harry Henty.[32] Birchmore, an 'old-time revolver man', established Kurundi Station, while Henty, a 'soldier-settler' who would later be shot by Murtarta Jampijinpa (Willaberta Jack), developed land at nearby Frew River.[33]

There were not many Whitefellas working on Kurundi Station in the 'early days'. Darby was one of a group of Warlpiri men and women living there, with over one hundred Warumungu and Alyawarr who worked in the stock camp, constructed yards, broke in horses and drove cattle up and down to Newcastle Waters. It was remote, undeveloped country, and mustering the herd could take weeks, even months.

We bin working around Kurundi Station. We get a big mob of cattle. All the time we work. We got to brand 'em, and we got to (go) mustering round. Bring 'em two way – horse and cattle. We get clothes, boots and whip, and leggings. No money, nothing. Nothing, long time ago. That's early days. We working for only clothes and tucker, and for meat. And tea and sugar. And boot and hat. No money, long time ago.

Well, we never turn around and fight for the white man. We travelling one mob. He got money, and he buy 'em. He sell 'em out cattle, and he get everything. He get everything: saddle, bridle, flour and blanket. That's the way, early days.

Whitefella, he's drinking. We never robbing him. (It's) only drink belonga him. Bottle of brandy, rum, and bottle of whisky. That's belonga him. They're drinking around – after cattle. We never robbing that white man. No, nothing. Keep away.

Aboriginal stockmen are the unacknowledged pioneers of the pastoral industry

R.M. Williams, who took over in the 1940s, reflected on his time at Kurundi:

Kurundi had its own Aboriginal tribe, a branch of Wailbri. They centred on that area and lived around the station, roaming, as is their way, as far afield as Lake Nash in the east and Hatches Creek to the south. These people were quite happy in the life they led on the station ...

We really liked the people of this tribe and I think it is a shame that they have been encouraged, by giving them food and money, to go and live in settlements where there is no work, no occupation and no encouragement, and where the young people drift into a life of uselessness. They were far better off learning a trade such as stockwork, which came naturally to their own way of life. Now they are the people in between; they do not have the opportunities to follow the ways of their ancestors, nor have they accustomed themselves to living with white people.[34]

Louise Dixon, who worked for George Birchmore, remembered a 'Darby Gardener' tending the garden around the homestead in 1935.[35] She recalled he wasn't Warumungu,

but could speak the language. When questioned about this, Darby said he did some gardening there and that it was he to whom Dixon was referring, but I think it unlikely as she recalled he was an old man. This demonstrates one of the problems of recording oral accounts of the past with men like Darby. It is the 'discourse of affirmation' that Stephen Muecke has written about with regard to his work with Paddy Roe.[36] It also indicates the difficulty of accurately constructing Darby's accounts of his droving days. However, the details of the journey — the places and the order of events — were important to him and can be relied upon.

While at Kurundi, Darby participated in a number of droving trips. A typical droving plant consisted of a number of drovers, a cook and a horse-tailer. Darby was either a horse-tailer, responsible for ensuring the safety and condition of the horses and often working at night, or a drover, responsible for finding the stray cattle and moving the herd along.

On one trip, Darby was sent to Oolloo Station, about 900km north of Kurundi Station. He collected a mob of cattle and travelled down the dry river stock route to Top Springs and then down the Murranji Track. He crossed the grassy plains and pushed through the infamous Murranji scrub, difficult country where cattle would often 'rush' (stampede), and on to Newcastle Waters. They completed their 1200km journey when they finally reached Alice Springs.

We go away riding horse, now. I go up to all that country right up to Darwin, longa Pine Creek. Big mob of cattle there, we get 'em, longa Oolloo Station. Jack Liddy and Mick Liddy. Two brothers (at Oolloo Station) bin have a lot of girls. Aboriginal girls there, riding horse.

That far we bin travelling, away from the McLaren Creek. Big mob of horse there, we bin take 'em to Oolloo Station, longa Pine Creek. That horse, he belonga old man Billy Carters. We bin go from McLaren Creek. No big road bin there, nothing. Only stock road before the war.

Alright, from there, we travelling right up to Katherine. We camp (at) that Station down one mile from Katherine – Manbulloo Station – and we get more horse there. From there, we're travelling right through. Follow that creek, now. We keep going, load out from Manbulloo, and we go right up to Claravale Station. We camp there.

Morning time, we go right up to Oolloo Station. We bin waiting there. They bin bring back big mob of cattle, and put 'em in the yard. Big mob of cattle! We got to take big bullock, cow and calf. We bin there about ten days waiting for cattle. Ten days! Got to chase 'em round right up to creek, and bring back from rock country.

After ten days, we're ready to go away. We bin follow that creek right round. Come back, longa Manbulloo Station. From Manbulloo Station, we turn it 'nother way. We bin watching there, long way. We bin couple of days there, keep 'em, feed 'em round, look after cattle. From there, we bin travelling right up to big waterhole they call Nelly's Hole.

We go after four days and camp longa Top Springs. Same day from Top Springs, we shift out that way, little bit sunrise. We bin camp there longa 'nother side Pussycat Plain Bore. We bin watch 'em there, and we bin feeding round, take 'em all the way very slowly. We bin give 'em drink, and we bin camp there again for the poor cattle. Proper poor cattle! Some fat, some poor.

Alright, we camp there about two nights. Morning time we feed 'em; afternoon time, we take 'em in the bush and we feed 'em around. After (the cattle) drink water, we bin shift out, longa that two hill. Government Bore there, right in the jump-up, this side from Pussycat Plain Bore. We bin camp longa jump-up, longa hill country.

We bin follow 'em right up to Murranji Bore, west from Newcastle Waters. We bin camp there. Three night I camp, digging round, feeding round, give 'em drink of water. (Cattle) quiet now, no more 'rush' (stampede). Big bullock, and cow and calf, we never bin brand 'em that one. We bin take 'em right through.

From there, camp longa road somewhere, longa desert, longa gidgee (stinking wattle) bore country. Hard timber that one. We bin west from Newcastle Waters. We bin camp there, longa plain country. From there, we bin get there early, longa Newcastle Waters. We bin stop there now, altogether. Ten week I stop there. I bin (horse) 'tailing' round again, dig 'em again, give 'em drink again. Look after 'em proper way.

Soon as everything is good bin come, we bin shift out. We bin take 'em right through – cut across – longa Eighteen Mile. And we bin leave 'em, longa yard. Oh, no! They bin galloping round everywhere,

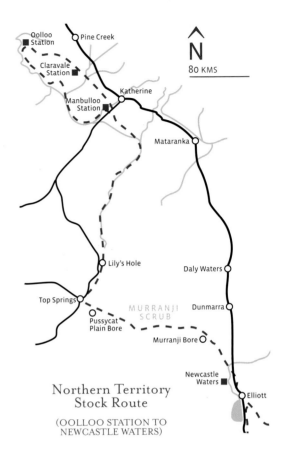

Northern Territory Stock Route

(OOLLOO STATION TO
NEWCASTLE WATERS)

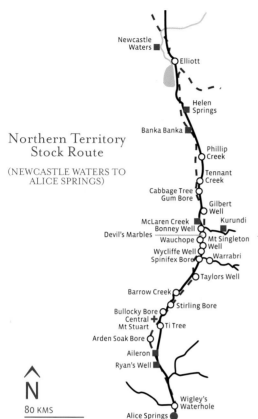

Northern Territory
Stock Route

(NEWCASTLE WATERS TO
ALICE SPRINGS)

Newcastle Waters
Elliott
Helen Springs
Banka Banka
Phillip Creek
Tennant Creek
Cabbage Tree Gum Bore
Gilbert Well
McLaren Creek
Kurundi
Bonney Well
Devil's Marbles
Mt Singleton Well
Wauchope
Wycliffe Well
Warrabri
Spinifex Bore
Taylors Well
Barrow Creek
Stirling Bore
Bullocky Bore
Central Mt Stuart
Ti Tree
Arden Soak Bore
Aileron
Ryan's Well
Wigley's Waterhole
Alice Springs

N
80 KMS

while we bin dip 'em. You know, that country got a lot of tick. You see 'em everywhere! Him biting all the time that bullock. Oh, no matter, we bin dip 'em in the water. Him not here, him longa that country. No good. Horse, too. That's why we bin dip 'em there, longa this side from Newcastle Waters.

We go right through and 'nother side bitumen (main north-south road) we camp, longa that big yard. From there, we got to go through the Banka Banka Station. Old station that one. From there, we bin go camp longa Banka Banka. From there we bin go right through, longa Morphett Creek. We bin camp there again. From Morphett Creek, we bin 'nother way now, longa bitumen all the way. Take 'em down (south).

Alright, we bin keep going right up to Phillip Creek. Missionary man bin there. Big mob Warlpiri bin there. We bin keep going – no matter that Warlpiri mob there, we bin leave 'em behind. We bin keep going to Telegraph Station – Tennant Creek Telegraph Station. We bin camp there about four night.

From there, we never bin shift out from that water – that's main water. We bin take 'em back again, longa grass country. Feed 'em round there. My boss bin coming there, now; that bullock man, drover man. Alright, him bin see 'em (cattle). Alright, he bin count 'em now: 'Well, you alright, old man.' Not old man, little bit youngfella me bin!

From there, blanket, flour, tea, sugar, everything him bin leave 'em there. Blanket, trousers, everything there. A lot of flour. Carry 'em flour, longa backpack. Load 'em up. A lot of work.

Tennant Creek – not Warlpiri peoples there – only Warumungu peoples, longa that country. We bin shift out now from Tennant Creek. We coming all the way now to Cabbage (Tree Gum) Bore. Camp there

two nights. We tailing round, feeding round grass for cattle. Number one that bullock!

We bin shift out again, right up to Gilbert Well. That bore bin there long time. That's Kurundi Station (and) we bin close up to Bonney Well. That station (cattle) – going to station – we bin cut 'em out there, leave 'em cow and calf (behind). Only big (male) bullock going right up to Alice Springs. Nother mob taking cattle – cow and calf – and I bin keep going, longa big bullock.

I bin take 'em from Bonney Well, right up to hill country, longa Marble Hill (Devil's Marbles). We bin camp there, and ten o'clock get into Wauchope Bore, give 'em drink of water there. We got to camp one night. From there, go right up to Mt Singleton Well. We bin there about five days, feeding round, look after 'em proper way. From there, we bring 'em in, longa Wycliffe (Well) Bore, and give 'em drink – plenty water.

And from there, we bin travelling right up to desert. No bitumen bin there, nothing. We bin (go) only stock road. Only new that bitumen. After war they bin make him. We bin take 'em right up to Spinifex Bore. We give 'em drink. I bin camp there about three nights, longa that bore. All night, tailing round, look after 'em proper way. Come back, give 'em drink, and take 'em again, longa grass. Lot of work I bin do 'em. Boss bin coming there again. Him bin bring 'em everything. Big canvas like this one. Tent there. Oh, big one! Flour, blanket, boot, leggings, you know.

From there, we're travelling after three days. And we go travelling right up to Taylors (Well). Big bridge there. No good water, longa that bore. You bin see 'em that windmill? Him all the time no good water. No matter, little bit we got to drink, and keep going after that one.

This side from Taylors, what they call 'new Barrow Creek', good bore there, and good water. That's where we get water. We got to fill 'em up canteens, horse canteen. Load 'em up.

Alright, that boss, he bin leave everything there for we. Canteen, too. Waterbag and leggings, and a lot of clothes. We bin working. I'm proper head drover man. Yeah, me! Got to think about no more rushing cattle. From there, take 'em back in the camp. Oh, everything cattle proper good now. Proper clean, and fat, too! Five days, we bin camp there, longa Barrow Creek Government Bore. No matter, we bin have a killer (bullock) there. Our killer, while we bin bring it – drover. We bin kill 'em there. Shoot 'em straight away. We bin go and get police (and) he bin shoot 'em that bullock, and we bin cut 'em up. Cut 'em properly. Everything, we never bin leave 'em. Bones too, we bin clean 'em up properly. Everything, we bin clean 'em up. Guts, too.

We bin load 'em up, longa big truck. Oh, we bin cook 'em everything! That *wirliya* (hooves), too. We bin cook 'em everything, head and all. And we bin travel, got 'em cooked one, now.

Which way we bin travelling? We bin camped right along Sixteen Mile Creek, long way from Barrow Creek. This 'nother side from Stirling Station. From Sixteen Mile Creek, long way now, we bin keep going, and we bin go right up to Stirling Bore – Stirling Station. Give 'em drink there, and we bin travelling 'nother way.

Only Kaytetye people, longa Stirling. Some Alyawarr people, too. That word there, I can talk. Lot of people there! I don't think we see 'em that mob (today). Always they sit down there.

We bin keep going. We bin camp down the road. From there, we bin go right up to Bullocky Bore. We bin camp two nights, and tailing round again. Bit of a desert there longa Bullocky Bore. From there, we go ready for 'nother side Ti Tree, longa that hill. We camp there, and morning time we take 'em into Ti Tree. We stop right longa dry camp, and we bin go right up to 'nother Government Bore. Give 'em drink there, now. We never bin camp, we bin go right through.

From Ti Tree, we bin camp longa road, and we bin take 'em (to) Arden Soak Bore. We bin camp there. Big windmill down there, working all the time. That station belonga Jack. Olden day station. That Jack, him bin have big mob of sheep, and he bin take 'em from there, right up to here, longa what they call Newhaven Station. From there, we bin keep going, and camp down the road. Long way again we bin travelling, right up to old station down Ryan's Well, 'nother side from Aileron. That Aileron 'city' there now, he's only fresh (new) one. We bin take 'em longa old Ryan's Well. We bin camp there about three nights, tailing round, and give 'em drink.

Alright, from there, we go through the gap. We take 'em right through, and we bin camp down the road, (at) Gillen's Well. We bin camp there about four days. Tailing round, feeding round. Oh, that bullock, he right now. Everything fat! (But) one big bullock lame. Well, I bin leave 'em there. They never bin shoot him. I bin just tell 'em: 'Alright, you can kill him behind.' Big bullock – he lame, he bin swell up.

No bitumen. Only like this one – dirt. We bin keep going, longa mulga country; we bin keep going, longa road. We bin keep going, and we bin camp longa Well Creek. Two horse bin working there, fill it up that trough. No windmill there. We bin camp two nights there. Whitefella call 'em Snake Well.

From there, morning time, we go right up to Sixteen Mile Creek, close up to Alice Springs. Right, we bin watch 'em there, and we bin keep going. Which way we bin take him? We bin take 'em right up to Wigley Wigley Waterhole. I bin take 'em there, longa big waterhole. All the time, everybody bin only take 'em there. We never bin camp there, we bin only just give 'em drink, and camp through the gap, west side. We never bin go to Bungalow (Alice Springs Hostel). No – west side – longa drover road we bin travelling.

That Charlie Creek (is) very deep. Bitumen there now – top one now – and old bitumen him go underneath the creek. From there, we bin travelling longa hill country, and take 'em right up to Alice Springs trucking yard, (where) that train stop. Before the war.

In his own words, Darby became a 'proper head drover man', often spending months on the road. It got him through what Dave Price refers to as his 'wild time':

> In the old days in the desert newly initiated, unmarried men were expected to live dangerously for a while … Before they had a wife and children to care for they could afford to take risks, to test their endurance and skills.[37]

Darby spoke of this time in his life with much enthusiasm. He recalled the names of waterholes, springs and bores and old stations and the people who lived there. He was also concerned with who owned the country — not just the pastoralists — but the Aboriginal owners. When telling stories, he would often point out that the Murranji country belonged to the Mudbara, or that Newcastle Waters was in Jingili country. While living at Kurundi and travelling through different Aboriginal countries on droving trips, Darby attended Alyawarr, Warumungu and Jingili ceremonies and received the *murru* (cicatrice) cuts on his chest.

News of the Second World War reached Darby when he worked at Kurundi, and he recalled some of the stockmen leaving to join the war effort. In the early 1940s, the army was camped on the main road, west of the Kurundi homestead and the Aboriginal stockmen like Darby would sometimes provide them with meat. Wolfram, a metal that was used in the production of weapons at the time, became quite valuable and was mined at nearby Hatches Creek. In between droving trips, Darby was sent to work in the mines. It was dangerous work, and while working in the shafts one day, a Whitefella dropped a hammer, which hit Darby and left a permanent scar on his forehead. He also remembered the police coming and arresting the German and Italian workers.

In the early 1940s, soldiers began arriving in Alice Springs in large numbers. Many men descended upon what had been a relatively small and isolated town. Large quantities

Ruins of Ryan's Well, an important watering point for drovers on the north-south stockroute. According to Darby, it was a 'whip' well where water would be hauled to the surface from a standing platform above the stone structure, dragged down the rails (foreground) by horses or bullocks.

of food began arriving in Central Australia in preparation for the possibility that the northern coast would fall to the Japanese.[38] Thousands of soldiers were stationed in Alice Springs, and a Labour Corps of Aboriginal workers was formed to unload supply trains and maintain the roads north and south.[39] In Central Australia, there was a general movement of Aboriginal people from the surrounding area to Alice Springs at this time, including many Warlpiri and Anmatyerr. Darby's friend Jimija Jungarrayi lived at the Bungalow (Alice Springs Hostel) at the Old Telegraph Station and worked with the Aboriginal Labour Corps. During the war, Darby visited Alice Springs and stayed at the Bungalow where he joined Jimija in the Labour Corps for a short time. He unloaded supply vehicles and collected firewood before returning to Kurundi:

Talk about for that last war time. We bin frightened little bit, while they bin make that big road right up to Darwin, right up to Alice Springs. Long time ago.

We bin know this trouble bin going on. War bin start, and same day we bin work longa cattle station. Muster 'em up cattle and bring 'em in, and grow 'em up proper way. Put 'em in the water, and riding horse. Proper way, we bin working.

Last war time, they fight for the Japanese. Long time ago, (they) nearly going to come right through. Our people – English man from Australia – all bin finish right up to bore. What to do? Big mob of people bin get shot. We're very sorry for that. Lot of youngfellas from out of the stock camp, we lose it.

We bin work round everywhere there, longa Darwin side. Right up to Katherine, Manbulloo Station and Top Springs. Bring 'em in cattle right up to Newcastle Waters. We bin travelling good. No argument, no trouble. That same day, that war bin come, and they bin big fight down longa bore. Lot of Australian 'boy'. We bin work round Hatches Creek; we bin working longa wolfram. They want to make 'em more bullets. That's why we bin working there.

Lot of white man bin there, and a lot of man they grab 'em and take away. That's Germans they take away. Policeman bin take away. They no want to see 'em. Take 'em away, put 'em (in) Alice Springs gaol.

That Army bin come through. Only two place they bin: Darwin and Katherine. They bin bomb Katherine and Darwin.

I seen 'em down there, longa Darwin, that place where that Japanese bin come along and bomb him. Big bomb they bin chuck it down right in the river, longside sea water. Some Aboriginal boy bin get killed. Cut it off bone here, while he bin running. No good altogether.

We bin mustering round there, now. We bin working for the boss, and we go mustering round the cattle. We got to take 'em down to yard, and they get 'em good fat one.

Alright, they kill 'em how many? Twelve cattle they got to kill 'em. They kill 'em one, two, three, four, five, six, seven, eight, nine, ten, eleven, twelve! That killer for Army boys. They got to have plenty meat for Army boys. We take it down and we leave (it) there. They got to put 'em in the big butcher's yard. They got to cut him. That's the way we bin only feed 'em, and look after 'em.

Same day, big war bin coming again. They bin bomb 'em Darwin, and they frighten all that Aboriginal boy. They bin take 'em right up to Adelaide. All that Aboriginal boy they going up that way. Big mob they take 'em, (in) what they call 'convoy'. They take 'em longa Army truck. They take 'em Aboriginal boy down Adelaide, from too much big war. No more keep 'em in Alice Springs. No, right through they send 'em in the train. And (when) that war bin finish right out there, they bin go back again. Send 'em back to country again. Go back to Darwin all that boy, now.

They got a mission everywhere. Yirrkala, all that country. Borroloola, all that country. Maningrida, all that country. Snake Bay, all that there. They bin send 'em whole lot, longa Adelaide. And they bin go back, sit down nothing, now. That war bin finish right out.

You know, while they bin here, they bin work down road. They bin think about country. Come back here now, after war, while they bin working for Army boys. Sometimes they have a big rain here, and go back in soakage water, sit down there. Oh, they're good worker, too. They look after proper way. They give it kangaroo, euro, and goanna. Everything, they give it.

That peoples, while we bin there, good mob, and work and cart wood, and give it good wage. And a lot of kangaroos they go catch 'em in the bush, and bring back and give it meat for all the old man and old girl. That's what they bin doing, long time ago.

We bin sitting 'round there, long time ago, longa Bungalow (Alice Springs Hostel). We bin sitting there. No talk for the wrong. We bin sitting good. Warlpiri people, Anmatyerr people, Arrernte people, and Pijapija (Pitjantjatjara) people. That's four all together, four peoples.

Central Australia, circa 1942. TOP LEFT Army trucks; TOP RIGHT Hospital tents; BOTTOM RIGHT 'Bitumen' highway, Devils Marbles.

We bin working round for war, helping (unload) food for the peoples. We shift 'em everythings.
We bin work through the camp, while that army bin start there. Army boys, they bin travelling. That's
long time ago.

During the Second World War, many Aboriginal people who had previously lived in
the bush or on remote stations worked in the Aboriginal Labour Corps. When the war
ended, there was some concern as to what would happen to the Aboriginal workers.
Should they be sent back to live a nomadic life, or did the government have some
responsibility to start settlements in their respective countries? Gordon Sweeney, Patrol
Officer with the Native Affairs Branch of the Northern Territory in the 1940s, recalled
that Warlpiri workers were in demand on cattle stations at the time. He also had concerns
about reports of the exploitation of Warlpiri workers at Bill Braitling's wolfram mining
venture on the Mt Doreen pastoral lease.[40]

In April 1946, the Yuendumu government settlement was established by the
Native Affairs Branch adjacent to Rock Hill Bore, approximately 50kms southeast
of Luurnpakurlangu (Mt Doreen). Initially, it was a ration depot and Warlpiri were
transported from Luurnpakurlangu, The Granites and Bullocky Soak in cattle trucks.

At this time, Darby was married to Lady Nakamarra, an Alyawarr woman, and they had
a son named Pilot at Kurundi. Joy Marks, daughter of George Birchmore, remembered
a young boy rolling into a fire not long after he was born and receiving the name Pilot,
as he was born the day a plane arrived.[41]

A few years later, Darby had an argument with some other men that involved his wife:

That *wurlkumanu* (Darby's wife) bin make trouble for me. Well, I bin leave ... I bin leave one boy, too.
That boy Pilot.

Darby had been thinking about going back to Warlpiri country for some time, so he
picked up his woomera, spears and boomerangs and left Kurundi Station, travelling
west to Wauchope and Bullocky Soak near Ti Tree, and eventually on to the border of
Anmatyerr and Warlpiri country where he came across the newly established settlement
of Yuendumu, on land belonging to the *Yurrampi Jukurrpa* (Honey Ant Dreaming). Darby
camped at Yuendumu hill before he came into the settlement.

Darby lived at Coniston. He left the country around Yuendumu when he was a boy. He went
over to Coniston where they made him into a man. He has one daughter there.
    Darby became a stockman. He used to walk everywhere. One old Jampijinpa, a cheeky man,
made Darby run away frightened right up to Kurundi Station. He stayed there for a long time

Warlpiri workers getting
ready to depart for
Alexandria Station 1955

working in the stockcamp walking around.

Well, one Nakamarra now. He got one Alyawarr woman. He was married now with one son. Darby sat down there for a long time. He got old there. He became an old man. He went right around through that Alyawarr country.

Lawa (nothing), he don't like 'em now Nakamarra. He said to himself, 'Well I better go back to my country. Yuendumu side.' His son was a big man now. He came to Yuendumu. He sat down there. DOLLY NAMPIJINPA DANIELS

Thomas Jangala Rice remembers Darby looking like a 'wild man' with dreadlocks, and walking into the settlement carrying a lot of spears. Dolly, Molly and Ruby Nampijinpa also remembered him arriving. They didn't know who he was – this rough looking man who had come from the east and begun working as a stockman at Yuendumu. Dolly remembered him:

Walking, walking, walking – that Darby running bugger! He used to walk everywhere. He was a stockman and a cook for all the stockmen.

Once his identity was established, Darby was given the nickname 'Kurundi' after the station where he had worked for over ten years. While he worked in the stockcamp for a

while, he soon headed to Papunya in search of a wife. However, he was unsuccessful until he later visited his family at Napperby:

They give me one girl from Napperby Station ... my brother (Jampijinpa) bin give it. 'You get 'em that one!', my brother bin telling me. (laughs) 'That's your wife!'

Jampijinpa was Thomas' father and had several wives, and as Darby was his younger brother, he had allowed him to 'marry' Napangardi. Dolly recalled the time:

He started work now at Yuendumu. Strong, solid man, too. He worked all over. Well, one Napangardi bin come from Napperby, our grandmother. He bin get 'em another Napangardi, now. Old lady. Middle-aged one. He find 'em girlfriend now, 'nother one ...
　　Darby used to meet his girlfriend in the bush. That Napangardi, 'nother one, him bin run away. He bin get another one, now. Two Napangardi bin fight from Darby.

When Darby returned to Warlpiri country, he observed his Warlpiri and Anmatyerr countrymen camped some distance from Yuendumu settlement. Like other members of his family, he camped in a humpy (bush shelter) to the north, the side closest to his country at Ngarliyikirlangu. Jeannie Nungarrayi Egan recalled how people used to camp several miles to the north, south, east and west of the community. In her words, 'We slowly came together.' Warlpiri had never camped together in such large numbers for long periods of time. So people lived in family groups, only coming in to the community to collect water and rations. At this time, Yuendumu was operating as a ration depot, and many Warlpiri and Anmatyerr were still living a semi-nomadic existence. Men, women and children would come in to the settlement for a midday meal, lining up with tin plates and cups. Ration days were on Tuesdays and Fridays, with tea, flour and sugar dispensed. Men worked clearing the airstrip and women collected firewood or washed clothes on sheets of corrugated iron.

A skilled and experienced stockman, Darby was in demand. He would travel 'up and down' from Yuendumu, sometimes visiting family at Napperby or working for Bill Braitling at Mt Doreen. When Darby shifted his camp back to Yuendumu, he would visit Luurnpakurlangu to get meat for the community kitchen:

We go right up to Mt Doreen, get a killer (bullock). And we got to make 'em all the time, boil 'em cabbage. I bin working (as) cookie, now. Cut 'em bones . . . cook 'em in the fire . . . boil 'em up bones for everybody. Big mob people bin here, too.

During the 1950s, many Warlpiri were encouraged to go, or were forcibly relocated, to the established settlements.[42] It was in response to the large number of Warlpiri at Yuendumu that Patrol Officer Brian Greenfield attempted to identify people prepared to move to the new settlement at Hooker Creek (now Lajamanu) to the north. Many of the people were reluctant to go and Darby was called upon to talk to them. Otto Jungarrayi Sims recounted the story:

A lot of people used to live here in Yuendumu. They used to have a Chief Protector (Superintendent) here and they used to get Darby. He was a sort of mediator for *Yapa* (Warlpiri) and the Chief Protector. He knew how to talk to them. He was there all the time helping . . . He's the one that fixed Lajamanu, when Lajamanu was nothing. Most of the Lajamanu people used to stop here. But it was too crowded and they made an agreement to make another community. So he was really involved in that too.

In 1952, the year Yuendumu Aboriginal Reserve was gazetted, two large trucks picked up about 130 people from The Granites, Mt Doreen, Yuendumu and Phillip Creek, and took them to Hooker Creek (Lajamanu).[43] They travelled on the Murranji track and arrived at Hooker Creek after five days, greatly increasing the population there that had previously numbered about forty. Although it was about a 500km journey, some of them walked back to Yuendumu. Abie Jangala walked back three times before he gave up.

According to Murray Barrett's records, Darby's son Edwin was born in 1954 at Napperby. He also had two daughters, Jessie who died in her first year in 1953, and Ruth in her second in 1957. Warlpiri don't like to talk about the death of young children, but between 1953–70, the infant mortality rate in Yuendumu was a high 24.7 percent of live births, with 16 percent of deaths occurring in their first year. This was a higher rate than that reported for any whole country to the United Nations in 1969, and was significantly higher than the non-Aboriginal rate of 1.82 percent in the Northern Territory.[44] Yuendumu Superintendent Ted Egan observed, 'There were no Warlpiri children from Yuendumu born in 1954, because they all died.'[45]

In 1954, some Warlpiri men were amongst a group that travelled to Toowoomba to perform a 'corroboree' for the Queen. The group included Darby and several other Warlpiri, and Nosepeg Tjupurrula, a well-known Pintupi man. They painted themselves with red ochre and wore hair-string belts around their waists.

The Queen also attended a 'corroboree' of a different kind performed by ballet dancer Beth Dean in Sydney. Inspired by the stories of Charles Mountford, Dean and husband Victor Carell, journeyed through Australia on a 'quest for knowledge among the aborigines'.[46] They visited Yuendumu in 1953, spending some months observing ceremonies, travelling to various sites and participating in the life of the community. They shared songs and dances, and researched material that would be used in Dean's performance of the 'Corroboree' ballet. They would later write a book about the experience and include a photo of a man, whom some people identified as Darby, with the caption: *A fine example of a fully initiated and self disciplined old man of Yuendumu.*[47]

In 1963, Darby saw the Queen again, this time at Alice Springs:

We bin only look from 'outside'. We never give it 'shake hand' for (her). A lot of children bin there.
We bin take a big mob of people, me and Jimija.

In 1958, Ted Egan (who later become the Administrator of the Northern Territory) took over as superintendent from Wally Langdon, a former policeman, who had been at Yuendumu for about six years. Ted described Wally as a 'no work, no tucker' man.[48] It was Wally who had organised Warlpiri to work in various occupations and arranged the 'work trips'. During this time, Darby briefly worked in Alice Springs as a butcher. He also travelled with a group of men to Gundagai in New South Wales and picked asparagus in what he jokingly referred to as 'Dog Dreaming' country because of the town's 'dog sat on the tuckerbox' story. Darby was surprised that the asparagus grew up again overnight — that no matter how many stalks they cut, there would always be more the next day. They

Otto Jungarrayi Sims

embarked on a big bus on the return journey 'flush' with money at Christmas time and drove through Melbourne, where Darby remembers camping in the 'bush' outside the Melbourne Cricket Ground.

Darby and his countryman Paddy Japaljarri Stewart were then sent to Queensland as part of the NT Welfare Branch's employment program in 1958.[49]

Old Fleming (missionary) bin say, 'All right, old man Darby you go to all that country right up to Camooweal droving cattle.'

As skilled stockmen they were paid award wages. They caught a bus from Alice Springs to Tennant Creek, then a truck took them across the Queensland border to Camooweal. They were working for Jack Stewart, to whom Paddy attributes his surname. They drove cattle back and forth between the Northern Territory and Queensland, and on to the railhead at Dajarra, which in its day was reportedly one of the busiest in the world.[50] Darby and Paddy returned to Yuendumu for men's ceremonies at the end of the year.

We bin travelling to Alice Springs, and we jump on the big bus with Paddy Stewart Japaljarri. Four fella Aborigine, and two white men – one Cookie, and 'nother Whitefella boss. His name Jack Stewart from Camooweal.

We bin travelling from Alice Springs. We bin go right up to Camooweal. Oh, we bin longa big waterhole, and we bin sit down there, west side from city. That man, Jack Stewart, he bin give it everything for we: saddle, everything to hobble 'em horse, and he bin grease 'em that bridle, too. Everything, we bin grease 'em. Everything ready for tomorrow.

From there, we bin go that way – north. We bin muster 'em back big mob of cattle and big mob of horse, right up to station called Morstone. Oh, lot of chestnut horse, black horse, we bin get 'em. And we bin (get) big mob of cattle, too. We bin rush 'em back this way (to Camooweal).

Five o'clock, we bin get up and walk away, and we bin camp right this side from Dajarra. Morning time, we take 'em in to the Government Bore, that water longa Dajarra. Properly dry, that bore. Too many cattle, I think. Oh, little bit water, he bin running longa trough.

One side sheep, another one cattle. One big (train carriage), and two double one, belonga sheep. Which way that sheep (going)? He got to go right up to Sydney, or might be Adelaide.

We bin truck 'em there. Only (now), that boy can't get up. He bin too much drink, too much grog. *Nguku*, we call 'em Warumungu side. I never bin drink, longa Dajarra, I bin watch 'em meself, right up to daylight! This mob bin drunk, whole lot, boss and all. Longa Dajarra, they never bin watch the cattle. No, poor bugger me bin watching, watching, watching up to daylight, and go back and have cup of tea. Right, then I got to turn around and watch 'em again. Got to go back and walk around again, walk around again. I got to come back and sit down to the fire, have 'em more tea. Make 'em self hot!

Long way, we bin go. We bin working hard, really hard. Today is easy one; and today is easy one for cattle, too. Truck 'em longa transport. Not like long time ago, push 'em along with horses, long way, right up to Mt Isa. PADDY JAPALJARRI STEWART

From there, morning time we take 'em cattle feeding round, longa grass. Oh, proper quiet cattle from Lake Nash. That's Alyawarr country.[51] Good, everything good. I never bin have trouble with that one, nothing. Every cattle, I droving good.

We bin coming back to Lake Nash. We bin there mustering round again, and we bin get a big mob again. Oh, all the fat ones. Take 'em (down) again. How many time I bin take 'em? Four time. Take 'em longa Mt Isa, and truck 'em longa Dajarra.

From there, we bin coming back now. We bin go right up to Camooweal, and we bin catch 'em big bus, and we bin coming back, whole lot. Oh, we bin get a lot of money – all the drover. I reckon the government bin take some, too.

In the 1960s, there was a push by the authorities to develop Yuendumu as a centre for pastoral enterprise, utilising the resources of the Yuendumu Cattle Company. Much of the reserve was fenced and yards were built. Bores were sunk and a well excavated to provide enough water for the expanding herd and a butcher's shop established. The aim was to have enough cattle to have a regular supply of meat for the settlement. A Yuendumu brand – YUT – or the Yuendumu Two Bob, was stamped on the cattle with a hot iron, in preference to the standard government brand.[52] Darby was a strong supporter of the cattle company and brought considerable experience and knowledge of the country to its day-to-day operation. As a head stockman, Darby oversaw much of the cattle company's operations, including the breaking in of horses and leading the Yuendumu droving plant when they brought in a mob from Haasts Bluff to increase the number of Yuendumu cattle to 680.[53]

In 1965, moves were made by the North Australian Workers Union to delete references to Aborigines in the *Cattle Station Industry (NT) Award*, as the provisions of the award allowed Aboriginal workers to be paid less than award wages. As a result of the application, equal wages for Aboriginal workers were introduced after a two-year period. According to Reeves' assessment in his report on the *Aboriginal Land Rights (NT) Act:*

The results were catastrophic … the Award changes led pastoralists to mechanise stock management, to employ European stockmen, and to sack Aboriginal workers on a large scale.[54]

In 1967, the year Aboriginal people were granted the same rights of citizenship as other Australians, the population at Yuendumu was approximately 917, twice the number of people living there in the early 1960s.[55] The increase in the population was largely due to the decrease in employment opportunities for Warlpiri and Anmatyerr on nearby cattle stations as a result of changes to the *Cattle Station Industry (NT) Award*. Aboriginal people had previously outnumbered non-Aboriginal workers on the stations in Central

Australia and, like Darby, are the unacknowledged pioneers who had worked alongside the Whitefella pastoralists to develop the country for pastoral enterprise. However, with the introduction of award wages many of the old stockmen and women were no longer wanted and returned to live in settlements and mission stations in their own country.[56]

Darby continued to work in various occupations, and although he was still physically fit, he was nearing retirement age and began to spend more time with the elders and concern himself with community matters.

In the late 1970s, Darby returned to the country west of Refrigerator Bore in search of a gold reef he had seen in the 1930s. Ed Kingston (Japangardi), a Baptist missionary at Yuendumu, recalls the trip:

One day Darby asked me to take him into the desert country as he had seen gold there in the early days when he was travelling with the camel trains. So he took water and tucker for a few days and I left him there and agreed to return for him later. We agreed that he should indicate his whereabouts by lighting a fire as there was a lot of undergrowth and tracks were difficult to see. When I returned a few days later, I noticed a huge pall of smoke when I was about 60kms away. Darby's fire had got away and the Tanami desert was blazing merrily. Somehow, I managed to avoid the flames in looking for his camp and in desperation I drove to the top of a sandhill to get my bearings. To my surprise I parked right next to Darby's swag. The old man appeared a while later and with a grin said, 'Good fire Japangardi.' He failed to find the gold and concluded that the sand had shifted over the years and covered it.[57]

Chapter Eight

Get

As the frontier moved north and west into the Tanami Desert, the local Anmatyerr and Warlpiri had increasing contact with Whitefella pastoralists and prospectors. By 1926, Central Australia had endured several years of drought and the Warlpiri and Anmatyerr became dependent on their more reliable waterholes. Many of these water sources were also used by the pastoralists who had pushed into the country, including Nugget Morton and B. Stanley Sandford at Broadmeadows Station, Harry Tilmouth at Napperby (and White Stone) Station, and Randal Stafford at Coniston Station. Warlpiri and Anmatyerr were forced to compete with the pastoralists and their cattle for access to water.[1] There were also conflicts over the spearing of cattle. Darby described the situation:

You know, hungry people bin only kill cattle belonga Whitefella. He not Aboriginal bullock that one – no, he's belonga white man. They bin carry round. That's why they bin only spear 'em. And a lot of Aboriginal 'boy' bin get shot, too, longa that country. Everywhere they bin get shot.

Kamanyarrpa survived and became known as 'Bullfrog'

They didn't catch Bullfrog. No, he was a winner. He escaped and lived free. He died in Yuendumu as an old man. JACK ROSS (*translation*)

His name Japanangka – old Bullfrog. He's my countryman! DARBY

In 1928, times were particularly tough and increasing numbers of Warlpiri and Anmatyerr came in to Coniston Station, and Stafford, while sympathetic to their plight, could no longer accommodate them all.

Darby was among those who had previously travelled to Coniston Station on Anmatyerr land, 80 kms east of the present-day site of Yuendumu. He was met by a large number of Warlpiri and Anmatyerr men and women who were camped in the creek near the homestead at Yimampi.[2] He learnt to speak English, and Stafford gave him the name Darby Ross. Whitefellas would often pass through, droving cattle or camels from the surrounding stations. With many of his countrymen at Coniston, Darby finished his initiation, the passage through which he became a 'proper man':

Whole lot, we bin sit down there, longa shade – in the creek … Finish now, *wati* (man) now. Plenty yam – bushtucker. Go away again now – about one year travelling.

Darby spent a year travelling after *Kajirri*, men's initiation ceremonies commonly referred to today as *Kankarlu*, or in English 'high school'. He travelled through Warlpiri country for some time, but it became increasingly difficult due to the lack of water, so he and his companions eventually travelled south to Hermannsburg, the Lutheran mission in Arrernte country. This was probably Darby's second trip to Hermannsburg. His accounts suggest that he went there at least twice prior to 1928, and that Pastor Albrecht was present on both occasions. He remembered a lot of people being there, that some were sick with colds and disease, and that a lot of people had died.

When asked about the reasons for his first trip to Hermannsburg, Darby recalled that it was known that Whitefellas had lived in the area for some time. He had heard these stories, and he was curious to see for himself. He had also heard that some of his family were living there. In her biography of Lutheran Pastor Albrecht, Barbara Henson quoted an interview with Darby:

First time to Hermannsburg. Old man (Albrecht), we heard about him. We bin get clothes like this, and rations. Big mob Aranda (Arrernte) there, safe there, all right to go there, oh yes, old man bin there. Other people used to walk there, bring news back. People came back and said there was soup, *mana* soup, flour soup. If they were hungry, they could go there and get soup. First time I went down I had a few whiskers, go by self. Country very dry.[3]

On one of these trips to Hermannsburg, Darby encountered many Arrernte and Warlpiri living there.[4] He listened to their stories about the Lutheran mission and the Whitefellas who were attempting to learn the Arrernte language and talked about their God. This intrigued Darby and he stayed in the area for some time. He suggested it was about 'ten months'.

In 1928, Darby decided to return again to Coniston. His Arrernte friends gave him some clothes and blankets, and he left Hermannsburg in the company of his grandfather (Japaljarri) and his donkey Toby. They headed north into what is now referred to as

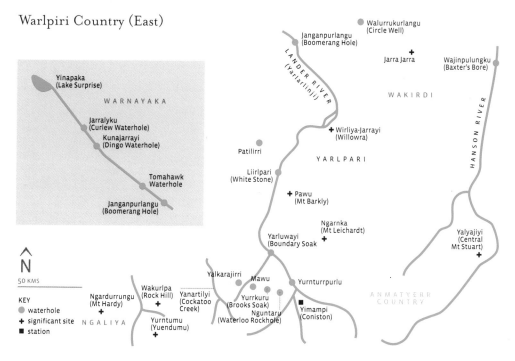

Walurrukurlangu
(Circle Well)

Janganpurlangu
(Boomerang Hole)

Jarra Jarra

Wajinpulungku
(Baxter's Bore)

LANDER RIVER
(Yarlarlinjji)

WAKIRDI

Yinapaka
(Lake Surprise)

WARNAYAKA

Wirliya-Jarrayi
(Willowra)

Jarralyku
(Curlew Waterhole)

Patilirri

YARLPARI

Kunajarrayi
(Dingo Waterhole)

Liirlpari
(White Stone)

HANSON RIVER

Tomahawk
Waterhole

Pawu
(Mt Barkly)

Janganpurlangu
(Boomerang Hole)

Ngarnka
(Mt Leichardt)

Yarluwayi
(Boundary Soak)

Yalyajiyi
(Central
Mt Stuart)

N

50 KMS

Yalkarajirri

Mawu

Yurnturrpurlu

KEY

● waterhole

+ significant site

■ station

Ngardurrungu
(Mt Hardy)

Wakurlpa
(Rock Hill)

Yanartilyi
(Cockatoo
Creek)

Yurrkuru
(Brooks Soak)

Nguntaru
(Waterloo Rockhole)

Yimampi
(Coniston)

ANMATYERR
COUNTRY

NGALIYA

Yurntumu
(Yuendumu)

Luritja country (although Darby said it was Arrernte), and on into Warlpiri country. The country was still very dry, so they camped at the larger waterholes. They were camped at one such waterhole at Karrinyarra (Mt Wedge) when the Whitefella Fred Brooks was camped out west of Coniston. Brooks, an old friend of Stafford, now in his sixties, was out collecting dingo scalps.

Brooks camped near the soakage water at Yurrkuru with two Aboriginal boys, Nyinanyanu Jakamarra (Skipper) and Yirran Pungerta (Dodger), who looked after his camels.[5] A large group of Warlpiri were also camped nearby. Among them were Padirrki Japaljarri (later known as George), Marungali Napurrurla and her husband Kamanyarrpa Japanangka (later known as Bullfrog and *Walypali-pakarnu* — literally 'Whitefella-killer').

On the morning of August 7, 1928, Brooks was killed by Kamanyarrpa and Padirrki. Darby claimed Kamanyarrpa's three wives were camped there, washing Brooks' clothes in exchange for food and tobacco. One of these women was Marungali, and Kamanyarrpa was waiting for her. When she didn't return, Kamanyarrpa and Padirrki went to bring her back.[6]

Kamanyarrpa hit Brooks with an axe and Padirrki attacked with a boomerang. They buried the body in a rabbit warren nearby then retreated into the hills. The first time Darby spoke to me about the Coniston Massacre was at Yurrkuru, the site of Fred Brooks' murder, and now also known as Brooks Soak.

Trouble bin going on here, long time ago. I want to tell 'em from Brooks Soak, west from Coniston, where they bin kill that old man. Fred Brooks his name. He bin have two camels and him bin starting greenhide bullock (making raw leather straps). From there, he bin get the water, and two (Aboriginal) boy bin after camels – morning time.

That old man (Brooks), him bin have 'em three girl – washing girls. They bin washing clothes for him. He bin keeping a couple of girls. They never go back, longa their husbands. They bin work, sleeping longa that Whitefella, while they bin kill that man. Name: Fred Brooks. That Fred Brooks old man get 'em big mob of dingo scalps. From there, that two boy bin come look about. And him (Brooks) bin cutting, and him bin make a lot of camel strap. He got to put 'em on here (neck) – chains (for camels).

From there, two boy bin after camels – and same day they bin come back and see him – while they bin kill him. His name: Japanangka – old Bullfrog. He's my countryman. He bin thinking about murdering from girl – three girls. 'Hey, what for that man keeping three girl?' 'Oh, *lafta* (have to) we talk today.' They bin talk, telling one another, all them poor boy – Aboriginal boy. They bin walking around there – got a spear. They bin coming to morning time. Before the dinner they bin kill him here – lunch time.

That two boy bin come back – have two camels. He bin look, 'Where that old man gone now?' Two boy bin look about for him. 'Oh here, they bin kill 'em everywhere. Look!' Boomerang – broken one. And nulla nulla (club) – broken one. And big spear – *wurrumpuru*. Big spear – man killer, that one. They bin see a lot of broken one there. And nulla nulla bin there too – broken one. And axe too – they bin use for cutting that old man. They bin split him right here (back of the head). That far we can tell this story.

When Nyinanyanu and Yirran returned with Brooks' camels and found him missing and signs of a struggle, they got word to Coniston, and arrangements were made to alert the authorities by telegraph from Ryan's Well.

Meanwhile, Alex Jupurrurla Wilson, a young man of about sixteen years (who eventually married Darby's niece), had been searching for Jimmy Wickham's infamous gold reef with the renowned old prospector Joe Brown, who had fallen ill in Warlpiri country.[7] Wilson left Brown in the care of Paddy Jakamarra and Kakalala Jampijinpa, and set out east for Coniston with news of Brown's illness.[8] He passed through Yurrkuru and discovered that Brooks had been killed. After arriving at Coniston, Wilson got word to Bruce Chapman, camped some miles to the south, and the two travelled to Yurrkuru and retrieved Brooks' body from the rabbit warren and buried it in a grave. Wilson and Chapman then returned to see Brown just before he died. They buried him near Ngardurrungu (Mt Hardy).[9]

Mounted Constable William Murray served in the Light Horse regiment at Gallipoli and France during the First World War. He joined the Northern Territory Police in 1919. He had no prior experience as a police officer and was not required to undertake formal training before accepting the position.[10] He held several posts before being appointed to Barrow Creek Police Station in July, 1926.

Reflecting upon the time in the 1980s during the Warlpiri Jila Well Land Claim hearings, and considering the involvement of Murray in the killings, Commissioner Maurice concluded:

Constable Murray was a product of his times. The evidence given in support of his actions, the Board's findings and the Commonwealth's acceptance of them amply demonstrate this. But they were times through which the claimants' parents and grandparents and other relatives had to live, and changes in the values and attitudes they reflect do not occur overnight.[11]

Visitors
Policemen

The Thornycroft Expedition in search of the 'Kookaburra' (aeroplane) 1929. Constable Murray is on the right.

Within a few days of the news of Brooks' death reaching Coniston, Mounted Constable William Murray arrived at the homestead with orders from Police Commissioner Cawood to attend the scene of Brooks' murder and to assist Joe Brown. Meanwhile, Walykuri Jakamarra (Woolingar) and Wiliyarrpa Japaljarri (Padygar) arrived at the Coniston homestead with dingo scalps.[12] Expecting to trade the scalps, they were instead arrested and chained to a tree. Walykuri managed to free himself and allegedly tried to hit Murray with the chain. Murray responded by shooting him in the head. He died two weeks later. Wiliyarrpa (the brother of Padirrki) would later travel to Darwin with another man, Yakirkra (Akirkra) accused of killing Brooks, and be found not guilty because of the lack, or inadmissibility, of evidence.[13]

At Coniston, Murray set about organising a party to assist him to investigate the incident. It included Alex Wilson, Murray's Arrernte tracker Paddy, Stafford and his station hands Billy Briscoe and Jack (John) Saxby, and two other Aboriginal men from Coniston known as Major and Dodger. They rode west from Coniston in the direction of Yurrkuru, following tracks to Nguntaru, a Honey Ant Dreaming site, only a few miles from Yurrkuru, where members of Darby's family were getting ready to travel to Patilirri for men's initiation ceremonies. Murray rode directly into the middle of their camp and demanded that weapons be dropped 'in the name of the King'.[14] The resulting violence included Murray and Saxby shooting to kill.[15] Darby's sister and brother-in-law were shot there.

The following story was recorded at Yurrkuru (Brooks Soak) with Darby sitting on the iron rail of Brooks' grave, feet resting on the concrete slab, and apologising for having to tell this 'hard' story.

Telling again, that two boy while they bin come back (and) look where they bin killing that old man. From there, they bin crying round; they bin seeing everything. Flour, everything while they bin pinching, and take away from him. And that two boy, they bin sorry for him (Brooks) – old man while he bin look, digging around everywhere.

Alright, from there, they bin running down and tell 'em Randal Stafford (at Coniston)... They bin sorry. Randal Stafford bin run; him bin go to right up to Ryan's Well. Station bin there. And from there, he bin send him wire for the Police. They want to get 'em more peoples, and he (Constable Murray) bin load 'em up, and bring 'em right up to Ryan's Well. And from there, they bin have 'em big truck. They bin load 'em up that one, and they bin coming from Alice Springs. They bin come through, and they bin coming to one day; they bin coming to Ryan's Well... And they bin go right up to Coniston, and that old truck, they bin leave 'em there.

From there, they bin get the big mob of horse, longa Randal Stafford... That police bin take 'em horse, and he bin carry with the rifle. And him (Stafford) bin say, 'That's all of my mob here.' Little mob.

Darby telling the Coniston story while sitting on Brooks' grave 1995

Darby   172

He never bin shoot 'em that mob, while they bin longa station all the time. They bin leave 'em; that policeman bin leave him. Randal Stafford bin stop him alright.

Another mob, while they bin living in the Brooks Soak – behind that hill. That's all they bin get there. Ready, look around again. They bin see 'em one Jakamarra, longa Mawu – waterhole. Alright, they bin kill that one Jakamarra, belonga that place. Alright, they bin shoot 'em that one, and they bin go around, 'Oh, big mob going that way!' They bin follow 'em up longa Waterloo (Nguntaru) rockhole – big rockhole. Big mob bin there . . . My sister, all about they get shot, too, there. And my brother-in-law. They finish (died) all up there. And from there, they (Murray's party) bin look, 'Oh, enough here.'

Oh, him bin put 'em heap. Little children and big boy; young man and big boy. Children. Oh, everything there! Women there, young girl; they kill 'em whole lot there.

From there, they bin camp down at Brooks Soak. And they bin camp there, longa scrub – somebody don't want to see 'em. That police bin there – camp in the bush. And from there, he bin watching that road. As soon as somebody come along, he get shot.

And from there, morning time, they bin follow that creek . . . and they bin go through to that 'nother hill there – Mt Leichardt (Ngarnka) – and they bin follow that creek. A 'thousand' people there, longa 'nother big waterhole. They bin have a 'business' (men's ceremony) there, while they want to go to Willowra (Wirliya-Jarrayi). And they get shot half way – about 'twelve hundred' peoples. They finish up there, half way. Oh, too much! Oh, big mob of youngfella, and big mob of old mans. Too much altogether.

And from there, they bin travelling. They bin see 'em another one, this side from Willowra. Our people bin there. They bin get shot, too. Girl and boy. Young kid, too. Children! Children, too. All the little ones, they bin get killed there. And some old man bin get shot.

Darby reflected on the events on a subsequent trip to Yurrkuru:

Alright, Whitefella bin come through, long time ago, and take 'em all the girls. Take away from Aboriginal peoples. That's long time ago. Not right at all. No, robber! Look like robber. Take away! That's why they bin get troubling – Aboriginal peoples, long time ago. Poor fella, they get shot for nothing. Get shot for nothing!

Lot of my mob is buried in the ground, now – while they bin get shot. They're buried underground. That's all the peoples, while they bin buried, long time ago. And we bin grow up 'nother lot behind (after).

We're very sorry we're telling this story. We no want more troubles. I talking here my word – Darby Ross Jampijinpa. We talk about we're very sorry for this people – children and girl while they bin get shot. We no want a like trouble like that one.

According to Darby, Warlpiri men, women and children were shot. The party burnt any weapons they found and buried the dead, which included Marungali. For obvious reasons, Nguntaru would later be referred to as Waterloo Rockhole.

Meanwhile, Kamanyarrpa and Padirrki were travelling west in the rocky country around Yalkarajirri. They then split up. Padirrki went east to Yurnturrpurlu, Kamanyarrpa west to Wakurlpa (Rock Hill) and on to Ngardurrungu (Mt Hardy). Pharlap Japangardi explains:

Old Bullfrog (Kamanyarrpa) hide himself longa Mt Hardy. Couldn't come down (from) there. Got 'em sugarbag (native honey) there, and watch 'em everybody white man coming now with horse. And he plant himself (in the) cave ... big mob on a horse, policeman and all other people. Old Bullfrog still on the hill ... They shoot 'em big mob, they shooting all around that eight-mile bore, this side from station. Old Bullfrog still on the hill watching. When shot go off, he go in the cave inside.[16]

Murray's accounts of the incident suggest that Kamanyarrpa was not known to him at the time and he appears to have treated everyone he met as potential perpetrators. Jack Jakamarra Ross agreed that 'the police party weren't looking for Bullfrog (Kamanyarrpa), they were just shooting anyone who was black'.[17]

After a day spent searching for others camped in the area, Murray and his party returned to Coniston. They left Stafford there, who was somewhat shocked by the events at Nguntaru, which had also alerted Warlpiri in the area to stay clear of the expedition. Murray's party then travelled north down the Lander river to Yarluwayi (Boundary Soak) and Six Mile Soak, before tracking down another group some distance away.[18] According to Murray, this encounter left another six people dead. Although Murray did not mention it in his report, Darby claimed the party then travelled to Patilirri (also known as Tipinpa) where the men's initiation ceremonies had begun. All the men were rounded up and shot.[19]

Murray's party then headed south towards Yurrkuru and travelled west to a soakage in Cockatoo Creek. On the way they tracked people in the hills and shot two men as they ran away. Murray shot another man at Mawu, a soakage a few miles west of Yurrkuru. Jack Jakamarra Ross relates the incident:

> There was an old Jakamarra – by himself – staring at a bird up in a tree at Mawu. He was throwing a boomerang at this bird as the police party came across him. They must have had trackers, because he didn't realise that someone was shooting at him. He was shot.[20]

The party encountered others, including a blind man, Rdakamuru, in the company of several women, who was questioned before being set free.[21] They headed south and west, possibly to Ngarntampi, or as far as Yipirri (near Mission Creek). More people were shot, and some arrested and taken back to Coniston, including Yakirkra.[22] Murray then took Yakirkra and Wiliyarrpa to Alice Springs to await the journey to Darwin for their trial.

Darby talked of 'two troubles' in this period. The first reprisals were the result of Brooks' murder on August 7, and the second followed an attack on Nugget Morton on August 28. At the time, Morton was a pastoralist living on the Lander River, near the site of the present-day Warlpiri community of Willowra, north of his main camp. Darby claimed Morton had ten 'girls' living with him, and that they used to ride his horses. Anecdotal evidence, including notes later collected by Ted Strehlow on patrol in 1937, after Morton had shifted to the east nearer Mt Peake Station, suggests he was not unaccustomed to having sex with these women.[23] The trouble with Morton appears to have been a direct result of his treatment of women, his aggressive nature, conflict over water sources and the alleged spearing of his cattle.[24] Morton was attacked at Janganpurlangu (Boomerang Hole). Perhaps because he was a solid man, though short and stocky as his nickname Nugget suggested, he managed to fend off his attackers, get his gun and shoot two of the men.[25] Morton, though injured, rode back to his main camp where he gave an account to his business partner Sandford.

Mounted Constable Murray was again sent forth and travelled through Coniston, ordering Wilson to join him, and then on to Tilmouth's camp at Liirlpari (White

Stone). He listened to Tilmouth's story of being attacked by Wangeriji ('Wangaridge') Jungarrayi, who had been working with him.[26] This occurred not long after the attack on Morton.

After meeting with Tilmouth, Murray continued on to Morton's camp, arriving at Broadmeadows in late September. He soon formed another party, including Morton, Wilson, and his young 'brother' John Cusack, and fourteen horses.[27] According to Murray's account, they followed tracks on the dry Lander River to Tomahawk Waterhole, shooting four people before returning to Janganpurlangu (Boomerang Hole). They then headed northeast to Walurrukurlangu (Circle Well) where they shot two men, and east to Wajinpulungku soakage (Baxter's Bore) on the lower Hanson river where they shot another eight men. Murray then returned to Alice Springs where he wrote a brief report, attempting to conceal the number of people who were killed.[28]

Darby suggested Murray's party went further afield than was noted in his official reports: down the Lander river to Kunajarrayi (Dingo Waterhole), Jarralyku (Curlew Waterhole), and right up to Yinapaka (Lake Surprise), where more shootings occurred before they returned to Janganpurlangu. While in the Hanson River area they also travelled through Jarra Jarra. Darby knew this because he was in a group that came across their remains one day while out riding horses. They had to excavate the graves with digging sticks, and they buried them next to the creek. Darby also spoke of bodies being burnt by Murray:

They bin go right up to Jarra Jarra ... Big mob again, he bin get shot. Oh, two heaps while they bin shoot 'em. Two heaps they bin chuck him ... Big mob of people buried under the ground.[29] Bones bin laying around there everywhere. And we bin bury 'em down the ground ... We bin bury 'em all the old man, and all the girl and children. Lot of peoples they bin burn 'em up to fire. Big mob of wood they chuck 'em underneath, and they burn 'em. Not right like that!

Dick Kimber's account of Walter Smith, a stockman who visited the area a few years later, suggests further evidence of massacres:

Walter was riding his camel along the Lander (River) when his attention was drawn to white objects. 'They were like paddy-melons. The skulls. A man felt sorry. There must have been two hundred of them – big ones, little ones, women, kids, everyone.'[30]

News of the events at Coniston soon reached the major newspapers in the cities down south where there was now more willingness to discuss humanitarian issues relating to Aboriginal people following reports of the 1926 Forrest River massacre in the

Kimberley. Several city papers carried the story, including Melbourne's *Argus*, which voiced the concerns of Methodist Minister Athol McGregor, who challenged the idea that the shootings were justified:

> My objection is not to constitutional justice, but to the shooting of 17 men and women by the police. No circumstances can justify the shooting of such a number, and was ever a battle fought in which 17 were hit and all died? So many settlers prefer a dead black to a live one that we must ask ourselves what did really happen.[31]

Many other sources, not least of which are Warlpiri oral accounts like Darby's, place the number of deaths at well over one hundred people, most not even remotely connected with the death of Brooks. Even Stafford considered it likely that twice the official number were killed.[32] In 1930, Lutheran Pastor Albrecht visited Pikilyi and was asked by Warlpiri living there why the Whitefellas had killed so many people. He had no answer for them. From his conversations, he concluded that it was likely up to one hundred people were killed.[33] Albrecht later wrote that the killing of Brooks was 'completely justifiable', at least with regard to Aboriginal Law.[34]

According to Darby, Murray's party shot men, women and children with little discrimination. The arrogance and confidence with which they did this is clear in Murray's response to a question about why he shot to kill, during the unsuccessful trial of Wiliyarrpa and Yakirkra:

> What could I do with a wounded blackfellow hundreds of miles from civilisation?[35]

In 1995, Darby travelled to the site of the old Coniston homestead. The buildings were not the ones he had known, but the ruins of Bryan Bowman's subsequent homestead. He pointed out some of the places he remembered, like the creek where Warlpiri used to camp. He stopped at Yurrkuru and sat on Brooks' grave and told the story as he had done many times before. He spoke of the killings with sadness and regret at the loss of so many lives. It left a very strong impression on him, one that he could not forget.

Nicolas Peterson, engaged in anthropological research in Yuendumu in the early 1970s, recalled Darby approaching him when police from Alice Springs were called to deal with an apparent riot at nearby Papunya. Darby expressed concern that if they came they might kill everybody.[36] At other times, Darby spoke more broadly of injustices committed against Aboriginal people in Australia. He had a strong belief, reinforced by his travels and interactions with other Aboriginal people, that they were not uncommon and had occurred all over the country from Tasmania to Melville Island:

Long time ago, it's only one man bin travel again: Captain Cook. Captain Cook him bin travelling from England. That's the one we bin see 'em on the video, down Canberra. That one we bin see 'em. We very sorry for the people, want to be level to white man. I reckon like still (Aboriginal people) behind the white man more and more. I've seen 'em every city, and Aboriginal people a little bit half, I reckon.

The indiscriminate manner in which the Coniston shootings were carried out struck fear into many Warlpiri and Anmatyerr.[37] They travelled far from the area, and grieved for lost family members. Oral accounts suggest that Warlpiri were the most affected. They went to places like Lirrakilpirri and Purturlu (Mt Theo) to the north, Kunajarrayi to the west, and Hermannsburg to the south. Jack Jakamarra Ross was camped at Rdakapirri near Mt Theo when he first heard the news:

> I remember this old Napaljarri woman coming towards us with a fire stick in her hand. She was naked and her body was covered with white ash. This meant that her sons had passed away. She told us to move on because there had been this trouble – that Whitefellas were shooting at Blackfellas ... She had abandoned her son somewhere out in the bush while on the run from the police and the trackers, and we saw her running towards us with the fire stick. We could hear her wailing from a long way as the sun was getting low. I asked her, 'Why are you crying?' Suddenly she hit me. I was wondering why she hit me, so I asked her again, 'Why are you crying?' She hit me again. That was twice. I was frustrated, but I asked her again, 'Why are you crying?' She said (using a hand signal), 'My son was shot.'[38]

Jack Jakamarra Ross

The Warlpiri who were still living in the desert stayed away for many years, and many did not return to the Coniston country. Yet, along with some of the other Warlpiri who had lived on the station, Darby returned and continued to work there. He spoke matter-of-factly about this, even though it is unlikely he could disconnect the places he visited, and the people with whom he worked, from the events in which many members of his family were killed.

Some years after the Coniston Massacre, Darby heard about the incident in which Murtarta Jampijinpa shot Harry Henty dead on December 15, 1928, at Kurundi Station. Due to his involvement in the events at Coniston, Constable Murray did not go out to search for Murtarta, also known as Willaberta Jack, until February, 1929. The following story was recounted by Darby and first appeared as *Warumungu Watikirli*, a booklet published by the Warlpiri Literature Production Centre in the 1980s. The English translation is by Mary Laughren.

Before the War, a white man called Harry Henty and an Aboriginal man called Murtarta Jampijinpa clashed over a woman. That Aboriginal man was Warumungu. Henty and Jampijinpa both fought over the one woman, over Napangardi who was said to be very beautiful. Napangardi was married to this Jampijinpa. She was also Warumungu – from that same place.

Jampijinpa and Napangardi were living at Kurundi Station where Henty was working. Napangardi used to work for Henty as a house girl. Jampijinpa was working in the stock camp.

Henty would detain Napangardi after work each evening. Jampijinpa would be waiting for her every night to come back from the white man's house. He got angry with the white man. The white man chased Jampijinpa away from the house. 'Clear out!' Jampijinpa said, 'No, I won't give you my wife. I'll take my wife away with me.'

The next night, the white man once again stopped Napangardi from going home. They slept together. Jampijinpa, who had been waiting in vain for his wife to come home, crept up to Henty's house. When he got close to the house, he saw the white man's rifle through the window. It was hanging there. He took it. Then he went around the house in search of the white man. The dogs barked at him as he was going around with the rifle, peering inside to see where Henty was. Henty heard the dogs barking and he got up. He looked around to see who was there. He opened a window.

Jampijinpa aimed the rifle at him. The white man came close to the window. Then Jampijinpa shot him through the neck – straight through with a single bullet. He shot him in the front, and the bullet went straight through and came out at the back of his neck. The white man fell down dead from the bullet. After that Jampijinpa took Napangardi away. 'Let's go to escape the whites. Many of them might come after us.' They ran away. They went to a rockhole called Kangaroo Hole. Jampijinpa built a humpy up on the rocks.

In those days there was no road there. Cars could not travel there. Only horses and cattle could move around there.

When the police heard that Harry Henty was dead, and that he had been shot by an Aboriginal man, they joined up to go after him. The boss policeman, who was named Murray, gathered together the other policemen to look for the Aboriginal man who had shot Henty.

They looked around for him on horseback for years. He kept eluding them. They used to go around to all the stations asking the people about the whereabouts of this Jampijinpa.

As for Jampijinpa, he stayed in the rocky hill country. He went along the hills from one waterhole to the next. Jampijinpa and Napangardi moved around together. They would walk on the grass, or where there were branches – leaves that had fallen down from trees – that's how they went. They would throw down spinifex to walk on, to prevent the others from following their tracks. They would also wipe out any tracks with branches.

They went around from place to place getting tea and flour when they were hungry. They would get rations from other Warumungu people. Jampijinpa had a lot of brothers-in-law.

At one place, there was a very nasty white man. Someone told him that Murtata had come for food. When he heard that, he set off after him, armed with a rifle. He went after Jampijinpa on horseback. 'Where's he gone? I'll shoot this villain today. He shot a white man.'

He went after Jampijinpa. After going a long way, he climbed up high on a hill. He caught sight of a humpy. 'That humpy, it belongs to that Aborigine.'

Then the white man took hold of his rifle. Pow! He shot to kill Murtata. He shot and missed. He put another bullet into his rifle, took another shot and missed. He put another bullet in, took another shot and missed again. Napangardi was also there, on the south side. She was crouching down in fear. Jampijinpa was terrified. 'Truly, he's going to shoot me. He's going to kill both of us.'

Having taken many shots at them, the white man ran out of bullets. Murtata and Napangardi crept away. When the white man failed to find them he went back to his place.

After a long time on the run, Murtata thought to himself, 'Will I give myself up? Yes, I might as well

Murtarta Jampijinpa

give myself up. The police will probably finish by shooting me.'

So, he just gave himself up to the police. He coolly surrendered to them. The police grabbed hold of him. They put a chain around Jampijinpa's neck. They handcuffed Napangardi.

After they had tied him up, that same Constable Murray took them to his car and tied them to it with the chain that was around Jampijinpa's neck. He forced both Jampijinpa and Napangardi to walk along chained to the car. He took them to Alice Springs, and after that, Jampijinpa was sent up to Darwin. They took him up to Port Darwin, on the coast.

In Darwin, at that time, was a Judge called Nicholls, who was a hanging judge. They took Murtata up there, but he won. The judge sent him back home to his country where he lived for a year. Then one day he was found dead. He is believed to have died as a result of being given poisoned flour by some white people who were probably trying to take revenge.

A Board of Enquiry was opened in late December, 1928. After travelling to many of the sites in January, 1929, the Board heard evidence in Alice Springs. Murray admitted seventeen people were shot after the murder of Brooks, and a further fourteen after the incident with Morton. Tilmouth admitted shooting one man. In all three cases the Board ruled the shootings justified, based on evidence given by Murray, 'Tracker Paddy', Stafford and other 'reputable settlers' including Morton, Tilmouth, Saxby and Briscoe.[39] They wrote: 'The Board is prepared to believe the evidence of all witnesses'.[40]

Researcher Mervyn Hartwig found no evidence that the Board investigated the reliability of witnesses, and drew attention to the Board's dismissal of evidence presented by missionaries, including Athol McGregor and Annie Lock.[41] The Board appears to have given no consideration to obtaining or recognising Warlpiri accounts, and found it 'impracticable' to take evidence from Wilson, stating it was not necessary and that Murray 'did not desire his presence'.[42]

Having cleared Murray of any wrongdoing, the Board explained why Brooks and Morton were attacked. Among their reasons were:

> (2b) unattached missionaries wandering from place to place, having no previous knowledge of blacks and their customs and preaching a doctrine of equality; (2c) inexperienced white settlers making free with the natives and treating them as equals;

To explain their conclusion that a punitive expedition had not occurred, the Board referred to the twenty-three Aboriginal people at Coniston who were allowed 'to go free'. According to Darby, it was Stafford who had stopped Murray from shooting the people who had been working on Coniston. In defence of the Police Constable, the Board also stated the following:

> Had he desired to disguise the number of natives killed, he could have done so in his official reports and evidence. Furthermore, if a massacre was intended, the Police Party could, as the evidence shows, have killed a hundred natives.

Visitors
Board of Enquiry

Chapter Nine

Good Old Days

Warlpiri acknowledge Darby as one of the last of the 'footwalk' people. He spoke of his carefree life as a boy, and his extended family's movements from place to place in search of food and water. Chance encounters and varying seasons resulted in a dynamic and unpredictable social life. When he discussed this early period of this life, Darby demonstrated a connectedness to people and place, and a very strong sense of how his identity was shaped in his early years.

Darby was born in Warlpiri country, in the Tanami Desert, in the early twentieth century. He walked hundreds of kilometres with his family in search of food and water and came to know the country intimately. The men would hunt for kangaroos and the women would dig for smaller animals and collect bushtucker. Food would be more plentiful after rain, when Darby's family would meet with other family groups. In these times, they would perform ceremonies and initiate their young men.

The Tanami Desert of Central Australia has been home to the Warlpiri people for *tarnngangku* (a long, long time). While estimates of the size of Warlpiri country vary, it covered an area of not less than 80 000 sq. km based on Darby's descriptions. He also suggested that the borders of Warlpiri country changed over the years — like when Warlpiri warriors fought over water sources with neighbouring tribes in the west. Anthropologists and older Warlpiri have indicated that Warlpiri people were divided into four sub-groups which roughly equate to a north, south, east and west subdivision of Warlpiri land: Warnayaka, Ngaliya, Yarlpari and Warrmarla. Darby referred to himself as a Ngaliya man.

It was a harsh climate, and people had to be tough to survive. They lived a semi-nomadic existence, reliant upon their accumulated knowledge of the country for their survival. A complex system of relatedness governed Warlpiri social life, permeated with *Jukurrpa* (Dreaming), which was present in the landscape and whose secrets were held by the elders. It was into this life and landscape that Darby was born in about 1905.

When Darby was born, Warlpiri did not record birth dates. Births and deaths were marked by the seasons, or droughts and floods, and the country in which they occurred. Darby recalled seeing Halley's Comet for the first time when he was very young (the earth passed through the tail of the comet in May, 1910). Darby's birth date was not recorded until years later, and has been written down as 1900, 1905, 1907, 1908 and 1910. His official birth certificate, which was presented to him in 2005, recorded it as 1905. He also shared New Year's Day as a common birthday with most old people at Yuendumu whose actual birthdays are not known. I estimate that Darby was born sometime between 1905 and 1908.

In the following story, Darby describes his life as a boy at various stages in the passage to manhood: his mother carrying him in a coolamon, learning to hunt kangaroos with the men, and hearing about Whitefellas travelling through the country.

Two little coolamons – (wooden) baby carriers. Little coolamons, we call 'em *parraja*. Make 'em plenty warm. No blanket, nothing. Alright, we're crying longa that little *parraja*. My mother give it *lampurnu* (breast milk). From there, no more crying more.

Little bit bigger now. And we walking round the knee now. Alright, 'Oh, that little boy gone over there.'

'Manta, warna kujaku!' (Pick him up, there might be snakes.)

Grandmother got to look after (me), mother belonga Nungarrayi (Darby's mother). Alright, that bushtucker, they feed him. They feed 'em we. Give it, and we eat 'em. That's the way they bin look after we, while we're crying round, hungry fella. No tea, no flour, nothing. Nothing at all. Alright, while we crying round there, they get 'em big mob of *yarla* (bush potato). They break 'em up and we eat 'em. Alright from there, little bit high now – coming up.

While we bin grow up, we going to shift out from that camp, go another way. We bin at old camp, and we bin shift out (to) another water, up near Rock Hill (Wakurlpa). We camping round there.

Little bit bigger now. Alright from there, they get 'em *marlu* (kangaroo). Might they got a big mob of dogs (dingoes). Might another mob bring back two kangaroo – two *marlu*. Everybody got to have a feast. Give it away – another mob, another mob, another mob, another mob. Oh, big mob peoples, might they give it little bit.

And from there, a little bit more high now, and we grow up more. Alright, they grow (me) up properly. And that little bit bigger, and we go out little bit long way now, longa single man's camp. And that's where we're playing, and lay down there. And mother and grandmother and another lot, bringing the food for everybody. And give it for we. And bush banana, we call 'em *yuparli*. They give it for we. Good tucker!

That's from long time ago. No cattle bin here; no horse bin here. No, we never seen the people travel up, got a big mob of camels. Before that *Kardiya* (Whitefellas).

Little bit high now we. He big boy now (Darby). (But) they talk longa that other boy. Bring him in four boy now, they got to go to 'business' (men's ceremonies). And from there, we bin grow up now. Look whiskers now! Little bit coming out from here (chin). We drink the water – rainwater. Oh, might be some big rockhole there; might be creek there. We might cook him longa that place.

Alright, we shift out for Rock Hill – Wakurlpa. We cook 'em longa that waterhole Mirijarra. And from there, we sitting round thinking about sugarbag – wild sugarbag (native honey). Cut 'em down (with) stone tommyhawk. Old man bin only cut 'em down, long time. He got to sharpen 'em again, longa big rock. And he got to rub 'em up again, and make 'em sharp. And he got to get 'em longa finger – that sugarbag inside. That's hard work. Only stone tommyhawks they bin use 'em. Which way they bin get that stone tommyhawk? Over there, not too far away, other side from Yuendumu.

And Whitefella bin come out while they bin walking around here. Through the town (where Yuendumu is now) he bin travelling here. They bin running away from that camel – that's wild peoples, Aboriginal peoples. And they bin run away, 'Hey, we got to go all the way now.'

'Look out, might him bite a we!' They bin only run, go to scrub country, longa mulga, sitting round inside the scrub. Oh, some fella might climb up the hill. Never see him (Whitefellas) before. While they bin making that telegraph line – he going right up to Darwin and Alice Springs – they (Aboriginal people) bin only frightened, run away in the bush.

Alright, little bit high now, we got whiskers now, longa single man's camp. We camping everywhere there, and playing, too. They bin only tie 'em up bushes – leaves – and we make 'em big ball. We wanna play longa that one. All the nakeds – no clothes.

And from there, all the man now, we walking around. They thinking about – whiskers long way now – they give it married now. That story from early days, from while we bin grow up, longa this country.

Darby's family were camped in the country to the north of the present-day site of Yuendumu. Ngarnayarlpirri, a rockhole that lies amongst a group of low-lying granite slabs, was Darby's birthplace. It is a Women's Dreaming site that is part of the story about the old man whose penis was chasing a group of women. The surrounding country is known as Ngarliyikirlangu, where many sites belonged to Darby's father and grandfather, and would one day be his responsibility. Several people have suggested other birth sites, and some interviews with Darby suggest that he was born near Pikilyi or Wanapiyi, places he visited as a young boy. However, on every occasion Darby and I visited Ngarnayarlpirri, he claimed, 'I bin born here.'

The landscape of Darby's country is dominated by large rusty granite boulders. They are the contested bush raisins of the Emu and Bush Turkey Dreaming, the eggs of snakes, body parts and the markings of those that created the country. Darby's family was living amongst them at the time of his birth as the country was holding water after rain. They collected the water in the rockholes at Warnirri-panu and Kunarurrpa, or by digging in the sand at Parirri. The men hunted rock wallabies and euros that lived in the hills, and kangaroos and emus that roamed the vast plain to the north.

Many of Darby's early memories are of kangaroo hunting. In this story, he describes how people would catch kangaroos (with the assistance of their dogs), then cook and distribute the meat to their families.

A long time ago, we bin sitting around in the bush, building humpies (shelters). Whitefella call them humpy, we call them *yujuku*. People are gathering plenty of wood. They make fire inside, and that humpy is warm.

Now, water is running everywhere, down the creek and along the flat, too. Water goes everywhere and makes green grass. That green grass grow up straight away.

They got a couple of dogs there. Mummy one – another one, boy one. Dingo one. He got pups.

When two kangaroo come up to the water – the boggy place – those dingoes got to catch him right there, (and) knock him down in the throat. That man got to follow those tracks. He says, 'Oh, him here!

Two fighting over there.' Two fella fighting: mummy one and old man.

Alright, he look back now. That man, he look every way for kangaroo. One time, chasing nearly ten mile, and another nearly four mile. He kill them, and bring them back, cut him in the side. He got to make a big fire – big mob of wood. He got to cook him properly.

He cook him – chuck leaves – and cuts him. Then eat him. He got to feed them dogs, too. Two dogs follow him all the way. He tell 'em (dogs), 'You follow this one, you follow this one.' (pointing to tracks)

All the way he follows, and he got to catch that kangaroo. Good dog that dingo. As soon as he see him (kangaroo), he is running. That old man catch him up quick, knock him down straight away. He can't bark, 'Arph, Arph.' He can't sing out, 'Hoooow.' Nothing! They knock him down that kangaroo. That old man, he run along and he kill him right there (back of the head). He drop him there, and cut him straight away (to check for fat). He's got to stitch him up to keep out the flies. That man has to cook for a long time. Two kangaroo there now cooking. Talk about fat! He got to break that backbone along a rock. He never had a tommyhawk – only rocks. That's long time ago. This time they use tommyhawks. Break up backbone and feed to those dogs. Just a little bit of bones. Good chew. Them dogs full up now.

From there, he is cutting down bushes with stone knife. Everything, he got to take back to camp, keep it for everybody. He carry him on a big, long stick. When he come back, people crying out, 'Hello, hello.' And clapping their hands, 'That's my uncle, bringing a lot of kangaroo!' They are singing out to him.

He's got to take those kangaroos along to single man camp. He leave them there, and another one got to work now, while that man bin sitting around the camp. That mob got to cut him up right.

'Got to keep this one's rib bones for all the girls.' Four rib bones, and some from leg – give him half and half. Everybody got to have the kangaroo.

Another man, he come along. He take a little bit of kangaroo for him(self), too. More people coming, and they got to have a feed. No cattle, no cheese, no nanny-goat – nothing. It's only kangaroo.

Everybody happy there, now.

In the next story, Darby describes the social obligations of hunting. He was camped with his family at Pikilyi (now also known as Vaughan Springs) during a period of wet weather, in a time leading up to initiation ceremonies.

That old man dog, he the boss. How many him kill 'em? One, two, three, four, and from there five. Him take that many. And they go – one, two, three, four, five, six – six man, they go, and they bring back that big mob of kangaroo.

And they got to keep it for grandfather.

And they got to keep it for mother.

This rockhole is Ngarnayarlpirri. All the women bin come through, hiding from Wutangula, from Kunajarrayi and Yipirri.
PADDY JAPALJARRI STEWART

And they got to keep it for grandmother.

And all the old man, they got to eat him.

And they got to make big fire there – lot of flies while he bin running through. They got to sit down in the middle of the fire. Another fire here, another fire here, another fire here, another fire here – from fly. Properly good one, they bin only make 'em.

Alright from there, everybody happy now. There, while they bin living from rain, they're camped longa that rock, too. Inside, they make 'em big smoke there – big fire, longa rocks. Longa Vaughan Springs (Pikilyi). And a big mob of women, they're camped. All the man, we camped. We walk up and down there – only two places. Mother and my sister there. My grandfather there. My grandmother again. Single man, they're sitting each side. Big mob of peoples, they sitting round there.

From there, soon as the rain finish, they go thinking about . . . Another three going that way, north – *yatijarra*. And another one, they going that way, sunrise – *kakarrara*. And this way they go, south – *kurlirra*. And from there they go west – *karlarra*.

Old man might go and get the boomerangs. Right after that, they ready to catch the young man – while they want to make him man. Alright, they catch him and they, 'Ooh, ooh, ooh, ooh.' (singing) All night and day. They singing there all night and day. Old man they are singing, too. They are singing whole lot. All the girls, they are dancing. They are singing out everywhere. Good one!

Darby was given the name Wanyu, after his paternal grandfather, with whom he also shared his 'skin' name Jampijinpa. Warlpiri society is divided into eight distinct groups identified by these 'skin' names. These groups determine the ideal relationships between members of each group. Darby, a Jampijinpa man, should marry a Napangardi woman, who is the 'right skin' for him. Their children then receive the Jangala (for males) and Nangala (for females) 'skin' names from their father and mother.

'Straight' wife, not 'wrong' girl. 'Straight' girl, they got to give it. Jampijinpa, he got to go Napangardi. Japangardi – give it Nampijinpa. Like my sister. That's 'straight' wife – he no want to make a trouble. They no want to (be) fighting around. They give it 'straight'. No more fighting. That's the way they bin only do 'em here, long time ago.

The ceremonies in which Darby participated served to further strengthen and define his relationships to others in the community. However, the system becomes even more complicated when the guidelines are not followed, as in the case of 'wrong skin' marriages, the negative consequences of which are a common theme in Warlpiri *Jukurrpa* (Dreaming). As a boy, Darby saw lots of fights over women. One particular incident involved an older brother who was jealous of his younger brother's new wife:

They give it married for him. And that 'nother (brother), him jealous. That two man got to fight. Get 'em big spear. Another one might carry the stone knife. From there, that young fella, he running down and cut his shoulder for him, his brother. Oh, no! That blood he run down right on the ground. Two brother fighting, now. Alright, 'You bin cutting me. You got a stone knife!' He cutting down the shoulder. Right in the back. Oh, (others) bin standing all around: 'Hey you, leave your brother. That's enough.' Oh, big fight! I bin only looking out the desert. Big fight bin only going on there.

And another fella he get 'em stone knife. Alright, him run now. And him bin pull 'em out that knife and cut him straight away. Right, finish and, 'Alright, you can keep that girl now.' (older brother) 'You right! You got 'em big girl and I got 'em little girl.' (younger brother) Alright, two finish for that fighting. That young fella right, while they bin give it a young girl for him. He sitting round there, got a sore back. And from there, 'Alright, me finish for you, my brother.' Alright, that (other) man, 'No, I don't want to come back and see you again. I got to go away from you.'

When he became a man, Darby was always careful to avoid the jealousy of his older brothers:

Alright, while me bin man, I never sitting round longside my brother. No I keep away from that one (his wife) – might (he) fighting me from (his) wife.

Throughout his life, and following Warlpiri tradition, Darby's father had ten wives who originated from areas to the east and west of his own country. As a boy, Darby visited many of these places with his extended family. His father had 'stolen' his mother from her country at Kunajarrayi, an important site of convergence for many *Jukurrpa* and a place where people would gather for ceremonies. He had taken his new wife away from her family and travelled south to Nyirrpi and Mawurrungu. When he returned to Kunajarrayi, it was to make peace and fulfil the obligations of a son-in-law to his wife's family. It was while they were camped in his mother's country (on a later trip) that Darby witnessed the killing of Napaljarri (Paddy Japaljarri Sims' sister) by Kampa Jakamarra. Napaljarri was Darby's cousin, and had been given as a wife to Kampa Jakamarra to settle a dispute he was having with a Jampijinpa man over another Napangardi woman (who was not 'promised' to Kampa nor was his 'right skin'). This occurred at Panma, southwest of Ngarupalya where Darby was camped with his family.

I bin see him, me bin big boy. Jakamarra (Kampa), he bin chasing round a Napangardi, over there, longa Nyirrpi. That old man Jakamarra and Jampijimpa bin fighting round all the time for one girl. And from there, they bin give a 'straight' wife for him (Jakamarra) – Napaljarri. Old man Jungarrayi (her father) bin give it. Big Napaljarri, my cousin, belonga Paddy Sims Japaljarri (her brother).

Well, he (Kampa) bin do wrong, and my cousin bin climb up the tree, longa Panma rockhole. That old man (Kampa) bin coming, now. Him bin have a big mob of spear and two boomerangs.

'Hey!' Him bin sing out like that (to Napaljarri in the) tree. He bin sing out, 'Come on Napaljarri. You and me gotta go!' Alright, my cousin bin start to cry, 'I no want you!' My cousin bin talking to him. Alright, from there, 'I no want to follow 'em you.' My cousin bin crying, longa big tree. Alright, he bin think about now – Jakamarra – he bin getting wild properly now. He bin just get 'em one spear, and him bin spear 'em through here (chest). He bin chuck 'em right longa that tree – wooooosh – right here – finish (die). My cousin, he bin spear through here. And (she) bin come down, just drop down the ground.

That Jakamarra bin run away, too. Which way he bin run? He bin go right up to Pitjantjatjara country, all around there, walking round. Cheeky man, that one.

That old man (Jungarrayi) – Paddy Sims' father – oh, crying! That old man bin cry properly. And my grandmother, (she) bin cry, too. And my Aunty bin crying round there. Oh, properly, that girl there finished (dead).

And from there, he never bin coming back, that mad Jakamarra. Him bin going for good. Oh, frightened from 'nother lot. And all the fathers there – Jungarrayi. All the Jungarrayi belonga that girl, they bin crying round everywhere.

And from there, him (Kampa) bin thinking about ten year. Ten year, walking around 'nother country. Pitjantjatjara country. Ten years!

From there, (he) bin coming back now. Him bin have a big mob of tobacco. That *pituri* (native) tobacco from hill. And he bin have 'em long hair. He bin coming back (to) Nyirrpi. I bin big boy now.

Three fella – one Jungarrayi, two Jampijinpa – they bin get to him. Oh, we bin very sorry for that old man, too – for that Kampa. They bin spear through here (chest), and him bin sticking out all the way. Can't pull 'em out! Oh, poor bugger. They bin chase him, now. Chase him, and they bin look. He bin get away alright. Blood bin running everywhere. Poor bugger! Big mob bin after him, now. All the Jungarrayi and Jampijinpa (men). That's all, there bin no Japaljarri there, now – from my cousin, dead girl, while they bin spear (her) through here.

Alright, they bin chase him, through from Nyirrpi. And like that, 'Hey!' That old man – grandfather – Japaljarri belonga me, 'You leave my *panji* (brother-in-law). I bin grow him up that one. You fella leave him!' Him bin tell 'em all the way. Never mind, they bin still chasing. And from there, that spear bin sticking out all the way behind, longa back. Big spear!

From there, they bin go right up that way. They want to go and have a look. They want to kill (hurt) him more. Alright, that old man (Kampa) there, they bin after him. One here, two there, three there, four there, five, six, and seven – they bin after him. Alright, they bin chasing, now. Poor bugger, they bin chasing him. He never bin stop back. No, that old man bin – him bin have emu feathers here – him bin hold 'em, and (then they) cut (that) old man.

My grandmother, (she) got no hair, (she) bin growl that mob, 'What your brother doing to my *panji* (brother-in-law)? That one, I bin grow 'em up.' They bin crying around. Alright, him (Kampa) bin there.

Paddy Japaljarri Sims was a young boy at the time his sister was killed by Kampa Jakamarra

Kunajarrayi

Him bin say, like that, good way. All of my mob, my nephews, him bin say good way, longa them. That Jakamarra, his name Kampa, he bin say good way, longa everybody.

Alright, him want to like have a toilet, poor bugger. Oh, him bin say, 'No, you fella wait! You fella wait, *bambai* (bye and bye) you fella kill 'em me.' Him bin say, good way longa them, and he never hit 'em. They bin wild, looking out everyway. They bin have spears and boomerangs. Everything they bin have 'em.

Alright, he bin nearly have 'em my uncle. He bin nearly going to spear 'em. Only poor bugger, one fella boy bin just get a spear through here. 'Ooooh!' Finish him! Right in the head, they bin finish him (Kampa). Oh, poor bugger drop down.

In another version of this story, Darby described Kampa returning to Warlpiri country and chasing Napangardi again (who was then married to Darby's older brother). Another Jampijinpa man warned Kampa that the Jungarrayi men were still upset over the death of their daughter Napaljarri. But he refused to leave. Darby's grandfather, old Japaljarri, watched as Kampa Jakamarra (his brother-in-law) was killed by the Jungarrayi men. They speared him in the side, they speared him in the back. Many men were involved, and they buried him in a rabbit hole. While discussing this story after the recording, Darby admitted to throwing a boomerang at Kampa and hitting him in the leg. At the time he was only a young boy.

Karrku, red ochre country

Darby was a Warlpiri man by birth, but like many of his countrymen, he had family connections in the Anmatyerr country to the east and the Pintupi country to the west. He was aware of his relationships and obligations to others from an early age. He had many brothers and sisters; he later recalled their names, and how and where they died. He outlived all his brothers, and his many nephews and nieces, whom he already called sons and daughters according to Warlpiri tradition, became his responsibility. He also outlived many of them.

When he was young, Darby would play the game of *purlja* with the other boys. He said it was like the modern game of Australian Rules football. They would make a ball out of hairstring or emu feathers and run around playing for hours. They grew up eating bushtucker: bush raisin, bush tomato, bush banana, bush onions and the staple bush potato. Different country and different seasons meant different foods. Darby remembered being excited about being given sugarbag (native honey), which could be found in the hollows of trees. It was like getting lollies from the store. They would eat a lot of kangaroo and goanna meat, and everyone was happy if they were really fat ones. They wouldn't eat them if they weren't *jara-kurlu* – if there was no fat on the intestines. If they were in the sandhill country to the west, they might get some bilbies or little wallabies called *mala*. Occasionally they caught a delicacy, like budgerigar that could be found in the hollows of trees. At times their diet was relatively monotonous, but in times

of plenty it was varied and provided nutritious food. Darby was fond of saying that there was no flour, sugar or tea in those days.

While the early white explorers often deplored the poor nature of the country, taking their tinned supplies on their long camel journeys, to the Warlpiri the Tanami Desert was just like a supermarket! Peter Latz, a Central Australian botanist and friend to Darby, who assisted him in his research, wrote:

> Surprisingly, the areas with the poorest soils, namely the spinifex areas, supply the greatest number of plant foods, at least on their fringes ... The uncertain rainfall of Australia's desert regions meant that Aboriginal occupants have had to be extremely opportunistic; the range of foods utilised in good seasons would have been quite different from those utilised in drought.[2]

In times of low rainfall, Darby's family had to travel further afield to find adequate supplies. This could take them out of country belonging to his family. Occasionally, they were forced to go south to the border with another tribe's country. They would light fires to announce their arrival. This was also the time when ceremonies might be exchanged with neighbouring groups, inter-tribal marriages arranged, and disputes settled. But this was of little concern to Darby when he was a young boy. Under the care and guidance of the older members of his family, he lived a relatively carefree existence, amusing himself along with the other boys, playing games and mimicking the men by hunting little birds and lizards. However, when he was about twelve years old, Darby left his mother's camp and entered the single men's camp, where he would be prepared for his initiation into manhood. His mother and grandmother continued to bring him food, but he now shared his fire with the other single men.

When Darby started to grow 'whiskers', he learnt to track and spear kangaroos with the old men. They would hunt together, but Darby would also hunt with his 'dogs'. He had four dingoes that would chase the kangaroos to him, or his companion, who would then spear them. After rain, the dogs might be able to catch the kangaroos over the boggy ground. Sometimes, the kangaroo would run a long way with the spear in its side and they would have to track it until it fell down. If they were far from their camp, Darby and his companions would cook the kangaroo where it lay, then carry it back to their families.

> That kangaroo, he running. He run all the way, and he drop down somewhere there. And two boy got to (go) after him. 'Nother one got to come back and cut 'em that meat ... and as soon they cutting down, they got to drink that blood, too. That blood make 'em good. Drink him, proper way ... We bring back plenty kangaroo. Give it for everybody.

When he was young, Darby heard stories about Whitefellas from those who had seen them working on the Telegraph Line to the east, or more closely observed them travelling through Warlpiri country on camels. There were also rumours of the Lutheran mission at Hermannsburg to the south, cattle stations to the east, and The Granites goldfield to the west. Yet Darby had no contact with Whitefellas in Warlpiri country at this time.

Wakurlpa, a few miles to the south of Ngarnayarlpirri, was given the name Rock Hill by the explorer William Gosse, who travelled south through the area in 1873, a month after Peter Warburton's expedition headed west through Warlpiri country in an attempt to reach the west coast of Australia. As Warburton travelled through Warlpiri country, he gave English names to various Warlpiri sites, including Karrinyarra, which he named Mt Wedge because he thought it resembled

a slice of cheese.[2] Gosse crossed Warburton's track on his way south, where he would 'discover' Uluru, giving it the English name Ayer's Rock. The explorers, and their companions, were the first of many Whitefellas who would enter Warlpiri country in the 'olden days'.

Some Warlpiri thought the white people were *mamu* (monsters) or *mirlarlpa* (spirits) who were revealing their human forms. They offered them bullock meat, but the people were unsure if they should accept these gifts as they thought they might be human flesh. Others offered flour, and again people were unsure, thinking it might explain the whiteness of these people – it was like the white ash that they themselves put on their bodies during mourning ceremonies. Darby described the early meetings, and the beginnings of relations between the Warlpiri and the intruders:

Early days. Some people, they never bin see white man. He (Warlpiri) too much – you know – myall (bush people). Never see 'em big mob of camels, 'Hello!' They bin only run away. They run away (to) the hill. Sitting round the mulga, longa scrub. And from there, soon as (Whitefellas) get long way, alright he'll come out again. They follow 'em that track – halfway. Some people bin look about for tobacco. Like they want to see the white man.

Visitors
Explorer

This story was recorded and transcribed in Warlpiri by Mary Laughren in 1977-78 for Yuendumu School's bilingual program. The translation is by Erica Napurrurla Ross.

Ngurlu (mulga seeds)

All the old people were digging for bush potato. They used to dig for bush potato, and would give it to others, or share it amongst themselves. All the old people would share their food. Oh, they were the good old days we were living!

The old men would go hunting for meat. They would kill *mala* (rufous hare-wallabies) and *pakuru* (golden bandicoots). Aboriginal people would hunt and kill them for food. They would share the food with other families. It was really good in those days when we used to share. We would give meat, and other people would give water – trading or exchanging for food. We would also give meat to single women's camp and single men's camp. The older people would teach ceremonies and Dreamings to the young men. They would paint them with ochre and feathers. They would say, 'We're going to teach you youngfellas so you can look after your country.'

They would teach them the Dreaming, and afterwards they would go hunting. They would go and get dried plants, chop them, and mix them with yellow and red ochre, then get the young blokes painted for ceremonies. The other people, men and women, would go hunting for goannas. They would also kill bullocks and other meat like *wampana* (spectacled hare-wallaby), *mala*, and *pakuru*.[3] Another kind of bandicoot was *kirlilpi* (desert bandicoot). It was like a *pakuru*, and people used to tread on them with their feet. *Kirlilpi* would run very fast, but *pakuru* would get tired.

The old people would go hunting and look for animals. They would catch them – people from this country – mulga country, and sandhill country – all those old people from this country.[4] All these people were from Mirawarri, Mikanji, Munkularri and Kurlurlunu. All these people belonged to Water Dreaming. They danced the Water Dreaming. The men dance for special ceremonies – like when they initiate young boys and they have to stay in the bush for a long time. The men and women would teach Dreamings and show them to their sons, nephews, and grandchildren. They would say, 'I'm telling you mob. I'm telling you the real story.'

It was really good in the old days. They didn't fight – nothing. Today there is always fighting. In the old days we didn't fight, it was really good Law. They used to send the young blokes hunting for meat; they used to teach the blokes the culture and Dreaming.

All the old women would go hunting for bush potato – all our mob. They would dig everywhere, digging holes everywhere. The old women would dig for bush potatoes, and would dig really deep – way down for the big potatoes – where there were lots of cracks on the surface. They would also dig for the young ones that were really white.

It was really good, and they would talk to *Wapirra* (God), 'Give us really good food and rain so there will be lots of bushtucker.' So, it rained and rained until it made the trees and grass grow. The rain made the plants grow, so the women collected seeds to make seedcakes, like damper. The rain made the plants, so there was plenty of bush potatoes growing everywhere.

The women would dig for bush potatoes and they would pile them up. They would give the young bush potatoes to the smaller children. All our parents would give us bushtucker. They would save the bigger bush potatoes for later. They used to have bigger ones in those days. Afterwards, they would go to another soakage, and they would say, 'Let's go! We should go west to Nyurripatu.'

Nyurripatu belongs to the Jupurrurla and Jakamarra 'skin' group. It is the centre for the Bush Potato Dreaming. They would dig for bush potatoes around Nyurripatu. They would go from there. They would go from every soakage for hunting. They would kill the animal called *pakuru*. They would step on them, and then they would cook them in the soft sand. Afterwards, it would rain – like it rains here today. But, nowadays it only rains a little bit. It was good in those early days, in the places where all those old people lived.

All the people, especially older people, would go hunting for meat, bush potatoes, and seeds. We would share it. We would get bush food – little berries like *marnikiji* (conkerberry) and *yawalyurru* (native currant) and *marrkirdi* (bush plum) – like marbles and put it in the coolamons. We would fill it right up; we would fill the coolamons with bushtucker.

The people would live at Nyurripatu, and the rain would fall and the grass would grow. The people would make shelters out of grass so that the rain wouldn't go through. It would be really dry. It was so good living in those days. Sometimes people would get lonely in the spinifex country and would say to one another, 'Let's go back to the mulga country.'

They were really good hunters, those dingo dogs, because the old men would 'sing' them to make them fierce. The dogs would chase the kangaroos through the wetlands until they got caught in a boggy place. They would be trapped and the men would follow and hear the dogs singing out, which meant they had caught the kangaroo. The men would follow the dogs' footprints, and they would say,

'Where is my dog? It must have caught a kangaroo.'

Then the men would follow from behind and would find nothing.

'Here is something which he must have followed.'

'This must have been the place where the kangaroo has been crawling along.'

So, the men would follow and find the dead kangaroo, which was mauled by the dogs. Then they would get the guts and clean it. The men would get a sharp stick to close the hole from which the guts were taken out. They would get the urine out, too. Then the men would pick up the dead kangaroo, swing it on their back, and take it back home.

In those days, they used to have good hunting dogs which belonged to those old people who have now passed away. Where did they get those good hunting dogs? They found them west at Kunajarrayi, Nyirrpi, Pikilyi, and Miyikirlangu; north at Nyurripatu, Yumurrpa, and Jila Well. They used to get those little dingoes when they were small pups. It was really good getting those dogs – male and female. They used to get two by two. They used to grow them up in pairs. They would say, 'That's my dog, that one.' Then they would take them home.

All those men would bring back kangaroo meat and hand out their share to their families. They would get stomach parts, tail, backbone and intestines. Then they would leave the meat so they could eat it in the morning. They would say, 'Let's leave the kangaroo meat for later, so we can eat it here in the camp.'

Afterwards, the older ladies would go hunting for bush potatoes. They would dig really deep down. What did they dig with? They would dig with a sharp stone. The older women would also carry sharp digging sticks with *palya* (resin), which they found in spinifex. The digging sticks were sharpened by stone knives, which made it easier for digging. The women would sharpen and sharpen and sharpen . . .

They would make a fire, and they would dig and cook the potatoes. Everybody would do that: in east camp, north camp, west camp and south camp. They would dig for bush potatoes for many hours, filling their coolamons before returning to the camp. Those bush potatoes taste like potatoes, but are really sweet. Who showed them where to find those bush potatoes? It was the old people.

I was a young man in those days. The old men would say to me, 'Give us some food.' And they would talk about the *mikawurru* (rain stones), while lifting the stone. Where did they get those from? Not from Puyurru or Lungkardajarra – but they would talk about it, and they would ask for things, 'Give use some food – bushtucker and meat. We haven't got any food.'

Then the women would look for seeds, because there was a lot of rain, and they knew that the rain brought a lot of bushtucker. The trees and grass grew from the rain. They would burn the grass with fire so that it was easier for the women to look for seeds – but nowadays there are cattle everywhere.

Yuendumu women out
hunting at sunset

In the scrublands, they would light a fire and burn the high grass. Then they would stay for a long time near waterholes and soakages, like Nyurripatu and Yumurrpa. There, the people would gather from surrounding places to get water.

Where did those men come from? Well, they came from the north. Places like Janami and Warlarla; north from Kulpurlunu and Yawuluyawulu. That's where those men came from, before joining one another at Yumurrpa and Nyurripatu. They would look and dig for bush potatoes. They would eat, eat and eat. Yes, that's how we lived in the old days!

Afterwards, the people would go camping in their own country. One mob would go west to Karnarri, others south to Kunajarrayi and Nyirrpi. A lot of people would go to Pikilyi, and north to Yawuluyawulu and Warnmankurlangu. Then they would go to Purturlu, living closely as neighbours. They wouldn't go to faraway places. No, they would live close to each other.

The people would come together when a person was really sick. If a person died, there would be people coming from every place, and there they would meet for 'sorry business'. If a group of people was coming, they would see smoke, and it would mean that people were burning the grass as a signal. The signal meant that the person was sick or might have passed away.

When those Jampijinpa and Jakamarra men from Munkularri passed away, people came to live in one big camp. They came in crying from every direction. The people would be dancing and crying at the same time. It was really good that people met one another at that time. But other people would argue among their family groups, saying, 'You weren't there to look after him. So, we will cut your back with a stone knife!' They used to cut their backs with stone knives as a way of being 'sorry' when they lost a loved one. There would be blood dripping from the stone knives – they didn't have Whitefella knives – they used stone knives in the old days. The men would try and stop a fight, pulling them apart if they had weapons like stone knives, spears and boomerangs.

If they fought, then stopped, the people would live happily in the one camp. The people would live in a camp with the relatives of those who had passed away. They would go on 'sorry' for weeks and weeks. Other people would come and join in the mourning ceremony. They would have a deceased person's things – like hair, clothes and blankets. They would have *wirinkirri* (hair spindle) for the deceased. Nowadays, things like this don't go on so much, but there is still 'sorry business'.

Some people would come for the mourning ceremony, and people would say, 'We do not think they are from this country.' The old people would cover themselves with white clay. They would hit or cut themselves with stone knives until they had blood pouring down. I am telling you about the old people. They were really well looked after before they passed away. They would have the 'sorry' ceremony, and they used to finish at night. When dawn was breaking, all the widows, sisters and in-laws would all 'finish' for the deceased. The people would then make another camp, away from where they had the 'sorry business'. Then the men and women would talk to one another about who was responsible for the death:

'Perhaps it was someone who did evil things, or it might have been an argument.' Then somebody would say, 'It must be someone!' So they would put the people who were accused in an open space. They would yell out, 'Hit them! Hit them because they have done something wrong.'

They would sort out the trouble, then they would talk about the deceased person's things. It is the old men who have to hold the deceased person's things – not the youngfellas – only all the old men. Then they would go hunting for bush potatoes. They would 'finish off' with bush potatoes. Nowadays, we have tea, sugar, flour, and blankets to 'finish off' in 'sorry' camp – so that we can talk again. It was forbidden for anyone to talk during 'sorry business'.

Today it is really sad because a lot of old people have passed away, and lots of white people have come to live in our country. There might be only three older men living here at Yuendumu now. The elders have passed away, and our people have gone away to live in places like Yarlalinji and Warntaparri, which is west of Yuendumu. They also moved to places like Nyirrpi. All our people went to faraway places. The people said to one another, 'We will meet again someday. We are going away to look for bush tobacco.'

This bush tobacco is a really *cheeky* (strong) one. They would gather bush tobacco and then would dry it in the sun. The people would go north and look for bush tobacco. Where would they go from there? They would go west. There would be waterholes and soakages in that area. They would live in an area called Warnirri-patu. They would all meet together in that place.

'Someone has lit a fire. It must be a stranger. Someone must have come from Pirlinyanu.' They would light a fire. They would signal by lighting fires. 'Someone may be coming.'

'Yes, I'm coming for tobacco and food!'

They would carry tobacco and food wherever they went, and would share it amongst themselves. The rain would fall and the tobacco would be dry, because they would keep it inside the hairstring, which was rolled into a round ball.

They would use *pakarli* (paperbark), which is like a vine in many ways. They would use it for footwear, for protection from the hot sand. Where would they get that *pakarli*? They would get it at Yarripirlangu, Kumarlpa and Palkakarrinya. They would carry *pakarli* from Waturlpunyu, a big camping place where a lot of people lived. They would give tobacco to those old people who would come from Pirlinyanu. They would share their tobacco and meat.

The people would start their journey at daylight, walking when it was cool. The old people would walk long distances to visit their relatives. They would kill *pakuru, wardapi* (goanna) and whatever else they could find. Oh, those old people were great hunters! We would also eat *minija* (feral cat), that lived in the mulga country by that time. We would give food to our sons, daughters, grandmothers and grandfathers. We would also share with other families.

We would say to ourselves, 'Maybe we will go to the east, or perhaps we will stay here.'

Everyone was living there, at Karnarri and Panma, a large rockhole in the spinifex country. People would also gather at Rilyi, a soakage. We would stay at Panma and dig for bush potatoes and bush tomatoes. We would gather bush tomatoes and pierce them with a stick, like a satay. We would have lots of food. Someone would say, 'There is lots of food here now. Enough for us to stay here and have a corroboree.'

They would have corroborees for young men. They would dance until dawn, when they would have a break before dancing again. The men and women would go hunting. That ceremony for those young men finished there at Panma. Then the people had a big ceremony called *Kirridikirrawarnu*. It involved tying branches on your legs and shaking your body.

The young men who were in the bush would go and live there for a long time. Then the men would tell the women to get ready for the young men who would soon come out. So the women would get the food ready for their return. That was how we were in the old days.

Once Darby was camped with his family at a place called Yarripirlangu.[5] At the time, he was still a boy and was becoming increasingly frightened about his upcoming initiation, so he decided to run away. He travelled north to Kirrirdi, and stayed there eating a goanna. The next day Darby headed east to Yamirringi, where he decided to spear an emu. Sitting next to the rockhole, he hid himself in a *yirntati*, a half circle of rocks and branches that kept him out of sight. An emu eventually came and Darby, concealed by the *yirntati*, speared it.

There is a rockhole and a wall with old paintings and engravings in the rock face at Yamirringi. It is near the Dreaming place where the *jajirdi* (western quoll) and *janganpa* (possum) fought a big battle. But they are no longer found in the area, and only perenties (large lizards) live amongst the rocks. It is still good country for hunting, although emus are seldom seen there now. The *yirntati* is still there, next to the rockhole, the same one that Darby hid in as a boy. Sometimes school kids from Yuendumu visit Yamirringi to listen to the *Jukurrpa* stories, or how the old people, like Darby, used to live. Darby would show them where people used to camp, mimicking their speech, and describing the women and children sitting next to fires waiting for the men to return from hunting. He would tell the story about the group of young Jampijinpa men who passed through Yamirringi on their way north to Yapirdi where they speared a Napangardi woman, in payback for the death of their brother, who was her husband.

From Yamirringi, the young Darby travelled south and west to Kurlayiwarnu, where he speared a rock wallaby in the hills. There were other people in the area and Darby met with them, although he was careful to avoid his *Lamparra*, his potential spouse's father, who would be involved in his initiation. Darby continued travelling south and west, visiting Palkakarrinya, Waturlpunyu and Yarripirlangu. He collected bushtucker and speared kangaroos for food with the people he met, before eventually heading north and west to the fresh waters at Pikilyi, where he remained for some time.

With rumours increasing about upcoming ceremonies, Darby became worried about his initiation again, and decided to travel north to Yarungkanyi where he might avoid being caught by the old men. But he found the country dry and decided to follow the line of the Water Dreaming east into Anmatyerr country and on to Yimampi (Coniston Station) where he met other members of his family and encountered the Whitefellas who were living there.

Not long after arriving at the camp at Coniston, an older Napangardi woman, his 'right skin', became interested in Darby:

Yuwayi, (she) bin chasing me, Napangardi, bin take me. (She) bin frighten me. I bin, 'What to do'!? Ha ha. His name Winnie. And *bambai* (bye and bye), I bin there ... (She) bin like me properly. Only, I'm not man – big *wee-hi* (boy) ... Youngfella – no whiskers – nothing. All right, I bin 'marry' 'em that Anmatyerr girl.

Warlpiri people often use the term 'married' to refer to intimate relationships. Jack Jakamarra Ross recalled Darby being chased by this woman soon after he arrived at Coniston. Darby was still an uninitiated boy at the time and this Napangardi woman was married to one of his older brothers.

Other Warlpiri accounts have alluded to stories of Darby being a bit of a 'lover boy' and upsetting his brothers, although they were sympathetic to his situation, taking into account that he was young and was heavily pursued by Napangardi. To some degree, they admired his courage at thinking he could get away with it. When questioned about it, Darby was quite circumspect and would only shake his head and laugh. However, at the time, it was the cause of much concern for him. Worried about 'jealous trouble', he was forced to camp on his own on top of a nearby hill because he feared for his safety. From his vantage point, he kept watch for any aggressors. They never came, but Darby was soon caught by the old men and initiated nearby. He remembers the time (laughing):

Palka-karrinya waterhole, Karrinyarra (Mt Wedge)

Lani-jarrija-rna (I was frightened). I no want to get a young man (initiated) ... We never bin properly know 'em. Well, that old man, he bin take me – young man while we bin run away – *wee-hi* (boy), you know. They bin make a 'young man' now ... Well, him properly *wati* (initiated man) now, me.

Country Can't Cry

In the following story, Darby is responding
to news of events overseas he has seen on
television. It reminded him of the Second World
War. This story is one of several recorded by
Darby, alone in his house, operating the tape
recorder. During these times, Darby spoke as
if he were addressing a wider audience:

European peoples, Aboriginal peoples – we're
living in one lot, now. All family. The white
mans, they're thinking about for war (in) 'nother
countries. We're very sorry for that. Fighting
for nothing. Got to (be) sitting good. No matter
where 'nother countries. That's our people,
everywhere. (They) no want to fight from
countries. That country can't cry for we! For
Aboriginal people, too. Nothing! He no want
to shoot. He not dingo! He not wild dingo.
Got to think about for this, all people

everywhere. The war, that's from anything,
while they fighting from countries. Country
can't cry for the we, nothing. Country – it's
the heart. That's the world. Country can't cry.
We want to live a good life.

They're bringing the war, they talk about
for war. Should be finish, long time ago. Our
people, last war (WWII) while they bin fight
here, they bin travelling right up to Darwin.
And big fight bin going on. That's all, we just
want to think about for this. We're not dogs;
we're not animals. That's a man; girl and man
and children. Children, he grow up. Father
and mother, got to grow him up proper way.

We no want to see trouble all the time.
Please, we're sitting round here right in the
centre, longa Central Australia. Please, leave
this trouble. We want a good life for everybody.
No matter (from) 'nother country. Sitting good,
work good. We no want fighting round from
anything trouble from country.

The world, he'll be finished anytime. We're
worrying for the people. Another people, they
got to take it easy way, got to take it slowly,
and got to take it good, and (not) think about
anything else. No more fighting. No more
thinking about for the hard something – war.
Poor people, might we finish, longa this country.

Endnotes

8 Annual Report 1970/71, Northern Territory Administration, Welfare Branch, p.59.
9 Translation from the Warlpiri, in Taylor 1988: 277.

CHAPTER THREE
Walking a Different Road (pp. 28–43)

VISITORS
Promoting Warlpiri Culture (pp. 40–41)
1 Interviewed by Dave Price 2005. English translation by Bess Nungarrayi Price.

2 Muecke 1997 cited in Healey, C. *Meanjin* 3/1999: 184.

VISITORS
Bush Mechanics and Satellites (p. 43)
3 Translation by Francis Jupurrurla Kelly reproduced in Michaels (1986: 1) and from a recording in the WMA archive 'The Invention of Aboriginal Television'.

CHAPTER FOUR
Painting Culture (pp. 44–67)

1 Congreve, in Kleinart and Neale 2000: 733. According to the art centre's website 2003: 'The name was chosen by a number of older men and women who saw the need for an art centre and endeavoured to form an organisation that represented their interests as artists but also recognised the importance of the cultural laws which are inseparable from the stories depicted in paint.'
2 In 2000, Paddy Stewart and Paddy Sims produced an award-winning series of thirty small bronze plate etchings based on the designs of the original *Doors*; and in 2005, Warlukurlangu Artists sold at auction a collection of paintings by Paddy Stewart and inspired by the *Doors*.
3 Letter from Edith Coombs to Warlukurlangu Artists 2001.
4 Interviewed by Louise Sullivan 1999.
5 Ross, T. 'The people and their home', translation of 'Yapa manu ngurrara', in *Warlukurlangu Artists* 1987.
6 Toyne 2000: 42–43.
7 Annexure, Objects of the *Warlukurlangu Artists Association* 1986.
8 Interviewed by Louise Sullivan 1999.
9 This and following quotes from an interview with Susan Congreve 1998.

CHAPTER FIVE
A New Ceremony (pp. 68–94)

1 I was unable to find an acceptable English translation or explanation for this term, but Bess Nungarrayi and Dave Price suggested that Darby was referring to 'sorry business' and that his use of 'party' and '*kula-tirnpa*' may refer to: '... the ritual gift giving that occurs at the end of "sorry business". People who have "worked" during the business are paid for their work with food, items like blankets (now money). In the old days it would have been more likely to be meat. Some of the deceased's belongings are distributed to kin on the basis of their relationship to the deceased. This may be what the old man means by "party" – the distribution of gifts, especially of food, a bit like our parties. *Kula-tirnpa* means "not dead" in this context and it may mean that the spirit was thought to be around still, and able to be communicated with until the final burial and chasing away of the ghost.' (pers. comm.).
2 Interview with Rosie Nangala Fleming 2003.
3 When discussing this with Darby, he drew a symbol in the sand that looked like the letter 'R'. I don't really know what he meant, but Dave Price suggested that he may have been referring to Chi Rho, which resembles a written 'R' and is a common symbol for Christ in Catholic iconography and is sometimes used by the Lutherans.
4 Meggitt 1962: 28, Bell 1983: 70 and Sweeney TS337 1980: 37.
5 Pat Fleming TS672 1991, T4: 9.
6 Tom Fleming 1977: 12–13.
7 Tom Fleming 1977: 15. Translation. Jordan 2003: 65–68 explores the way in which baptism may be understood by the Warlpiri to reflect initiation.
8 Tom Fleming 1977: 30.
9 Pat Fleming TS672 1991.
10 Jordan 2003: 40.
11 For this and the following examples, see Tom Fleming 1977: 30–32.
12 Interview with Kath Kingston 2000. For further information on the development and meaning of Christian *purlapa*, see Jordan 2003: 118–128.
13 For this and following examples, see Reece 1986.
14 The Lutherans at Hermannsburg used the Arrernte equivalent of *Jukurrpa* (*Altjira*) as their word for God.

Note: Where a quotation is not referenced, it is from the author's personal collection of interviews and tapes.

CHAPTER TWO
Dreaming, Life and Law (pp. 6–27)

1 Ross, in *Warlukurlangu Artists* 1987: 9.
2 This and following translations from material associated with 'Jardiwarnpa: a Warlpiri Fire Ceremony', provided by WMA.
3 Transcript from public meeting with the Select Committee on Constitutional Development at Yuendumu 11 April 1989. The translation provided is not completely accurate when checked against the original spoken Warlpiri and English, and I have edited it slightly. The meeting was held to discuss the issue of incorporating land rights legislation into the proposed Northern Territory constitution (and other related issues) as part of the process leading up to the referendum on Statehood.
4 Pat Fleming TS672 T3: 10.
5 Interview with Darby Jampijinpa Ross, 20 June 1990, translated by Alice Napanangka Granites for WMA.

VISITORS
Recorders and Filmmakers (p. 23)
6 Today, the series of films, produced by the Australian Institute of Aboriginal Studies (now AIATSIS), are occasionally viewed by men in closed sessions at WMA in Yuendumu.
7 Barrett 1965, LA68, A1, B5, AIATSIS 65/12.

VISITORS
Missionaries (pp. 82–87)

15 Henson 1992: 68.
16 Henson 1992: 106. When Albrecht visited Pikilyi in 1930, he thought the country was 'unoccupied' Crown Land, and while he was aware that the pastoralist Bill Braitling was in the vicinity, he did not know that he had already claimed the area. Henson, 1992: 58.
17 Marcus 2001: 7.
18 Marcus 2001: 193. Strehlow was employed by the Native Affairs Branch.
19 Hill 2002: 336–7.
20 Hill 2002: 338.
21 Strehlow 1959: 185.
22 Albrecht to Charles Duguid, cited in Henson 1992: 90.
23 Steer 1996: 15.
24 Henson 1992: 166.
25 Reece's expedition diary, 30 June 1944. Luurnpakurlangu translates as Kingfisher country.
26 Strehlow 1959: 188.
27 Sweeney TS337 1980: 35.
28 Sweeney TS337 1980: 37–38. Warlpiri oral accounts also refer to arranged marriages as a way conflict between families was resolved in the new social structure.
29 Jordan 1999: 2. It is perhaps because of the Baptists' contribution that there is a misconception that Yuendumu was once run as a 'mission'. Jordan 2003: 131–132 documents the realisation of the Baptist missionaries in the 1990s that it was time that the ceremony that they had introduced be examined in its own cultural context, and the responsibility of finding their own way be handed over to the Warlpiri – that it was 'time for us to get out of the way and give them some space'.
30 Steer 1996: 67.
31 Steer 1996: 68.
32 Reece in *Oceania* 1970: 1.
33 Reece 1986. It appears as if Reece was using the term *Jukurrpa-warnu*, which Warlpiri associate with *Jukurrpa* (literally 'associated with *Jukurrpa*'), as a vehicle to fit the Christian God into a Warlpiri worldview. There is little evidence (as far as I can see – prior to Christian influence) that the Warlpiri believed in a supreme being, although Darby contradicted this view occasionally when telling stories about his early life in the bush.
34 Tom Fleming 1977: 4.
35 Tom Fleming TS106 1990: 7.
36 D.D. Smith TS844.

37 Pat Fleming TS672 1991, T3: 1. Jordan 2003: 148 writes: 'Tom Fleming did not share the common attitudes of the missionary of his day towards Aboriginal culture.'
38 Tom Fleming TS106 1990: 3.
39 Pat Fleming TS672 1991, T4: 7.
40 Jordan 2003: 5–6.
41 Tom Fleming 1977: 31. See Jordan 2003: 34–36 for further examples.
42 From a description by 'J.' in field notes taken by Swain in 1984, presented in 'The Ghost of Space: Reflections on Warlpiri Christian Iconography and Ritual' in Swain and Rose 1988: 462.
43 Swain 1988: 460 has argued that '...the Warlpiri feel Christian myth cannot be located in their country without the consent of the mythic custodians'.
44 Swain 1988: 455.
45 Swain 1988: 453.
46 Ross 'The Way We Used to Live', BRDU 1977–78, translation.
47 Tom Fleming 1977: 16.
48 Interview with Lloyd Ollerenshaw 2002.
49 Darby said he went to the 'number two' ceremonies, not the 'number one' ceremonies that he called *Juju*, which can be interpreted in a simplistic way (but not completely accurately) as representing Satan or a devil, and the elements of Warlpiri ceremony that Darby considered to be inconsistent with his Christian beliefs.

Warlpiri Warriors (pp. 95–97)

1 Annual Report 1959/60: 47, Northern Territory Administration, Welfare Branch.
2 Letter from Dick Kimber 2003.

CHAPTER SIX
Yuendumu: Living on Yurrampi (pp. 98–129)

1 Giese NTRS 226 TS755 Tape 22: 13.
2 *Yuendumu Tjaru* 1970: 29.
3 Keys 2000: 119.
4 Baarda 1994: 205.
5 Reynolds 2000: 214–215. Reynolds 211 researched the origin of pastoral leases in Australia and asserted that the 'Colonial Office created pastoral leases to allow for the mutual use of the same land – the pastoralist had a right to conduct his pastoral enterprise, the Aborigines to use the land in their traditional manner.'
6 Francis Jupurrurla Kelly, Bush Mechanics website 2002.

7 Reeves 1998: 23.
8 *ibid.*
9 Coombs and Stanner 1974: 3–4.
10 Coombs and Stanner 1974: 20.
11 Coombs and Stanner 1974: 21.
12 WMA, *Council Election Speeches* 1984.

VISITORS
Government (pp. 108–109)

13 Wave Hill Station was owned by Vesteys, a multinational company that had a questionable reputation for its treatment of workers.
14 In 2001, Whitlam attended the Yeperenye Festival in Alice Springs where, to the accompaniment of Paul Kelly's song 'From little things, big things grow', one of Lingiari's descendants returned the favour by pouring sand into Whitlam's hands in recognition of his role in setting the agenda that led to the acknowledgment of land rights for Aboriginal people in the Northern Territory. Malcolm Fraser was also there, but only received a brief round of applause as acknowledgment for his government's role.
15 Annual Report 1958/59: 11, Northern Territory Administration, Welfare Branch.
16 Cited in Leichleitner and Nathan 1983: 18.
17 Reeves 1998: 26. At around the same time, Nugget Coombs and Walter Stanner visited Yuendumu on behalf of the Council of Aboriginal Affairs. In their report, they described Yuendumu as resembling many other 'bush towns' in Central Australia, and while somewhat pessimistic about the situation, felt obliged to offer some hope with a series of recommendations for the community, including greater 'Aboriginalisation'. See Coombs and Stanner 1974.
18 Reeves 1998: 27.
19 Reeves 1998: 28–32. While the Labor Party (ALP) are often acknowledged as the champions of Land Rights, it is not known how the Warlpiri would have fared under the Whitlam government's legislation. They may have been worse off – it was the ALP who later failed to establish the principle of national land rights in the 1980s. Dave Price, pers. comm.
20 Inalienable, community freehold title is significantly different to standard freehold title. It has been the subject of much debate because of the economic implications of collective ownership and subsequent governments have considered changing the act to facilitate individual ownership of property by Aboriginal residents.
21 Interview with Rosie Nangala Fleming 2003.

22 Jarrardajarrayi is the place 'where the lover passed' and the story associated with it is about elopement.

VISITORS
Naturalists (pp. 114–115)

23 Report by Finlayson, expanded upon by Hetzel and Frith, cited in Leichleitner and Nathan 1983: 26. For further information, see Gibson 1986 and Johnson et al. 1989.
24 Brands 1987. See Johnson et al. 1996.
25 Hiddins 1999: 75.
26 Transcript from public meeting with the Select Committee on Constitutional Development at Yuendumu 11 April 1989.
27 ibid.
28 Dave Price. Notes from a meeting with Thomas Jangala Rice and Jeannie Nungarrayi Egan 2005.

VISITORS
Researchers (pp. 120–125)

29 There has been considerable debate by researchers about the way in which Aboriginal people have been labelled according to language groups, and whether or not this is simply convenience or an accurate reflection on the way in which Aboriginal societies were once organised. For further information, see Burridge's 1973 argument for 'unspecified larger groups' when referring to 'pre-contact' times.
30 Although Mervyn Meggitt wrote the classic structural-functionalist ethnography on the Warlpiri (Desert People), he did not work with Darby, and I have not included references to his work. Despite the popularity of his work amongst first-year anthropology students, criticisms of his ethnography often point out that he failed to adequately deal with the issue that he was researching amongst a settled people, and that his account of the Warlpiri inaccurately presents them as living in a 'timeless vacuum'.
31 Munn 1973: xv.
32 Pers. comm. 2001.
33 Barrett 1976: preface.
34 Barrett 1976: 157. Bess Nungarrayi Price translates 'wilka ngarunu' (wirlki ngarnu) and 'murumuru kulgalga' (murrumurru kurlkarlka) as 'jaw-bone eater' and 'sore jaw or gums' respectively.
35 Barrett 1976: 159.
36 Strehlow in Barrett 1976: 162.
37 Barrett 1976: 160.
38 ibid.

39 Pat Fleming 1991: 2, 4 TS672. Barrett 1976: 273 refers to this document as Fleming, D., Barrett, M. and Fleming, T. 'Family Records of the Yuendumu Population'.
40 According to Pat Fleming, a Dr Brock from Adelaide visited the community in 1952 and gave approximate ages to everyone at Yuendumu. Fleming 1991: 2 TS672.
41 Barrett 1976: 266.
42 Simpson, Nash, Laughren, Austin and Alpher (eds.) 2001: intro.
43 David Nash 2001 'American's work spoke to Warlpiri', obituary, The Australian, 4 December 2001.
44 Pers. comm. 2005. Bess Price's father and Darby were of similar age and grew up together.
45 1973 audio recording by Darby to Ken Hale. Transcribed by Ken Hale and translated by Bess Nungarrayi Price.
46 When Peter Bartlett interviewed people at Yuendumu for the CAAMA oral history project in 1983, he encountered further evidence of Darby's enthusiasm. While most interviewees contributed one or two recordings, Darby made nineteen recordings over a period of six weeks.
47 1972 audio recording by Darby to Ken Hale. Transcribed by Ken Hale and translated by Bess Nungarrayi Price. Bess thought that Darby was referring to the Vietnam War.

VISITORS
White Toyota Mob (pp. 126–127)

48 Muecke 1997: 38 referring to Gillian Cowlishaw's metaphor for the failure of the DAA to establish a 'non-welfare economy'.

CHAPTER SEVEN
Proper Head Drover Man (pp. 130–163)

1 Kuruwarri refers to markings that 'are', but also represent, elements of Jukurrpa.
2 McGrath 1987: 23.
3 Charles (Pat) Chapman NTAS TS529: 6. The water in one well was reportedly 47 percent salt. See Jones, 1987: 197.

VISITORS
Pastoralists and Prospectors (pp. 137–141)

4 Hartwig 1960: 3.
5 Terry 1931: 227. See Baume 1933: 82 for further information.
6 Strehlow 1959: 312.
7 Terry 1931.
8 Terry 1931: 228.

9 Evidence of Saxby to Board of Enquiry 16 Jan. 1929 (cited in Cribbin, 1984: 136–138). Oral accounts describe Saxby as an expert marksman.
10 Latz TS819 1996:16–17.
11 Latz TS819 1996: 17.
12 Through the research of Simon Japangardi Fisher and Lisa Watts, Warlpiri were surprised to discover that the Braitling family later held the lease 'in perpetuity'.
13 Watts and Fisher 2000: 84. Jack Ross interviewed by Simon Fisher in 1998.
14 Cited in Watts and Fisher 2000: 163–164. Anecdotal evidence suggests that Braitling was as much interested in the potential of mining in the area as he was in meeting the terms of his pastoral lease. See Tom Cole TS29:10.
15 Reece cited in Watts and Fisher 2000: 207.
16 Les Penhall TS303 1982, T1: 2 and Hill 2002: 371.
17 Gordon Sweeney TS337 1980: 36. When Strehlow visited Luurnpakurlangu in 1940 as a patrol officer, he found an alarming incidence of venereal disease (Hill, 2002: 339–340, 366). Reece also heard anecdotal evidence from Warlpiri that Braitling was sleeping with two young girls.
18 Frank Baarda TS714 1991, T1: 8.
19 Lily Ah Toy, TS8706 1996: 7.
20 Watts and Fisher 2000: 155.
21 See Davidson 1905.
22 To Warlpiri these boulders are the bodies of the Janganpa (Possum) men who were scattered as Yarripiri (The Serpent) fell from the sky into the earth there while they were dancing. Bess Nungarrayi Price, pers. comm.
23 Elias 1996: 2.
24 Braitling in Meggitt 1962: 21.
25 Kimber, Alice Springs News, 10 September 2003.
26 'Historical Time Line Relating to the Southern Warlpiri', prepared by Dave Price.
27 Elias 1996: 4.
28 Jones 1987: 196.
29 Baume 1933.
30 Meggitt 1962: 25.
31 Charles (Pat) Chapman TS529: 5. Chapman was the son of Charles Chapman Snr.

32 Joy Marks TS280 1980: 1–2.
33 Murphy Japanangka TS862 1997: 5–18 and Warden 2003.
34 Williams 1986: 103–104.
35 Louise Dixon TS39 1980: 9.
36 Benterak et al. 1996: 258.
37 Dave Price (unpublished manuscript).

38 In 1942, the Japanese bombed Darwin, Wyndham and Broome, and Aboriginal patrols were organised along the north and west coasts. Darby heard that some Aboriginal men had been killed by bombs at Bagot near Darwin and that a convoy of trucks had evacuated the Aboriginal survivors to Adelaide.

39 According to Corporal Eric Brown (pers. comm.), stationed in Alice Springs in 1942, the Aboriginal Labour Corps, of about 1000 men, did a large part of the hard work in Central Australia during the war years and have been largely unrecognised for their efforts unlike their colleagues in the North. He claimed they were paid a small amount for their labours: ten pence a day compared with five shillings a day the white soldiers received. However, the old men like Darby and Jimija were proud of their work with the army.

40 Gordon Sweeney TS337 1980: 35. He had also heard the suspicions that Braitling was denying Warlpiri access to water.

41 Joy Marks TS280 1980: 19–20.

42 Bell 1983: 71.

43 Greenfield TS637 1990, T3: 7.

44 Middleton and Francis 1976: 16–17.

45 Ted Egan TS676 1991.

46 Carell and Dean 1955: 3.

47 Carrel and Dean 1955: 145.

48 Ted Egan TS676 1991: 5.

49 Annual Report 1958/59: 34, Northern Territory Administration, Welfare Branch.

50 Simpson 1996: 127.

51 This was once Bularnu country, but they have since disappeared, possibly because they had nowhere to hide from the colonisers on the grass plains of their country. Dave Price, pers. comm.

52 Ted Egan TS676 1991: 13–14.

53 Annual Report 1960/61: 33, Northern Territory Administration, Welfare Branch.

54 Reeves 1998: 23.

55 Middleton and Francis 1976: 12. While citizenship of Australia (previously Britain) was formally extended to Aboriginal people in Australia in 1949 with the *Nationality and Citizenship Act 1948*, they were effectively excluded from exercising these rights by state and territory laws. The Department of Aboriginal Affairs was also created following the referendum.

56 Many of the smaller family-run properties also supported the Aboriginal workers' families prior to the changes. Anecdotal evidence suggests that the employment of some Aboriginal workers became complicated by the changes that led to their legal access to alcohol.

57 Letter from Ed Kingston 12 November 2000.

CHAPTER EIGHT
Get Shot for Nothing (pp. 164–183)

1 *Lander Warlpiri Anmatjirra Land Claim* 1980: 8 and Read 1991: 33–34. Darby claimed that pastoralists often established their water supplies using pre-existing water sources, such as soakages, by digging them out or letting the cattle 'make a big mess' and rendering the water unfit for human consumption.

2 When Ted Strehlow 1959: 319–320 visited Coniston Station in 1932, he estimated that 80 percent of the women camped there were from Karrinyarra (Mt Wedge) in Warlpiri country.

3 'First time to Hermannsburg', Darby Jampijimba, 1984, in Henson 1992: 42. *Mana* may mean *marna* (grass).

4 Many Warlpiri travelled to Hermannsburg at this time. Some of their descendants continue to live there and are said to have 'grown up Arrernte'. Pers. comm. Dave and Bess Price 2002.

5 Hartwig 1971: 2. Accounts of the events surrounding the death of Brooks, the attack on Morton and the travels of Murray's party vary. There is considerable discrepancies between Murray's official account, the finding of the Board of Enquiry, the written historical record and Warlpiri oral accounts. Many people have attempted to write historical accounts relating to these events, and I am indebted to them for their research. However, it is clear to me that there will never be one single authoritative account of these events. Where possible, I have recorded the events as told by Darby; other accounts may describe the events differently. However, in reconstructing this story, other material was consulted, and where possible discussed with Darby, or otherwise compared with other accounts and decisions made regarding its inclusion. While Darby was not an eyewitness to many of these events, the story is included here because of the effect it had on him – members of his family were killed – and also because of the wider implications for the Warlpiri in its aftermath.

6 Tim Japangardi Langdon, BRDU 1978: 18, claimed that Brooks used to take women to sleep with them while threatening their husbands with his rifle and that the Warlpiri planned the murder of Brooks so that he would stop taking their women. In his account, they waited until Brooks had dug out the soakage and returned to his tent. Then they attacked. However, other oral accounts suggest that Brooks didn't sleep with the women, because of his old age and

good reputation, but that they provided some company for him. Kimber writes of the possibility of a revenge attack from suggestions by Walter Smith, and Darby, who told him: 'That old Brooks, him bin have a brother. Old policeman. Him bin shootem three brother belong Bullfrog.' Kimber investigated this, and while he found that a policeman by the name of Charles Brookes had served in the NT at the time, he was not a relation of Fred Brooks. However, on the evidence of trusted Warlpiri informants, Kimber believes that a police murder of Warlpiri prisoners did occur southeast of The Granites in about 1912. See Kimber, 'Centre's Rough Frontier Justice' in *The Alice Springs News*, 8 October 2003.

7 The gold reef was reportedly discovered by Jimmy Wickham during a prospecting journey in the Tanami. It later became known as Wickham's Find and was a much sought after prospect, although Wickham and others were never able to relocate it. Brown persisted after most had given up. Wilson's white prospector father and Aboriginal mother had taken him to the Tanami goldfields as a young boy from Western Australia.

8 Hartwig 1971: 3–4.

9 There is conflicting evidence over the roles of Wilson and Chapman in these events, complicated by Chapman's death soon after. See O'Brien 2002: 15, Cribbin 1984: 27–30, Read 1991: 37–38, and Hartwig 1960: 21. Hartwig's 1971: 3–5 account is the one to which Darby held. Langdon's (Read, 1991: 37–38) and other oral accounts suggest that Brown died when Wilson was with him and that Wilson and his companions buried him. There is also some confusion about where Brown was buried. It is possible that he was buried near Luurnpakurlangu which appears to have been the original 'Mt Hardy', known at one stage as 'Joe Brown's Mt Hardy' before Braitling renamed it 'Mt Doreen', and gave the name 'Mt Hardy' to a hill further to the east.

VISITORS
Policemen (p. 171)

10 Evidence of Murray to Board of Enquiry 16 January 1929 (cited in Cribbin, 1984: 146). This was not unusual in the Northern Territory at the time (see Clarke, 1974: 1). For further information, see O'Brien 2002.

11 *Jila (Chilla Well) Warlpiri Land Claim* 1988: 5.

12 Hartwig 1971: 6.

13 *Argus* 14 January 1929: 11. Wiliyarrpa was later known as Mussolini and died in Yuendumu in the early 1970s.

14 Cribbin 1984: 55. This request was later questioned by Methodist Minister Athol McGregor, who was quoted as saying, 'Common sense tells us that one cannot call on a black to stand in the name of the King, as English to them is only noise.' (*Argus* 14 January 1929: 11.)

15 However, Saxby later gave evidence to the Board of Enquiry stating he was uncertain as to whether he had hit anyone. Cribbin 1984: 136–137.

16 Pharlap Japangardi, interviewed by Murray Barrett in 1955. See also Langdon (BRDU) 1978: 19.

17 Ross, interviewed by Grant Japanangka Granites in 2003. English translation.

18 Hartwig 1960: 24.

19 Hartwig 1971: 11 also refers to interviews conducted at Yuendumu in 1971 when 12 Warlpiri stated on five occasions this was the case. Saxby also told Terry 1931: 303 he visited 'Tippenbah' with Murray. See also Jampijinpa's eyewitness account in Read 1991: 44–46.

20 Ross, interviewed by Grant Japanangka Granites in 2003. English translation.

21 Ross pers. comm. and Langdon (BRDU) 1978: 19.

22 Also known as 'Yakilkra' and 'Lajikujantu Jakamarra' according to Hartwig 1971: 13.

23 This information was communicated to Strehlow by Don Campbell from Mt Peake Station. Strehlow's biographer Barry Hill 2002: 288–289 refers to an entry in Strehlow's diary. 'He told me about happenings.' These included Nugget keeping a Western Australian lubra there for his stockwork: she had tried to run away but Morton had got her back each time and inflicted a severe hiding as a deterrent against further attempts to run away. Strehlow recorded that Nugget was now employing as 'stockmen' one or two other little native girls, nine or ten years of age, whom he had raped … 'Probably,' Strehlow concluded, 'the story is true, other station owners have hinted at the same thing previously.'
    Morton was also implicated in further rapes, but Hill 2002: 290 writes that Strehlow was unable to bring Morton to account, noting that 'the evidence was evidently too difficult to gather'. When Strehlow visited Mt Peake in 1932, Mrs Campbell suggested that Morton had kidnapped Lill, an Aboriginal girl from the Top End, and forced her to stay with him. See Strehlow 1959: 103–104.

24 Morton was reportedly a former circus wrestler and boxer, and had at one time assaulted Wilson after he protested about Morton taking his wife away from him.

25 One of the men shot was called 'Walgardu' Jangala according to Hartwig. There is also Warlpiri evidence (Hartwig 1971: 14) that 'Walgardu' was the husband of

one of the women Morton was sleeping with.

26 Vaarzon-Morel 1995: 43 and Hartwig 1971: 16. Tilmouth was also involved in other incidents, possibly a result of ill-feeling towards the pastoralist who chose to make his camp near a sacred site.

27 Ross, pers. comm. Murray's own account of the party did not mention Cusack, but referred to a 'small native boy' (cited in Cribbin, 1984: 142). Dick Kimber pointed out that some Warlpiri accounts, such as Darby's, incorrectly claimed John Cusack was a member of the party, and suggested that the boy was more likely Kaytetye or Anmatyerr. As I have attempted to present Darby's version of events, I have included Cusack as a member of the party.

28 Hartwig 1960: 29–30.

29 Other Warlpiri have spoken of more killings by Murray and Morton than have been officially recorded. See Hartwig 1971, Read 1991 and Vaarzon-Morel 1995. Wilson, who accompanied them, and was not called before the Board of Enquiry, later spoke of several unrecorded incidents. Darby also spoke of Anmatyerr and Kaytetye people being killed by Murray in the area west of Barrow Creek.

30 Kimber 1986: 109.

31 *Argus*, 14 January 1929: 11.

32 Strehlow 1959: 314.

33 Henson 1992: 58.

34 From a letter 18 April 1960 from Albrecht to Mervyn Hartwig, cited in Henson 1992: 290.

35 *Argus*, 14 January 1929: 11.

36 Nicolas Peterson, pers. comm. 2001.

37 There is a number of oral accounts that suggest Warlpiri people continued to be killed covertly by Whitefellas in the 1930s.

38 Ross, interviewed by Grant Japanangka Granites in 2003. English translation.

VISITORS
Board of Enquiry (p. 183)

39 'Finding of Board of Enquiry 1929', cited in Cribbin 1984: 152–155.

40 *ibid.*

41 Hartwig 1960: 51.

42 'Finding of Board of Enquiry 1929', *op. cit.* It is not unreasonable to conclude that police commissioner Cawood, who was on the Board of Enquiry and had been responsible for Murray's actions at the time of the shootings, would have had an interest in excluding Wilson's evidence, and any Warlpiri or Anmatyerr accounts. Murray's tracker Paddy was the only Aboriginal witness who testified, and unlike all the other witnesses, he was not questioned directly.

CHAPTER NINE
The Good Old Days (pp. 184–211)

1 Latz 1995: 22–23. Further information on Warlpiri bushtucker, including extensive documentation on their Warlpiri names and uses, can be found in Latz's *Bushfires and Bushtucker*, the definitive book on the subject to which Darby contributed.

VISITORS
Explorers (p. 201)

2 Anne Mosey, pers. comm.

3 Warlpiri is rich in synonyms and it may appear that Darby is referring to the same animal when the Warlpiri word is different but the English translation is the same. However, Darby claimed that *milpa-rtiri* and *wampana* were separate species.

4 Ngaliya Warlpiri were sometimes referred to as *manja-wardingki* (people of the mulga).

5 Information for this story is from Ross 1977 'Nyurruwiyi Yupujurla' and pers. comm. 1999.

Bibliography

BOOKS, JOURNALS, UNPUBLISHED MANUSCRIPTS, NEWSPAPER ARTICLES

Baarda, W. (1994) 'The impact of the bilingual program at Yuendumu, 1974 to 1993', in Hartman and Henderson (1994) *Aboriginal Languages in Education* (IAD Press, Alice Springs).

Barrett, M.J. (1976) *Dental Observations on Australian Aborigines: collected papers and reports 1953–1973* (Faculty of Dentistry, The University of Adelaide, Adelaide).

Baume, F.E. (1994, 1933) *Tragedy Track: the story of The Granites* (Hesperian Press and North Flinders Mines Limited, Carlisle).

Bell, D. (1983) *Daughters of the Dreaming* (Allen and Unwin, North Sydney).

Benterak, K., Muecke, S. and Roe, P. (revised edition 1996, 1984) *Reading the Country* (Fremantle Arts Centre Press, South Fremantle).

Brands, J. 'Plucked from the brink', in *Territory Digest*, Vol. 9 No. 2, June 1987.

Burridge, K. (1973) *Encountering Aborigines: Anthropology and the Australian Aboriginal* (Pergamon, New York).

Carell, V. and Dean, B. (1955) *Dust for the Dancers* (Ure Smith, Sydney).

Clarke, H.V. (1974) *The Long Arm: a biography of a Northern Territory Policeman* (Roebuck, Canberra).

Connellan, E.J. (1992) *Failure of Triumph: the story of Connellan Airways* (Paradigm Investments, Narwietooma Station, NT).

Coombs, H. and Stanner, W. (1974) *Program for Yuendumu and Hooker Creek*, Council for Aboriginal Affairs report (Australian Government Publishing Service, Canberra).

Cribbin, J. (1984) *The Killing Times: the Coniston massacre 1928* (Fontana Books, Sydney).

Davidson, A. (1905) *Journal of the explorations in Central Australia by the Central Australian Exploration Syndicate 1898–1900*, South Australian Parliamentary Papers, no. 27 (SA Government Printer, Adelaide).

Elias, D. (1996) *Golden Dreams: The Warlpiri and an Economy of Difference*. Seminar paper presented to Department of Archaeology & Anthropology, Faculty of Arts, Australian National University, 23 August 1996.

Fleming, T. (October 1977) *An outline of the history of the Australian Baptist Home Mission in the Northern Territory*, unpublished manuscript.

Gibson, D. (June 1986) *A biological survey of the Tanami desert in the Northern Territory* (Conservation Commission of the Northern Territory, Technical Report, Number 30).

W.C. Gosse's Explorations, 1873, Australian Facsimile Editions No. 71 (1973), Reproduced by the Libraries Board of South Australia from a copy held in the State Library of South Australia, (Libraries Board of South Australia, Adelaide).

Hale, K. (1995) *An Elementary Warlpiri Dictionary* (IAD Press, Alice Springs).

Harris, J. (1990) *One Blood: 200 years of Aboriginal encounter with Christianity: a story of hope* (Albatross, Sutherland).

Hartwig, M. C. (1960) *The Coniston Killings*, thesis presented as part requirement for the Honours Degree of Bachelor of Arts in The University of Adelaide, unpublished manuscript.

Hartwig, M. C. (c. 1971) 'Coniston Massacre', unpublished update to BA Honours thesis. (The text indicates some research for this thesis was undertaken in March, 1971. Copy sighted at Yuendumu and provided by Robin Japanangka Granites was incomplete.)

Healey, C. *Meanjin* 3/1999: 184.

Henson, B. (1992) *A Straight-out Man: F.W. Albrecht and Central Australian Aborigines* (Melbourne University Press, Melbourne).

Hiddins, L. (1999) *Explore Wild Australia with the Bush Tucker Man* (Penguin, Ringwood).

Hill, B. (2003) *Broken Song: T.G.H. Strehlow and Aboriginal Possession* (Random House, Milsons Point).

Johnson, K., Burbidge, A. and McKenzie N. (1989) 'Australian Macropodoidea: status, causes of decline and future research and management', *in Kangaroos, Wallabies and Rat-kangaroos*, edited by G. Grigg, P. Jarman and I. Hume. (Surrey Beattey and Sons, New South Wales).

Johnson, K., Gibson, D., Langford, D. and Cole, J. (1996) 'Recovery of the Mala *Lagorchestes hirsutus*: a 30-year unfinished journey', in *Back from the Brink: Refining the Threatened Species Recovery Process*, edited by Sally Stephens and Stephanie Maxwell (Australian Nature Conservation Agency).

Jones, T. (1987) *Pegging the Northern Territory: a history of mining in the Northern Territory, 1870–1946* (Northern Territory Department of Mines and Energy, Darwin).

Jordan, I. (8 Dec. 1999) 'Brief History of Baptist Ministry to the Indigenous People of Central Australia', http://www.bwa-baptist-heritage.org/bap-ab.htm.

Jordan, I. (2003) *Their Way: Towards an Indigenous Warlpiri Christianity* (Charles Darwin University Press, Darwin).

Keys, C. (2000) 'The House and the *Yupukarra*, Yuendumu, 1946–96', in Read, P. (ed.) *Settlement: A History of Australian Indigenous Housing* (Aboriginal Studies Press, Canberra).

Kimber, R. G. (1986) *Man from Arltunga: Walter Smith, Australian Bushman* (Hesperian Press, Carlisle).

Kimber, D. (2003) 'Real True History: The Coniston Massacre', part one, in *The Alice Springs News*, 10/09/03.

Kimber, D. (2003) 'Centre's Rough Frontier Justice: Revenge Murder, Wrong Man Dies', part five, in *The Alice Springs News*, 08/10/03.

Kleinart and Neale (eds.) (2000) *The Oxford Companion to Aboriginal Art and Culture* (Oxford University Press, South Melbourne).

Latz, P. (1995) *Bushfires and Bushtucker: Aboriginal plant use in Central Australia* (IAD Press, Alice Springs).

Laughren, M. and Hoogenraad, R. (1996 draft) *Warlpiri Word List* (CADP and IAD, Alice Springs).

Leichleitner, D. J. and Nathan, P. (1983) *Settle Down Country: Pmere Arlaltyewele, a community report for the Central Australian Aboriginal Congress* (Kibble Books, Malmsbury).

McGrath, A. (1987) *Born in the Cattle* (Allen and Unwin, Sydney).

Marcus, J. (2001) *The Indomitable Miss Pink: a life in anthropology* (UNSW Press, Sydney).

Meggitt, M.J. (1962) *Desert People* (Angus and Robertson, Melbourne).

Michaels, E. (1986) *The Aboriginal Invention of Television in Central Australia 1982–86* (Australian Institute for Aboriginal Studies, Canberra).

Michaels, E. (1994) *Bad Aboriginal Art: Tradition, Media, and Technological Horizons* (Allen and Unwin, St Leonards).

Middleton, M.R. and Francis, S.H. (1976) *Yuendumu and its children: life and health on an Aboriginal settlement* (Department of Aboriginal Affairs, Canberra).

Muecke, S. (1997) *No Road: Bitumen all the way* (Fremantle Arts Centre Press, South Fremantle).

Munn, N. D. (1973) *Warlpiri Iconography: Graphic Representation and Cultural Symbolism in a Central Australian Society* (Cornell University Press, Ithaca).

O'Brien, J. (2002) *'To infuse an universal terror': the Coniston killings of 1928*, History Department, Northern Territory University, June 2002, unpublished paper.

Read, P. and Read, J. (eds.) (1991) *Long Time, Olden Time: Aboriginal accounts of Northern Territory History* (IAD, Alice Springs).

Reece, L. (1970) 'Grammar of the Wailbri Language of Central Australia', in Elkin, A.P. (ed.) *Oceania Linguistic Monographs no.13* (University of Sydney, Sydney).

Reece, L. 'What the Warlpiri Aborigines Believe about the Origin of Everything', *Creation Magazine*, 8.2, March 1986.

Reeves, J. (Q.C.) (1998) *Building on Land Rights for the Next Generation: The Review of the Aboriginal Land Rights (Northern Territory) Act 1976* (ATSIC and the Commonwealth of Australia, Canberra).

Reynolds, H. (2000) *Why weren't we told? A personal search for the truth about our history* (Penguin, Ringwood).

Ross, T. 'The people and their home', translation of 'Yapa manu ngurrara', in Warlukurlangu Artists (1987) *Yuendumu Doors: Kuruwarri* (Aboriginal Studies Press, Canberra).

Simpson, B. (1996) *Packhorse Drover* (ABC Books, Sydney).

Simpson, Nash, Laughren, Austin and Alpher (eds.) (2001) *Forty Years On: Ken Hale and Australian Languages* (Pacific Linguistics, Canberra).

Steer, P. (1996) *It happened at Yuendumu*, self published, Melbourne.

Strehlow, T. (1957, 1959) *Land of Altjira*. Final revision started March 11, 1959. – copy held at Strehlow Research Centre, unpublished manuscript.

Strehlow, T. (1971) *Songs of Central Australia* (Angus and Robertson, Sydney).

Summer Institute of Linguistics, Australian Aborigines and Islanders Branch (1986) *Kriol Dictionary* (First draft, Darwin).

Swain, T. (1988) 'The Ghost of Space: Reflections on Warlpiri Christian Iconography and Ritual', in Swain and Rose (eds.) *Aboriginal Australians and Christian Missions: Ethnographic and Historical Studies* (Australian Association for the Study of Religions, Adelaide).

Swartz, S. (1997) *Warlpiri Yimi Kuja Karlipa Wangka* (Summer Institute of Linguistics, Berrimah).

Taylor, P. (ed.) (1988) *After 200 years: photographic essays of Aboriginal and Islander Australia today* (Aboriginal Studies Press, Canberra).

Terry, M. (1931) *Hidden Wealth and Hiding People* (Putnam, London).

Toyne, P. (2000) *The internal colonisation of the Warlpiri and its resistance through educational practice*, PHD thesis, La Trobe University, unpublished manuscript.

Vaarzon-Morel, P. (ed.) (1995) *Warlpiri Women's Voices: Warlpiri karnta karnta-kurlangu yimi*, (IAD Press, Alice Springs).

Warburton, P.E. (1875, 1981) *Journey across the Western Interior of Australia*, facsimile edition, (Hesperian Press, Victoria Park).

Warden, J. (2003) 'The Death of Harry Henty', draft paper, National Museum of Australia.

Warlukurlangu Artists (1987) *Yuendumu Doors: Kuruwarri* (Australian Institute of Aboriginal Studies, Canberra).

Watts, L. and Fisher, S. (2000) *Pikilyi: Water Rights – Human Rights*, joint Masters thesis, Faculty of Aboriginal and Torres Strait Islander Studies, Northern Territory University, unpublished manuscript.

Williams, R.M. (1986) *Beneath Whose Hand: The Autobiography of R.M. Williams* (Pan Macmillan, Sydney).

Wycliffe Bible Translators (1992) *Yimi-nyayirni-wangu God-kurlangu* (The Bible Society in Australia, Canberra).

Yapaku Association (n.d., limited distribution) *Yapaku Yunparninjaku* (Summer Institute of Linguistics, Darwin).

Yuendumu Tjaru: for the people of Yuendumu (1970) (Yuendumu Social Club, Yuendumu).

GOVERNMENT REPORTS

Annual Report 1958/59, Northern Territory Administration, Welfare Branch.

Annual Report 1959/60, Northern Territory Administration, Welfare Branch.

Annual Report 1960/61, Northern Territory Administration, Welfare Branch.

Annual Report 1970/71, Northern Territory Administration, Welfare Branch.

Claim by the Warlpiri and Kartangarurru-Kurintji (1979) Report by the Aboriginal Land Commissioner, Mr Justice Toohey, to the Minister for Aboriginal Affairs and to the Administrator of the Northern Territory (Australian Government Publishing Service, Canberra).

Jila (Chilla Well) Warlpiri Land Claim (1988) Report No. 26, Report by the Aboriginal Land Commissioner, Mr Justice Maurice, to the Minister for Aboriginal Affairs

and to the Administrator of the Northern Territory (Australian Government Publishing Service, Canberra).

Lander Warlpiri Anmatjirra Land Claim to Willowra Pastoral Lease (1980), Report by the Aboriginal Land Commissioner, Mr Justice Toohey, to the Minister for Aboriginal Affairs and to the Administrator of the Northern Territory (Australian Government Publishing Service, Canberra).

Transcript of Public Meeting at Yuendumu (11/4/1989) for Select Committee on Constitutional Development (S. Hatton and B. Ede).

Yurrkuru (Brookes Soak) Land Claim (1992) Report No. 43, 'Findings, Recommendation and Report of the Aboriginal Land Commissioner, Mr Justice Olney, to the Minister for Aboriginal and Torres Strait Islander Affairs and to the Administrator of the Northern Territory. (Australian Government Publishing Service, Canberra).

INTERVIEWS

Australian Institute for Aboriginal and Torres Strait Islander Studies (AIATSIS)

Pharlap Japangardi, interviewed by Murray Barrett, June 1955. BARRETT_M01 collection, archive tape LA072a. Courtesy Audiovisual Archive, AIATSIS.

Pharlap Japangardi, interviewed by Murray Barrett, 1965. BARRETT_M01 collection, archive tape LA068. Courtesy Audiovisual Archive, AIATSIS.

Northern Territory Archives Service (NTAS)

Lily Ah Toy NTRS 1983 TS8706 interviewed by Jane Bathgate 1996.

Frank Baarda NTRS 226 TS714 interviewed by Francis Good at Yuendumu 1991.

Charles (Pat) Chapman NTRS 226 TS529 interviewed by Ronda Jamieson 1989.

Tom Cole NTRS 226 TS29 interviewed by Helen Wilson 1984.

Louise Dixon NTRS 226 TS39 interviewed by Hilda Tuxworth 1980.

Ted Egan NTRS 226 TS676 interviewed by Francis Good 1991.

Pat Fleming NTRS 226 TS672, interviewed by Francis Good 1991.

Tom Fleming NTRS 226 TS1026 self-taped 1990.

Harry Giese NTRS 226 TS755 Tape 22 interviewed by Peter d'Abbs April 1991.

Brian Greenfield NTRS 226 TS637 interviewed by Jeremy Long 1990.

Murphy Japanangka NTRS 226 TS862 interviewed by
	Nicholas Gill at Ngurrutiji, Gosse River NT 1997.
Peter Latz NTRS 226 TS819 interviewed by Meredith
	Campbell 1996.
Joy Marks NTRS 226 TS280 interviewed by Hilda Tuxworth
	1980.
Les Penhall NTRS 226 TS303 interviewed by Mary
	Stephenson 1982.
Darby Ross NTRS 219 TS782 interviewed by Francis Good
	at Juka Juka 1991.
Darby Ross NTRS 219 TS793 interviewed by Francis Good
	at Ngarliyikirlangu 1991.
D.D. Smith NTRS 226 TS844 interviewed by Meredith
	Campbell 1996.
Gordon Sweeney NTRS 226 TS337 interviewed by Don
	Dickson 1980.

Warlpiri Media Association (WMA)

Interview with Darby Jampijinpa Ross, 20/6/90, translated
	by Alice Napanangka Granites for Warlpiri Media
	Association's Jardiwarnpa Warlpiri Fire Ceremony
	Film Project proposal for AIATSIS Grants, Warlpiri
	Media Association 1990.
Video interview with Jack Jakamarra Ross and Harry
	Japangardi Jones at Yuendumu (September 2003) by
	Grant Japanangka Granites and Anna-Lisa Nangala
	Egan for Warlpiri Media Association. English
	transcription by Grant Japanangka Granites and Liam
	Campbell.

Yuendumu School Bilingual Resource Development Unit (BRDU)

'The Way We Used to Live', Darby Jampijinpa Ross,
	recorded and transcribed in Warlpiri by Mary
	Laughren, Yuendumu 1977–78, © Yuendumu BRDU.
	Translated and edited by Erica Napurrurla Ross and
	Liam Campbell.
'Nyurruwiyi Yupujurla', Ngarrurnu-nganpa Darby
	Jampijinparlu (Ross), Yirrarnu George Jampijinparlu,
	Yuendumu School 1977.
'Yurrkuru-kurlu', Ngarrurnu Tim Japangardirli (Langdon),
	Yirrarnu George Jampijinparlu, Kuruwarri kujurnu
	George Jampijinparlu, Yuendumu School 1978. English
	translation by Mary Laughren and George Jampijinpa.
'Warumungu Watikirli', Yirri-puraja Darby Jampijinparlu,
	Yirrarnupala pipangka David Nash Jungarrayirli manu
	Lloyd Spencer Jungarrayirli, Yardapala yirrarnu Neville
	Poulson Japangardirli manu Mary Laughren
	Napaljarrirli, Warlpiri Literature Production Centre
	Inc. 1984.

OTHER MEDIA

Audio and video recordings with Darby Jampijinpa Ross
	at Yuendumu and surrounding areas 1995–2004,
	recorded and transcribed by Liam Campbell.
'Jardiwarnpa: a Warlpiri Fire Ceremony', episode four of
	'Blood Brothers', presented by Warlukurlangu
	Artists, Warlpiri Media Association and City Pictures,
	© 1993 Australian Film Finance Corporation, Ned
	Lander and Rachel Perkins, screened on SBS
	television 27/7/93. Transcript provided by Warlpiri
	Media Association. Translators: Kay Napaljarri Ross,
	Jack Jakamarra Ross, Erica Napurrurla Ross, Rosie
	Nangala Fleming and Alice Napanangka Granites.

Project participants

THOMAS JANGALA RICE
Kirda (owner)

Thomas is Darby's brother's son. In Warlpiri society, he is considered to be Darby's son, and he took the role of *kirda* in the project, taking responsibility for Darby's stories. Darby taught Thomas much of the cultural information relating to the *Jukurrpa* (Dreaming) that is the responsibility of the Jampijinpa and Jangala skin groups to which both men belong. Thomas' involvement in the project was essential to maintaining community ownership and a Warlpiri perspective.

Thomas is a successful artist whose paintings can be seen in the National Gallery of Australia, South Australian Museum, The Holmes à Court Collection and the Akademie der Künste, Berlin. Thomas was among the men who travelled to San Francisco and Melbourne to create ground paintings for the openings of the 'Spirit Country' exhibition.

Thomas is married to Jeannie Nungarrayi Egan who was a senior teacher at Yuendumu School and one of the longest serving teachers in the Northern Territory. Their enthusiasm for the project stems from their desire to record and preserve Warlpiri Law and Culture for future generations.

PADDY JAPALJARRI STEWART
Kurdungurlu (guardian)

Paddy (aka Cookie) is most well known for his roles in the creation of the Papunya mural and the *Yuendumu Doors*. He is a founding member of Warlukurlangu Artists and has served as its chairman on several occasions. He accompanied Paddy Sims to Paris for the 'Magiciens de la Terre' exhibition and has become one of Yuendumu's most prolific artists. In 2005, he sold a collection of paintings based on the *Yuendumu Doors* at auction for a record price.

When asked about his biographical entry, Paddy had this to say (translation):

In the old days, we would walk around here. We used to live in our homeland. We would worry about getting food, and we would talk about going hunting: 'We might go to Wangarla.'

Then our mother and father would come with meat. They would find bushtucker: goannas, kangaroos, honey ants, bush raisins, bush bananas, or bush potatoes. Good one. That's how we would live in the early days. Old Darby, he knew.

Paddy and Darby worked and travelled extensively together throughout the Northern Territory. At Darby's request, he fulfilled the role of *kurdungurlu* on this project, verifying the content of stories, particularly those of an historical and culturally sensitive nature.

JACK JAKAMARRA ROSS
Kurdungurlu (guardian)

Jack was renowned for his enthusiasm for telling stories and extensive knowledge of *Jukurrpa* (Dreamings). Thomas identified Jack as an important participant in this project. Darby's stories also mention him and Jack had stories of his own to contribute to the text. Jack participated in many of the bush trips and Thomas consulted him to verify the information Darby recorded.

Like the other men involved in this project, Jack was a strong supporter of Warlukurlangu Artists and exhibited his art and craft extensively. In 1999, he travelled to San Francisco as a guest of the Gantner-Myer families to create a ground painting for the 'Spirit Country' exhibition. Jack also featured in Warlpiri Media's *Bush Mechanics* television series.

Like Darby, Jack saw a lot of changes in his lifetime. He had mixed feelings about Whitefellas, and would talk about the importance of holding on to *Jukurrpa* and the strength in Warlpiri Law and Culture. He was well respected by all who knew him. He passed away during the final phase of the project, and although no longer with us, will always be remembered by everyone at Yuendumu.

PADDY JAPALJARRI SIMS
Kurdungurlu (guardian)

Paddy was identified as an important contributor to this project by Darby and Paddy Stewart. Darby knew Paddy's family as a young man and Paddy had many stories of his own to tell of that time, as well as verifying the information in many of Darby's stories. He fulfilled the role of *kurdungurlu*, taking us to his country at Kunajarrayi (which he shared with Darby's mother).

When asked about this biographical entry, Paddy told the story of when he was camped at Kunajarrayi as a young man. It was the first time he saw an aeroplane. It was high in the sky and looked like a big black bird: 'Look like devil. Might be devil!'

Since then, Paddy has learnt all about Whitefellas. In the early days of Yuendumu, he was known as Paddy Garden because he worked in the market garden. He has fond memories of 1989, when he went to Paris for the celebrated 'Magiciens de la Terre' exhibition and created a ground painting installation with other Warlpiri artists.

Paddy became one of the strongest supporters and most successful of the Warlukurlangu Artists. A gentleman painter, most days he can be found sitting on the back veranda with a canvas at the art centre. He works with bright colours and is proud of the *Jukurrpa* that his paintings depict.

Paddy is the head of a large family, with whom he shares his house, and hopes that they will follow his example and learn their *Jukurrpa*.

SCOTT DUNCAN
Photographer

From his early childhood in the Virgin Islands, to his Emmy award-winning world cinematography, Scott Duncan has been following a path in the pursuit of amazing locations and stunning images. With a camera always at hand, he consistently explores new ways of seeing the world.

Scott was first introduced to the artists of Yuendumu while working on a documentary project for the Sydney Olympic Games. Captivated by the landscape and the local people, Scott returned many times to Warlpiri country, photographing, visiting and just listening.

Educated at the School of Visual Arts in New York with a BFA in Photography, his continued journey as artist and storyteller is constantly driven forward by his passion for world travel, art, and research.

LIAM CAMPBELL
Writer

Liam first met Darby in 1989 as part of a language and cultural exchange program in high school. He returned to Central Australia a few years later, eventually moving out to Yuendumu to record stories with Darby.

He has lived in Yuendumu for the past ten years working as a youth worker, art coordinator and on various collaborative media projects. This book formed part of his studies through the Centre for Australian Indigenous Studies at Monash University.

It has been a journey of discovery, and along the way Liam has made lots of friends and family at Yuendumu. He misses Darby and Jack, and hopes that, through the efforts of those involved in the project, they will be remembered by everyone at Yuendumu, and that others will get a chance to share their experiences and learn a little about Warlpiri life and culture.

Acknowledgments

This book is the result of a journey I took with Darby, but it has involved many (so many) other people, most of whom knew Darby, and whose stories crossed paths with his at some point.

For their friendship and personal support (and houses to stay in!) over the years Frank and Wendy Baarda, Sara Boniwell, Carson Japanangka Brown, James Japanangka Brown, Peggy Nampijinpa Brown, Steven Japanangka Brown, Anna Cadden, Vic, Marg and Bridie Campbell (my father, mother and sister), Linda Chellew, Andrew Cowen, Daryl Grahek, Cecily Napanangka Granites, Michael Harries, Graeme Horne, Crocodile Japangardi Johnson, Jimmy Japanangka Langdon, Lucky Nampijinpa Langdon, Molly Nampijinpa Langdon (my other mother), Tara Leckey, The Malmsbury Mob (Bouchers, Holmes, Knolls, Nous, Shogrens and Thommos) – 'Do your Dreams!', Johnny Japangardi Miller (my other father), Michael Morgan, Anne Mosey, Django Nou, Natalie O'Conner, Karissa Preuss, Ronnie Reinhardt, Gordon Jangala Robertson, Colin and Merran Smith, Andrew Japaljarri Spencer, Isobel Napaljarri Spencer, Joel Sprake, Andrew and Vesna Stojanovski, Barb, Emma, Morris and Rebecca Stuart, Malcolm Wall, Andrew White, Neil Jupurrurla White and Colin Youl.

For their support of the project, either by providing support letters, photos, anecdotes, quotes, advice, interviews, reading sections of the manuscript, or assisting in the process of research and development Cecilia Alfonso (WAAA), Chris Anderson (Newmont), Brett Badger, Murray Barrett, Robert Barrett, David Betz, Joe Jangala Bird, Christine Bosua, Eric Brown, Senator Ian Campbell, Bethune Carmichael (BRDU), Susan Congreve, Jack Jangala Cook, Edith Coombs, Andrew Cowen, Dick Cowen, Robert de Crespigny, Dolly Nampijinpa Daniels, Françoise Dussart, Jeannie Nungarrayi Egan, Robert Edwards, Ted Egan, Derek Elias, Jol Fleming, Rosie Nangala Fleming, Cathy Flint (NTAS), Michael Frankel, George Jangala Fry, Francis Good (NTAS), Robert Graham, Robin Japanangka Granites, Matt Grimm (SDF), Alana Harris (AIATSIS), Les Hiddins, Melinda Hinkson, Robert Hoogenraad, Tiger Japaljarri, Wes Jay (Woodlands Media), Michael Jensen, Ken Johnson, Phillip Jones (SAM), Ivan Jordan (ABMS), Tony Juttner, Tom Kantor (WMA), Francis Jupurrurla Kelly, Ed and Kath Kingston (ABMS), Stephen Kitto, Tim Klingender (Sothebys), Beverly Knight, Peter Latz, Mary Laughren, Annette McCarthy (DEH), Bill McKell, Lara McLellan (AIATSIS), Sally McMartin (Newmont), James Japangardi Marshall, Andrea Nungarrayi Martin, Samson Japaljarri Martin, Howard Morphy, Stephen Muecke, Nancy Munn, Yasmine Musharbash, David Nash (ANU), Daisy Napanangka Nelson, Carolyn Newman (NTAS), Justin O'Brien, Yasmine Musharbash, Uni Nampijinpa Martin, Jenny Moore (JPM), Lloyd Ollerenshaw, Nicolas Peterson (ANU), Cobra Japangardi Poulson, Ivy Napangardi Poulson, Helen Read, Liz Reed (CAIS), Scott Reid (JPM), Kimberley Roth, Helen Read, Eddie Jampijinpa Robertson, Edwin Jangala Ross, Erica Napurrurla Ross, Kay Napaljarri Ross, Victor Jupurrurla Ross, Lynette Russell (CAIS), Judith Ryan (NGV), Rick Shapter (Australia Council), Graeme Shaughnessy (Strehlow Research Centre), Bessie Nakamarra Sims, Otto Jungarrayi Sims, Jilly Nakamarra Spencer, Maxine Nungarrayi Spencer, Lucy Stewart (ArtsNT), Jo Stubbings, Louise Sullivan, Steve Swartz, Leon Terrill (CLC), Banjo Jungarrayi Tex, Sandy Jangala Tilmouth, Peter Toyne (MLA), Robbie and Connie Nungarrayi Walit (WMA), James Warden (NMA), Shorty Jangala Watson, Lisa Watts, Lindsay Japangardi Williams, Warren Japanangka Williams, Adrian Winwood-Smith and Felicity Wright.

The organisations which supported the various stages of this project with finances or in-kind support include Aboriginal and Torres Strait Islander Board of the Australia Council for the Arts, Centre for Australian Indigenous Studies (Monash University), Cultural Development Fund of NT Arts and Museums (ArtsNT), Department of Environment and Heritage (Commonwealth Government), JPMorgan, Newmont Australia, NT History Award (2001, NTAS), Queens Trust for Young Australians, Save As, Scott Duncan Films, Splitting Image, Yuendumu School's Bilingual Resource Development Unit and the Yuendumu Community Government Council. Of special mention is the committee of Warlukurlangu Artists which enthusiastically supported our project and allowed us to administer it through their organisation during the development stage.

There are a few people to whom I am further indebted for their inspiration, encouragement, belief and hard work
My parents, Vic and Marg, always supportive, understanding and loving in so many ways. Anna Meltzer for her love and support as I struggled to pull everything together. My friends and family at Yuendumu who have always welcomed me and made me feel at home. Colin Youl for introducing me to the Warlpiri language. Colin Smith for his friendship with both Darby and myself. The staff of Hetti Perkins, who always made me feel welcome and took care of Darby in his final years. Dick Kimber for his enthusiasm and encouragement every time we met. Pouneh Hatami for sharing her heart, encouragement along the way, and her acceptance of my commitment to walking a different road. Dave and Bess Nungarrayi Price for their inspiration (25 years of marriage!), friendship, and reading of the manuscript. Simon Japangardi Fisher and Rita Cattoni at Warlpiri Media for supporting the project. Rod Davies, Warren Smith, Mick Smith, Peter Warren and everyone at Splitting Image. Carmen De La Rue for helping us understand and negotiate the production process. Sandy Cull for her beautiful design and for making this the project she went out on her own with. Bruce Sims for his experience and sensitivity with the text of Darby's story and investing so much time into making it happen. Phil Bosua — without whom this book may never have been made — for his hard work, belief in the project and ability to think big. Scott and Diana Duncan — for their friendship, sensitivity, generosity, and their life-long commitment to making beautiful custom images.

The project team   Thomas Jangala Rice, Jack Jakamarra Ross, Paddy Japaljarri Stewart and Paddy Japaljarri Sims. It was my privilege to work with these men — to go on hunting trips, select photos, discuss Darby's stories, visit country (and some other countries!), and share a Toyota with. This book represents the end of a long process of shared experiences documenting country and stories.

Lastly to Darby   For the journey of understanding — life experience, the sacredness of land, love of people, belief in Wapirra and the importance of humour. He always called me Japanangka or nephew (I don't think he even knew my English name!), and I called him Jampijinpa or Uncle. He made me family. Old Darby, whose life story I hope, as I believe he would have hoped, gives us reason to believe that not only can we learn to live with each other in this country, but also respect and grow in understanding of the things that matter, move us, challenge us, and celebrate the differences between us. Just like Darby and I did.

List of abbreviations

Copyright and photography credits

Sponsors

PRODUCTION

Australian Government

Department of the Environment and Heritage

This project was made possible through funding support from the Australian Government under the *Sharing Australia's Stories* national heritage grants programme. DISCLAIMER: The views expressed herein are not necessarily the views of the Commonwealth or the Minister for the Environment and Heritage, and the Commonwealth does not accept responsibility for any information contained herein.

This project was sponsored by the Northern Territory Government through the Department of Natural Resources, Environment and the Arts and the regional arts fund of ArtsNT.

This project was supported by Newmont Australia.

RESEARCH AND DEVELOPMENT

This project was proudly supported by JPMorgan.

This project has been assisted by the Australian Government through the Australia Council, its arts funding and advisory body.

Scott Duncan Films
www.scottduncanfilms.com

Warlukurlangu Artists
www.warlu.com

Warlpiri Media Association Inc.
www.warlpiri.com.au

Audio CD

The following texts are transcriptions to accompany the audio CD. The references to the main text are to similar sections, where there are edited versions, not the same as these literal transcriptions.

TRACK 1

Thank you this story while we talk here today. They want to like listen to this. My name Darby. I talk here today.

TRACK 2 (p. 191)

All that country they bin only go hunting. And they bring back a big mob of kangaroos. They're running everywhere. That dog got to catch him – that dingo one dog. Four, five, six might they get a kangaroo.

That old man there dogs, he the boss. He kill 'em. How many him kill 'em? One, two, three, four, and from there five. Him take that many. And they go, one, two, three, four, five, six – six man. They go, and they bring 'em back that big mob of kangaroo.

And they got to give it for grandfather.
And they got to give it for mother.
And they got to give it for grandmother again.
And mother they got to give it.
And all the old man they talk right, they got to eat him.
And they got to make big fire there. Lot of flies while he running through. They got to sit down in the middle of the fire. Another fire here, another fire here, another fire here. From fly. Yeh, properly good one they been only make 'em.

Alright from there, everybody happy now.
He talk,

'Alright, thank you!'
They talk one another, Warlpiri. Not English. Warlpiri they talk.
Alright,
'Oh, good one!'
Oh, good mob while we bin there.
Right after that, they're ready want to like catch a young man. Young man while they want to make him man. Alright, they catch him and they,
'Ooh, ooh, ooh, ooh.'
All night and day. They're singing there all night and day.
Singing. And from . . .
'Ooh, ooh, ooh, ooh.'
With the sticks?
Yeah. Oh, properly.
The big old man, old man they are singing, too. They are singing whole lot longa there – all the girls – they are dancing to all the girls. They are going,
'Ooh, ooh, ooh, ooh.'
They are singing out everywhere. Good one!

TRACK 3 (p. 193)

That old man bin coming now. Him bin have a big mob of spear and two boomerangs. Well,
'Hey!'
Him bin sing out like (to) that tree there, gum tree. He bin sing out,
'Come on Napaljarri, you and me got to go! Come on Napaljarri, you and me got to go.'
Alright, that my cousin bin start to cry,
'I no want you.'
That my cousin bin talking to him, longa that old man, Jakamarra.
Alright, from there,
'I no want to follow 'em you.'
That my cousin. Him bin say,
'Hey, come up, come up!'
Him bin run now. He want to like get hold of him (her). And that my cousin bin climb up the big tree, longa bloodwood tree.
Oh, him bin talking. Alright, Jakamarra bin there standing around, looking around,
'Come on, you and me go. You and me go!'
That Jakamarra, he's a (unclear) . . . my cousin, sister belonga what-do-you-call-em Paddy Sims.
Alright, *bambai* (bye and bye) he bin get wild properly, now. That Jakamarra, he bin get wild properly now. He bin just get 'em one spear, and him bin spear through the here. He bin chuck 'em right longa that tree. Spear there. Yeh, spear 'em. Alright, he bin have a woomera (spear thrower), and that's why him bin chuck 'em . . .

Your cousin?
Yeh, my cousin.
He speared your cousin?
Him bin spear through here (chest). And he (she) bin come down and got a spear now. Drop down the ground.
That Jakamarra bin (unclear) run away. Which way he bin run? He bin go right up to Ernabella, all around there. Walking round. Cheeky man, that one.
Yeh, that Jakamarra. We call 'em Kampa. You got to write 'em (down) that one too.
Alright, from there, him bin start . . . (crying) That old man bin cry properly. And my grandmother. Grandmother, him bin cry, too. And my aunty, yeh my aunty, bin crying around there. Old man bin killing that (girl). And grandmother, aunty bin kill (hit) 'em self (in the) head. Oh, properly, that girl there finished (dead), right longa ground.
Good story, this one. That's olden days, long time ago.

TRACK 4 (p. 193)

Two bin fighting, now.
Oh, they been standing all around. They bin hold 'em,
'Hey, you leave your brother, you leave your brother. That's your brother.'
'That's enough of you two fella, two bin fighting.'
Oh, blood running everyway from back. Oh, shoulder, anything there cutting one another . . .
Oh, big fight! I bin only looking out the desert. Big fight bin only going on there.
And another fella he get 'em knife, that stone knife. Not a Whitefella knife, an Aboriginal knife. That knife from bush, from desert.
Alright, he run now. And him bin get 'em, pull 'em out that knife and cut him straightaway.
All just the same,
'Go on give it. You cut 'em your brother.'
Alright, that two bin only fight.
Right, finish and,
'Alright, you can keep that girl now.'
They say,
'You right? You got 'em big girl and I got 'em little girl.'
Alright, two finish for that fighting.
Bambai (bye and bye) him go away now that man. He no come back more. Him go to another place.
And from there, that young fella right, while they been give it young girl for him. He sitting round there, got a sore back. While they, his brother bin cutting down.
And from there,
'Alright, me finish for you, my brother.'
Alright, that youngest man,
'No, I no want to come back and see you again. I got to go away from you.'

TRACK 5 (p. 170)

That trouble bin going on here, long time ago. I want to tell 'em from Brooks Soak, this side from Coniston, west from Coniston, where they bin kill that old man. Fred Brooks his name. Old man. He bin have two camels and him bin starting greenhide bullock (unclear, making raw leather straps).

And from there, he bin (unclear) in the water, and two boy bin after camels – morning time.

It's only me telling story, good word. This one from early days.

No money while they bin living round there everywhere. While we bin sitting around here, too. We tell 'em to him, and they bin getting that old man (Brooks). Him bin have 'em three girl, washing girls. They bin washing clothes for him. And him bin keeping a couple of girls. He (they) never go back, longa their husbands. They bin work, sleeping longa that Whitefella old man, while they bin kill that man. Name: Fred Brooks. This old man, that Fred Brooks old man bin want to like get a big mob of dingo scalps. Dingo scalps.

And from there, that two boy bin come look about. And him (Brooks) bin cutting, and him bin make a lot of camel hobble strap for camel, while he want to put 'em on here (chains).

From there, two boy bin after camels, and same day they bin come back and see 'em him, where they bin kill him. His name, old man, Japanangka, old Bullfrog. He's my countryman. Him bin thinking about for murdering from girl – three girls.

'Hey, what for that man keeping 'bout three girl?'

'Oh, *lafta* (have to) we talk today.'

They bin talk to him, telling one another, all the poor boy, Aboriginal boy. They bin walking around there – got a spear. They bin coming to morning time. Before the dinner they bin kill 'em him. Before the dinner. They bin kill him just lunchtime.

And that two boy bin come back – got two camels. And him bin look,

'Where the old man gone now?'

Two boy bin look about to him.

'Oh here, they bin kill 'em everywhere look!'

Boomerang – broken one. And nulla nulla (club) – broken one. And big spear – *wurrumpuru*. Big spear, like you know, man killer, that one. They bin see a lot of broken one there. And nulla nulla bin there too – broken one. And axe too, what they bin use for cutting that old man.

They bin split him right here.

That far we can tell you this story.

TRACK 6 (p. 172)

Telling this story, good word. That number one story.

And that police (Murray) bin take a horse, and he bin carry with the rifle. And him (Stafford) bin say,

'That's all of my mob here.'

Little mob. He never bin shot 'em that mob, while they bin longa station all the time. They bin leave 'em; that policeman bin leave him. Randal Stafford bin stop him alright.

Another mob, while they bin living in the what-do-you-call-'em, the Brooks Soak, behind that hill. That's all they bin get there. Ready, look around again. They bin see 'em one Jakamarra longa Mawu, they call 'em waterhole down Mawu. Alright, they bin kill that one Jakamarra belonga that place. Alright, they bin shoot 'em that one, and him bin run, they bin go around,

'Oh, big mob going that way!'

They bin follow 'em up, see him longa Waterloo rockhole, longa big rockhole. Big mob bin there. *Bedy* (about) 'ten hundred' peoples, 'ten hundred' peoples. Big mob. My sister, all about they get shot, too, there. And my brother-in-law. They finish (died) whole lot there.

And from there, they (Murray's party) bin look,

'Oh, enough here.'

Oh, him bin put 'em heap. Little children and big boy; young man and big boy again. Children. Oh, everything there! Women there, young girl; they kill 'em whole lot there.

From there, they bin camp down at Brooks Soak. And they bin camp there, camp longa scrub – somebody they no want to see 'em. That police bin there, camp in the bush. And from there, he bin watching that road. As soon as somebody come along, he get shot.

And from there, they bin go there morning time, they bin follow that creek, and they bin go through to that 'nother hill there – Mt Leichardt – and they bin follow that creek, right up to creek. A 'thousand' people there, longa 'nother big waterhole. They bin have a business (men's ceremony) there, while they want to go to Willowra. And they get shot halfway – about 'twelve hundred' peoples. 'Twelve hundred' peoples. They finish (die) there, halfway. Yeh, too much! Oh, big mob of youngfella, and big mob of old mans. Too much altogether. 'Twelve hundred' too much!

And from there, they bin travelling. They bin see 'em another one, this side from Willowra. Our people bin there. They bin get shot, too. Girl and boy. Young kid, too. Children. Children, too. All the little ones, they bin get killed there. And some old man bin get shot.

TRACK 7 (p. 146)

Alright, from there we start again go away, riding horse now. And I go right up to all that country right up to Darwin, longa Pine Creek. Big mob of cattle there we get 'em, longa Oolloo, Oolloo Station . . .

Alright, we bin take 'em back again, longa grass country. Feed 'em round there. Feed 'em round. My boss bin coming there, now; that bullock man, drover man. Alright, him bin see 'em (cattle). Alright, he bin count 'em now. Alright, he bin count 'em, count 'em, count 'em, count 'em:

'Well, you alright, old man.'

Not old man, youngfella, little bit youngfella me bin.

Alright, from there, blanket, flour, tea, sugar, everything him bin leave 'em there. Blanket, trousers, everything there him bin leave. And a lot of flour. Lot of horse, too. Carry 'em in flour, longa backpack. Load 'em up. A lot of work . . .

Alright, him bin leave everything there for we. Canteen, too. Waterbag and leggings, and a lot of clothes. We bin working. Alright, from there, I'm proper head drover man. Yeah, me! Got to think about no more rushing cattle. No more.

TRACK 8 (p. 88)

One more thing I wanted to ask you. It's about that story when Jesus (was) up at Yuendumu Hill?

Yeh, that's him. That one, that true word. Him bin come here. Him bin coming got a big cloud.

Big cloud?

Yeh, I'll tell 'em one more.

Him bin coming to big cloud. And Him bin (sound effects) lightning. Just like alongside of me. Not the proper lightning, nothing, only belonga Father. Him camped out there, longa 'nother side from Yuendumu. 'Nother side from Yuendumu, this side from Yuendumu hill. That side. We might go round there any time, I'll show you.

And another one (time), Him bin travelling moonlight, longa *kirntangi, kirntangi*. Moon, we call 'em *kirntangi*. Only little spear he bin have him. Spear.

That Father bin coming through the gate. Him bin come out from through the gate. Big gate over there. Long way down, longa heaven. The Father bin coming to me, now. Straight ahead. And Him bin coming right up to moonlight. Moon bin here, this way. Yeh, moon bin there. This way moon coming.

Kakarrara? (east)

Yeh – *kakarrara*; and He bin here. Right there.

And from there, Him bin look down to me. Oh, Him bin making me paralysed!

Junga? (true)

Yuwayi (yes), Him bin making me paralysed. What

to do? Oh, I bin,

'Oh, look this!'

I bin shivering. I never bin sleep after that, while that Father bin come, while He bin make proper, oh everything cold down here. He bin making everything. Yeah, that's why me pray for everybody. *Yapaku* (for people). That's why. That's true word.

TRACK 9 (p. 212)

European peoples, Aboriginal peoples – we're living in one lot, now. All family.

The white mans, they're thinking about for the war. They think about for war in 'nother countries. We're very sorry for that. Shooting for nothing. Fighting for nothing. Got to (be) sitting good. No matter where 'nother countries. That's our peoples, everywhere. No matter 'nother country. Our peoples. We think about for him might take a good life.

That Whitefella (unclear) law, while they talk about for (unclear) law. War fighting. He no want to fight from countries. That country can't cry for we! For Aboriginal people, too. Nothing! He'll be hard thing, this old law. We no want this law, or fighting. No, sitting good. Work good. While we here, we think about for good life, everybody's.

He no want to shoot. He not dingo! He not wild dingo. Got to think about for this, all peoples everywhere. The war, that's from anything, while they fighting from countries. Country can't cry for the we. Nothing. Country – it's the heart. That's the world. Country can't cry. We want to live good life. Everybodys. All this, while we talk here today. This morning, while we talk here, we no want to think about for, think about for peoples, good life. Take a good life. Sitting good. We no want something hard law.

They're bringing the war, they talk about for war. Should be finish this long time ago, our people's last war while they bin fight here. They bin travelling right up to (unclear) bore, through to Darwin. And big fight bin going on right up to (unclear) bore and Darwin. That's all we just want to think about for this.

We're not dogs. We're not animals. That's a man. Girl and man, and children. Children main one, he grow up. Father and mother got to grow him up proper way. We no want to see trouble all the time. Please, we sitting round here right in the Centre, longa Central Australia . . .

This world, he'll be finished anytime. He'll be life all the time. That's ground and here, longa this world while they walking around, drive round everywhere. And we worrying for the people. Another people, they got to take it easy way, very easy. Slowly. He got to take it slowly. And he got to take it good. And think about no anything else. No more fighting. No more fighting around more. No more thinking about for the hard, something war.

Poor people, might we finish longa this country. This the world, he'll be life all the way. He'll be life all the way, this the world. We only sitting good. No trouble. We want to take a good life, for this, while we here today.

The Lord watching war. That Lord Jesus Christ, he'll be coming back not long. For the here, longa this world. Thank you for this, while we talk here for the Father. Father and Son and Spirit.

TRACK 10

Ngarlu Jukurrpa, Darby Jampijinpa Ross at Yuwmurruluwarnu, 1997.

In this excerpt, Darby sings and tells a *Jukurrpa* story in Warlpiri. In the story, Jungarrayi attracts a wrong skin woman to him – a Napangardi (mother-in-law) – by singing and spinning hair string on his thigh. The song and the rhythmic sound of the spinning draws her to him. She is mesmerised by the song. She comes from the west; he is on the eastern side. She follows the sound of the singing. He spots her behind a ghost gum and then follows her to the western side of the place called Ngarlu. She stops to urinate, and then he catches up and has his way with her there. The song that he was singing becomes a *yilpinji* (love song) that men use to attract women.

TRACK 11 (p. 78)

Easter *Purlapa* (Corroboree, excerpt) Yuendumu Baptist Church, circa 1980.

TRACK 12 (p. 103–104)

Nguru Warlalja (Our Family Home Land), Gordon Jangala Robertson, live recording for PAW Radio.